FAREWELL

TO SPORT

PAUL GALLICO ·

FAREWELL *Paul Gallico* TO SPORT

Essay Index Reprint Series

BOOKS FOR LIBRARIES PRESS
FREEPORT, NEW YORK

INTERNATIONAL STANDARD BOOK NUMBER:

0-8369-1926-2

LIBRARY OF CONGRESS CATALOG CARD NUMBER:

74-128244

PRINTED IN THE UNITED STATES OF AMERICA

To Westbrook Pegler, Grantland Rice, Damon Runyon, Harry Salsinger, Mark Kelly, Alan Gould, Jim Dawson, Dan Parker, Davis Walsh, Joe Williams, Hype Igoe, Bob Considine, Bill Corum, Henry McLemore, Stu Cameron, Ralph McGill, John Kieran, Jim Kahn, and all the rest of my friends and companions on the sports pages of America, this book is dedicated with nostalgia and my sincere affection.

PAUL GALLICO

TABLE OF

CONTENTS

FAREWELL

TO SPORT

I

MINE EYES

HAVE SEEN

THE GLORY...

FROM THE summer day thirteen years ago when as a wide-eyed, open-mouthed novice, a rank cub who had never seen a prizefighter before, I was sent to Jack Dempsey's camp at Saratoga Springs, New York, to write stories about his training for the defense of his title against the challenge of Luis Angel Firpo, to another summer evening not long past, when in the vast Reichs Sports Stadion in Berlin the Olympic flag crept down the masthead and the perpetual flame died and vanished from the great black tripod, my last assignment—this is the first time that I have had a chance to stop for a moment and think over the things that I have seen and reported in the wildest, maddest, and most glamorous period in all the history of sport. I am able to do this, because I am saying good-by to sports-writing.

It was an incredible period, this dizzy, spinning, sports reel of athletes, events, records, personalities, drama, and speed, a geared-up, whirling, golden world in which a lifetime was lived in five years, or sometimes it seemed even overnight, as heroes and heroines, champions and challengers burst upon the scene, shone like exploding star shells, and often vanished as quickly.

I have for these past years had a ringside seat where men and women have, with their bodies, performed the greatest prodigies ever recorded. I saw the abysmal, unreasoning fury of Dempsey and Firpo fighting like animals and sat in a blinding cloudburst and watched Gene Tunney annihilate an unbeatable Dempsey. I saw Red Grange weave his twisting patterns up and down football fields, and followed in the galleries of Bob Jones as he played his smooth, superb golf shots that have never since been matched.

Bill Tilden banged his unreturnable cannon-ball service across the net, and Jim Londos stood brown and glistening with oil and sweat under the hot candelabra of the wrestling pits. Tex Rickard was a bland, thin-lipped, Stetson-hatted gambler and an organizer of prizefights on a gigantic scale, and again Tex Rickard was a painted corpse on a bier lying in a state far beyond his worth in the center of Madison Square Garden, which he built.

Babe Ruth stood up to bat on his thin, match-stick ankles, his head characteristically cocked a little to one side, slowly waving his bludgeon, and old Grover Cleveland Alexander, his oversized cap comically perched on top of his weatherbeaten head, prepared to pitch to him. Gertrude Ederle rode up Broadway standing in the back of a car with her arms outstretched with joy and happiness, into a blizzard of torn ticker tape and newspaper and telephone-book confetti. Primo Carnera, 278 pounds, fought Tommy Loughran, 183 pounds, under a Miami moon, and Giorgetti and Brocco and Spencer rode their flimsy bikes eternally around the wooden saucer of the six-day races.

What a world! What heroes and heroines! How the black ribbon streamers of the celebrating headlines poured from the high-speed presses! The death wagons roared around the Indianapolis speedway track at two hundred and twenty miles an hour, and Helen Wills was something leggy with two long brown pigtails tied with bows that bounced and shook as she ran, and then she was a grown woman, cold, calm, commanding, absolute queen of her tennis world.

Army played Navy at football before a hundred thousand people, and Paavo Nurmi dog-trotted around and around the oval running-track, in his methodical and devastating assaults upon Time, assaults that created records that no one would ever break until one day a dark-haired miler from Kansas named Cunningham ran a mile race at Princeton, not against opponents who were left far behind, but against the moving finger of a giant electric split-second clock set up at one end of the stadium. This then was to be the most dramatic foot-race ever run, and so it was until the day two summers ago when a black-shirted New Zealand medical student with straw-colored hair and a skinny body ran that same Cunningham and the greatest field of runners ever assembled into the ground in the Olympic equivalent of the mile.

Dynasties fell, nations collapsed, politics changed, dictators appeared, countries were torn apart by revolution, there were distant wars, but all I saw were the eight-oared shells glistening in the late afternoon sun at Poughkeepsie, shattering the shining surface of the water with their blades, crawling like enormous water-spiders down the reach of the Hudson; prizefighters lying twitching on the canvas while their opponents waited for them to get up, their arms following the spread of the ropes out from the ring-posts in the corners; horses streaming in gay, changing patterns around the dirt tracks, their heads bobbing in rhythm and counter-rhythm, with a million dollars and more riding on their velvet noses. In my world there were only ball games played in the hot, sweating Indian-summer days, when every move made by the figures in white and gray outlined against the brown and green diamond was greeted by nerve-shattering, hysterical roars from seventy thousand people, or there would be eight naiads in black silk swim-suits threshing the blue waters of a pool between cork-roped lanes, and lovely bodies arched from high platforms into the cool water below.

Hockey-players wheeled like birds in flight on the silvery ice, armored football-players crashed their heavy bodies against one another or kicked the ball spinning up into gray sky; fencers slashed and lunged, runners threw themselves at tne tightly stretched bit of string at the finish line, jumpers scissored over bars set at unbelievable heights—it was a world at play, a fantastic competitive cosmos in which nothing ever seemed more important than who won, what was the score, who did it, and how.

Moments of beauty are remembered inseparably with athletes performing in the arenas. There were Herb Pennock's pitching motion, and the gleam in the eyes of Helen Wills looking up at a tennis ball in the air during her service, and her lovely neck line, and the smooth swiveling of Dempsey's shoulders as he punched a rataplan on the light bag. I find myself suddenly thinking of Maxie Hebert and Ernst Baier skating the pair at Garmisch, in a snowfall that made the scene resemble an old print, or of R. Norris Williams's backhand half-volley, or the six-round bout between Jimmy Slattery and Jack Delaney, the most brilliant and graceful prizefight ever boxed between two men.

There were Georgia Coleman poised on the springboard, her yellow hair, capless, shining in the California sun, and Dorothy Poynton's magnificent and graceful swan dive off the high tower, in which for a moment she became an exquisite white bird poised on some unseen current of air; the tremendous and awe-inspiring flotilla of vessels of every description that dotted the Atlantic Ocean off Newport, seen from the air, as they followed the America Cup races, and Aldo Nadi, the world's greatest fencer, himself a living rapier in brilliant darting movements of attack and parry. The most perfect thing in human locomotion ever to please the eye was the foot-running of Ben Carr of Pennsylvania until one saw Jesse Owens running, not on the track, but over the top of it. Or I see Eleanor Holm Jarrett, herself a lovely creature, swimming the back-stroke, her fresh young face wreathed in green and white foam; Tommy

Hitchcock leaning under the neck of his mount in full gallop to make a polo shot, Benny Howard rounding a pylon at two hundred and fifty miles an hour in Ike, one of his tiny white form-fitting racers, Pepper Martin sliding into second base. . . .

They were queer fascinating folk who peopled this weird world and who became my temporary companions as the seasons brought them round, each in turn, almost as though they were papier-mâché figures pasted on a slowly revolving cyclorama. It seems as though I never knew days, weeks, months, winter, spring, summer, and autumn, but only sports seasons. The baseball season opened April 14, moved steadily through the summer, and then merged, via the world series, into the football season. There would be the indoor and the outdoor boxing season, the indoor track meets with their regular performers, the hockey season, the winter golf circuit and the summer tournaments, the indoor and outdoor tennis periods, the racing meets apportioned off by the jockey clubs in batches of three weeks to a track, the spring and fall six-day bicycle races, all coming round year after year regularly, as if driven by clockwork, with their costumes and paraphernalia, their lingo, their camp followers, and their famous characters.

I have to think of course of Jack Kearns, smart, dapper, the perfect wise guy, groomed and scented, the finished modern type of fight manager; and the late Leo P. Flynn, old, white-haired, leathery-faced, one corner of his mouth exhibiting a small permanent orifice from talking and spitting out of it, calluses on his under forearms from leaning on the ropes and side-talking advice into the cauliflower ears of the fighters he used to call his bums—he was any casting director's vision of the perfect old-time fight manager. Then there were curious egg-headed Humbert Fugazy, the little Italian banker who fancied himself a fight promoter and who was always building dream stadiums that never materialized except on paper; and tough, cocky little Gene Sarazen, the *enfant terrible* of golf, and his running-mate when the white-flannel troupe came round, gay, smart, cynical, Vinnie Richards, the bad boy of

tennis. Knute Rockne, bald, quizzical, had a magnificent sense
of humor, and Bill Duffy, dressed up like a tailor's model, had
strange eyes and was a dangerous man. Fat Harry Mendel, the
perennial press agent of the six-day races, appeared as surely as
death and taxes twice each year, and one was glad to have
known small, quiet Miller Huggins, who always seemed patiently tired from the strain of managing the Yankees when
they were the greatest slugging club in the history of modern
baseball. And there were men of mystery such as Hugo Quist,
the secretive manager of Paavo Nurmi, or men of romance,
flamboyance, and ballyhoo like C. C. Pyle, inventor and promoter of the great coast-to-coast foot-race, nicknamed by
W. O. McGeehan "the Bunion Derby."

All the things they did and said over that exciting period
were news. The names come crowding back again—Jim Farley,
chairman of the New York Boxing Commission, always playing his bland political game, the late John McGraw, with his
gnarled face and bulbous nose, and the lean, ascetic-looking
(but tough) Connie Mack; good-natured buoyant Helen Hicks,
the husky girl golfer, and the great ball-players of the era, Cobb
and Speaker and Sisler, Walter Johnson and Lefty Grove and
the famous Dean boys, Dizzy and Daffy. There were more
fighters than I can think of—the dark, shuffling, pawing Paul
Berlenbach of the numbing punch, the hysterical Sharkey,
Baby-Face Jimmy McLarnin, who always managed to look like
a choir-boy while he was knocking you out; the brilliant, bounding Johnny Dundee; weird unorthodox Harry Greb, and the
brave Mickey Walker; Tunney, the enigma; Carnera, the misfit
circus freak who became heavyweight champion; Schmeling,
the only German who ever learned how to fight with his fists;
Harry Wills, the perpetual championship contender; and Joe
Louis, one of the finest and deadliest fighting machines ever developed. It seemed that never at one time had so many great
performers and fascinating people been gathered together
under one tent.

The breathless rapidity with which the scene would shift

left you little or no time for thought or reflection upon this mad, whirling planet of play. One afternoon you might be at the tennis tournament at Forest Hills, between matches drinking an iced tea at little iron tables set out on the close-clipped green lawn, beneath gay, colored umbrellas, surrounded by beautifully dressed women and soft-spoken men in summer flannels; and the next you might find yourself sitting at a spotted, rickety wooden table in a frowsy, ribald fight camp, gagging over a glass of needle beer and eating a steak sandwich, surrounded by lop ears, stumble-bums, cheap, small-time politicians, fight managers, ring champions, floozies, gangsters, Negroes, policemen, and a few actors thrown in for good measure.

It would be a ball game one day and the Kentucky Derby the next. You had hardly got the sound of the galloping hoofs, the paddock trumpet-call, and the muffled, unforgettable "They're off!" out of your ears, not to mention the gambling fever cooled in your veins, when you were standing in a gallery on a hillside, overlooking green, scrupulously manicured fairways, pitted with irregular white patches, listening to the soft "snick" of the cleanly hit golf ball. And hardly were you used to the jargon of the golf tournament—"Jones has gone crazy, he's even threes for five holes . . . What did Hagen turn in? . . . Diegel has to birdie the last two to tie . . . Sarazen's two under coming into the eighth, but they say Cruickshank's burning up the back nine"—when you find yourself perhaps at Indianapolis, wandering about the beehive-busy motor pits with the heavy stink of gasoline and burning oil always in your nostrils, and your head ringing with the constant thunder of exploding motors.

It was a wonderful, chaotic universe of clashing colors, temperaments, and emotions, of brave deeds performed sometimes against odds seemingly insuperable, mixed with mean and shameful acts of pure skullduggery, cheapness, snide tricks, filth, and greed, moments of sheer, sweet courage and magnificence when the flame of the human spirit and the will to triumph burned so brightly that it choked your throat and blinded your eyes to be watching it, and moments, too, of such villainy, cowardice, and depravity, of such rapaciousness and malice that you felt hot and ashamed even to find yourself reporting it.

The swimming of the English Channel by Gertrude Ederle in the face of the most awesome handicaps of wind, weather, sea, and human hatred and jealousy was as matchless and wonderful a triumph of courage and indomitable will—uselessly applied, if you must, but beautiful, nevertheless, as the building of Primo Carnera into the heavyweight championship of the world was a dark, foul, noisome thing, infamous from beginning to end, completely sordid and corrupt.

I have seen the coming of the million-dollar gate, the seventy-thousand-dollar horse-race, the hundred-thousand-dollar ball-player, the three-hundred-thousand-dollar football game, the millionaire prizefighter, and the fifty-thousand-dollar golfer. I have witnessed an era of spending in sport such as has never been seen before and which may not be matched again, when the box-office price for a single ringside seat for a heavyweight championship prizefight was fifty dollars, and fetched as high as two hundred and fifty dollars a pair from speculators. In my time more than a million dollars passed through the betting windows at a racetrack in a day. Babe Ruth drew a salary of seventy thousand dollars a year, and Gene Tunney was paid a million dollars for a single fight lasting half an hour. Non-champions were paid as high as thirty thousand dollars for a six-round bout, and a horse could win four hundred and forty thousand dollars in a single year, and did. And I have seen the bubble collapse as sharply and completely as did the great stock boom, and watched prizefighting go downhill from a million-dollar industry back to the small-time money from which it came.

Too, I witnessed the amazing growth of American football from a game that was always popular and well attended, to the greatest money industry and gate attraction of all sports, greater than prizefighting, baseball, hockey, or any professional sports, the total football receipts for one season far surpassing those of any other sport. And I watched the game degenerate into the biggest and dirtiest sports racket the country has ever known, far sootier even than prizefighting, which has never pretended to be on any level higher than a pigsty.

Somehow or other, all of these things managed to happen in those years between 1923 and 1936, years which saw not only the greatest champions that our games have ever known, but an astounding plethora of men and women challengers and runners-up who were nearly as good as the champions.

At one time, for instance, fighting for the tennis supremacy held so long by Tilden as an amateur, there were such players as Little Bill Johnston, Dick Williams, Frank Hunter, Vinnie Richards, Manuel Alonso, Borotra, Cochet, and Lacoste. Contemporary with Helen Wills Moody was Suzanne Lenglen, perhaps the greatest of all the women players at the peak of her form, as well as Molla Mallory, Mary K. Browne, Helen Jacobs, Betty Nuthall, Dorothy Round, and Kay Stammers.

Bob Jones was such a stand-out in the golfing world that he made people forget the greatest troop of professional and amateur golfers that ever lived and played at one time, headed by Walter Hagen and including such players as Gene Sarazen, Mac Smith, Tommy Armour, Chick Evans, Frances Ouimet, Johnny Goodman, Billy Burke, George von Elm, Leo Diegel, Bobby Cruickshank, Olin Dutra, Horton Smith, and dozens of others.

An age that was first dazzled by the speed and showmanship of Charlie Paddock at one hundred yards also knew Ralph Metcalfe, Eddie Tolan, Ralph Locke, Frank Wycoff, and finally the greatest sprinter of them all, Jesse Owens. The era is remembered chiefly by the running of Paavo Nurmi, but it also had Willie Ritola, Glenn Cunningham, Bill Bonthron, Jack Lovelock, Joie Ray, Gene Venzke, Eric Ny, Luigi Beccali, and a lot of other boys who could step that mile.

Ederle's feat in swimming the English Channel made her the outstanding girl swimmer of the post-war era, but those same years saw the most dazzling array of women swimming and diving stars ever assembled, including Aileen Riggen, Helen Wainwright, Helene Madison, Jo McKim, Lenore Kight, Dorothy Poynton, Kit Rawls, Georgia Coleman, Sybil Bauer, Agnes Geraghty, and Helen Meany. They not only could swim and dive better than anyone else in the world, but most of them were stunning to look at as well.

Red Grange and Knute Rockne are the best-remembered football names of the period, but during that fantastically prodigious time there were also Pop Warner, Gil Dobie, Alonzo Stagg, and Fielding Yost, equally great football coaches, and among the famous players, Albie Booth, Chris Cagle, Ernie Nevers, the famous Four Horsemen of Notre Dame, Stuhldreher, Layden, Miller, and Crowley, and later Frank Carideo and Joe Savoldi of the same school, Bronko Nagurski, Stan Kostka, and Benny Friedman and Harry Newman, the great Michigan players.

Every sport, it seemed, at least to us reporting it, had the greatest champion of all time at the head of it and at the same time the greatest competition to make him and keep him champion. There was Earl Sande, matchless as a money-winning jockey, Sonja Henie, probably the greatest girl figure-skating champion ever, Johnny Weissmuller, who was all by himself while he swam, Eleanor Sears, who was unbeatable at squash, Gar Wood, the champion of all speedboat drivers, Peter De Paolo who was National Automobile race driving champion for three years in succession, Glenna Collette, who whipped the women's golf field the way La Moody dominated tennis and who was contemporary with probably the greatest girl golfer that ever played, Miss Joyce Wethered of England; and we have yet to develop a polo-player to compare with Tommy Hitchcock.

That, then, was the marvelous era that is past, and those a few of the people who performed in it. Some of them are dead. Few of them are active any longer or retain their titles. It seems to me that I am quitting in good time. And yet in all those long days of endless excitement I found myself usually too busy reporting to do much evaluating. Why did we love Dempsey? What was it made us call Miss Wills, later Mrs. Moody, "Our Helen"? Why did we spend dollars into the millions to see ham fighters and very often fake prizefights? What makes us go to ball games to the number of ten million spectators a year? Why do we stand for dirty football? What makes women athletes such wretched sports? Why are Negro athletes? What made Gene Tunney tick?

Sports-writing has been an old and good friend and companion to me. One does not, it seems, barge ruthlessly out of such a friendship. Rather one lingers a little over the good-by, sometimes even a little reluctant to leave, and uncertain, turning back as some old, well-loved incident is remembered, calling up again the picture of vanished friends, having one's last say, lingering as long as one dares before that final, irrevocable shutting of the door.

II

WHO DO YOU

THINK YOU ARE

—DEMPSEY?

THE MOST popular prizefighter that ever lived was Jack Dempsey, born William Harrison Dempsey, June 24, 1896, at Manassa, Colorado, and heavyweight champion of the world from July 4, 1919 to September 3, 1926. It has been generally forgotten that for a long time he was also one of the most unpopular and despised champions that ever climbed into a ring.

And, curiously, it is possible to place one's finger upon the exact time and place, almost, when the switch occurred and the cult of Dempsey-worshippers was born—a public love and idolatry that have transcended anything ever known in the ring and perhaps, for that matter, in any sport.

It was, I suspect, some time between the hours of one and two o'clock in the morning of September 4, in 1926, in a room at the Ritz-Carlton Hotel in Philadelphia. It was about then that he returned there minus the heavyweight championship of the world, which he had left with Gene Tunney at the Sesquicentennial Stadium a short while before. They had fought for half an hour in a torrential rain and Tunney had battered the supposed invincible champion almost beyond recognition.

14

He was not alone. Seconds, hangers-on, reporters crowded into the room behind him. A lovely woman came to him with pity and tenderness and took him into her arms and held him for a moment. Lightly she touched his face with her finger-tips. One side of that face was completely shapeless, red, blue, purple in color, wealed, welted, and bruised, the eye barely visible behind ridges of swollen flesh.

She said: "What happened, Ginsberg?" Ginsberg was Estelle Taylor's pet name for her husband.

Dempsey grinned out of the good corner of his mouth, held her off for a second, and then said: "Honey, I forgot to duck."

From that moment on, everybody loved him.

John L. Sullivan, the Boston Strong Boy, was reputedly the most popular heavyweight champion of all times, but this is not so, because in Sullivan's day (his last fight was in 1892) prizefighting was neither respectable nor widespread in its appeal. It was long before the days of Tex Rickard, million-dollar gates, new-laid millionaires with an itch for publicity, and the freedom of post-war manners and morals which made it possible for a prizefighter to aspire to and eventually marry a society girl and be accepted in her class as a human being. It was before the days of high-pressure newspaper publicity and prize-fight ballyhoo and also before the time when Sweet Charity learned, to borrow one of boxing's own expressive terms, how to put the bite on prizefighting as a quick and at first infallible money-getter. In the old days the sport was socially outlawed. Women—that is to say, ladies—did not go to the boxing pits and therefore Sullivan's popularity was limited strictly to the class then known as "sports."

But nearly everyone in every walk of life seemed to love and admire Jack Dempsey. There was hardly any class to whose imagination he did not appeal. He was and still remains today in the minds of millions of people the perfect type of fighting man.

He was, as fighters go, a pretty good performer, though not nearly so good as legend and kindled imaginations pictured him. He had great truculence, pugnacity, and aggressiveness, a valuable and unlimited fund of natural cruelty, tremendous courage, speed and determination, and good, though actually, not extraordinary, hitting powers. He was never a good boxer and had little or no defense. His protection was aggression. He was not, for instance, ever as good a fighter and boxer as the Negro Joe Louis is today, notwithstanding Louis's defeat by Schmeling. Dempsey's entire reputation was based, actually, on two fights, the one in which he knocked out gigantic Jess Willard at Toledo, to win his championship, and the thrilling, atavistic brawl with Luis Angel Firpo, the big Argentine, at the Polo Grounds in New York, September 23, 1923. But they were sufficient, for they marked Dempsey as a giant-killer, a slayer of ogres. He became one with David, Siegfried, and Roland. And it is interesting to note in connection with this that Dempsey's period of unpopularity, even though he was branded a slacker during the war, really dates from the day in 1921—July 2, to be exact—when he knocked out the French-man Georges Carpentier, at Boyle's Thirty Acres, in Jersey City, in four rounds. Carpentier was hardly more than a heavy middleweight. He probably didn't weigh more than 168 pounds for the fight. He was a little man, much smaller than Dempsey. And he was a war hero. This fight also marked the first of the million-dollar gates.

But Dempsey was a picture-book fighter. By all the sons of Mars, he looked the part. He had dark eyes, blue-black hair, and the most beautifully proportioned body ever seen in any ring. He had the wide but sharply sloping shoulders of the puncher, a slim waist, and fine, symmetrical legs. His weaving, shuffling style of approach was drama in itself and suggested the stalking of a jungle animal. He had a smoldering truculence on his face and hatred in his eyes. His gorge lay close to the surface. He was utterly without mercy or pity, asked no quarter, gave none. He would do anything he could get away with, fair or foul, to win. This was definitely a part of the man, but was also a result of his early life and schooling in the hobo jungles, bar-rooms, and mining camps of the West. Where Dempsey learned to fight, there were no rounds, rest intervals, gloves, referees, or attending seconds. There are no draws and no decisions in rough and tumble fighting. You had to win. If you lost you went to the hospital or to the undertaking parlor. Dempsey, more often than not, in his early days as hobo, saloon bouncer, or roustabout, fought to survive. I always had the feeling that he carried that into the ring with him, that he was impatient of rules and restrictions and niceties of conduct, impatient even of the leather that bound his knuckles.

But all of these characteristics added to the picture of a man who could swing his fists and slug bigger, heavier, stronger men into unconsciousness. It crystallized something that all of us at one time or another long for—to be able to "up" to someone, a giant, a bully, a tough guy, without qualm or tremor, and let him have it.

All the great legends of the ring are built upon the picture that the average man has of himself as he would like to be, a combination of D'Artagnan, Scaramouche, the Scarlet Pimpernel, and—Jack Dempsey. If we could, we would all be gentle, soft-spoken creatures, tender with women, cool and even tempered, but once aroused—"Whap!" A lightning-like left or right to the jaw. Down goes truck-driver or footpad or hoodlum. We mentally dust our hands, readjust our cravat, smile pleasantly, step over the body of the prostrate victim, and carry on. Just like that. The most popular thing a sports-writer can say about a prizefighter, the good old stand-by, is that outside the ring you would never take him for a pug. No, sir, more like a bank clerk or a business man. Just as quiet and gentle—loves birds and flowers, and you ought to see him with his kiddies on his knee. Look back into the files. Sharkey cultivated petunias. Schmeling would lie for hours in the grass and watch a mother bird feed its young. Tunney retired in a rowboat to some secluded portion of a mountain lake and read a good book. Joe Louis studied the Bible (or at least he was trying to learn how to read so that he could study the Bible if he wanted to) and

was good to his mother. . . . But what killers when aroused!
Could that soft-spoken fellow with the well-cut clothes, the
rather queer, high-pitched voice, and the perfect manners be
the Jack Dempsey who clouted Jess Willard until he resembled
nothing at all human, and floored Luis Firpo eleven times before he knocked him out? How wonderful to be so quiet, so
gentlemanly—and yet so terrible!

Actually, for many years, Dempsey was inclined to be as
cruel outside the ring as he was in action within. I have seen
him in a playful wrestling match in a training camp, with one
Joe Benjamin, a lightweight who used to be kept around as a
sort of a camp stooge and jester (every big fighter always has a
camp butt or jester), bring up his knee into Benjamin's groin
and leave him squirming with pain. Gus Wilson, who came
over from France with Carpentier as trainer and remained here,
became one of Dempsey's good friends and even trained him.
But in friendly roughing, Dempsey once hit him what he
thought was a playful tap on the side and Gus went to the hospital and the damaged kidney was removed. Estelle Taylor
loved Dempsey, but all through their married life she lived in
constant terror of him. It must have been a good deal like being
married to a catamount.

To me this always added to the picture rather than detracted
from it, because I like my prizefighters mean. Cruelty and absolute lack of mercy are an essential quality in every successful
prizefighter. I have never known one who wasn't ruthless and
amoral. It is childish to believe that this can be put on and off
like a mantle. The gentle lambs outside the ropes are never
much good within, and vice versa. The managers and press
agents for prizefighters were not long in discovering what the
public wished to think about the comportment of their tigers
in street clothes. For the most part, the stories about their
sweet and lovely natures are untrue. Much later, when they
are older and retire from the ring, the mean streak may become
more deeply submerged, as it has in the case of Dempsey. But
the life that a prizefighter lives while in daily training is hardly

conducive to softening his character. His brutality and viciousness are carefully cultivated, fed, and watered like a plant, because they are a valuable business commodity. He practices
daily cruelties upon spar boys who are paid to accept them un-
complainingly. There never was a meaner man than Dempsey
with his sparring partners unless it be the cold and emotionless
Joseph Louis Barrow.

Dempsey used to have such big, inept hulks as Farmer Lodge
in his training camps. He slugged them and slogged them. If
he knocked them down, he waited until they got up and then
knocked them down again. If it looked as though they were
about to collapse from the effects of the punching he was giving them, he would hold his hand just long enough to let them
come back a little—and then slug them again.

The average boxing fan or person familiar with the beauties
of the game will inquire at this point: "Well, what are sparring
partners for?" This is unanswerable, but there are degrees of
permissible brutality, especially with injured men. But wounds
or no wounds, taped ribs or none, fresh cuts, bad eyes, bruised
lips or no, when they went in to spar against Dempsey they expected no mercy and got none. When his trainer called:
"Time," he set out to beat them into insensibility, and generally did. Most fighters, in training, will let up when they have
hurt a rehearsal mate with a punch to the extent that he begins
to come undone at the seams and wobbles a little. There is
nothing to be gained by knocking him out unless a bunch of
the boys from the press have arrived from town, when it makes
good copy for them and will sometimes affect the betting odds.
They have even trained Joe Louis to hold back a little when he
gets a spar boy going, but Dempsey never eased up in all his
life, so far as I ever saw or knew. The first signs of their eyes
glazing a trifle or that sudden little leaning forward of the body
and shaking of the knees that telltales a lethal punch, and he
would leap forward, his lips drawn back over his teeth, and rain
his hooks upon them until they collapsed slowly and slid to the
floor. He treated each and every one of them as his personal

enemy as soon as he entered the ring. He seemed to have a constant bottomless well of cold fury somewhere close to his throat.

Dempsey is accused by many of having been a foul fighter, and the same is fervently denied by the Dempseymaniacs. Dempsey himself never denied it, to my knowledge. In point of fact, under the strict interpretation of the modern rules of ring combat, he was a foul fighter, rough, anxious to hurt, and careless of his punches. But psychically Dempsey actually never was a foul battler, because in his simple way he recognized no deadlines on the body of his opponent and certainly asked for none to be enforced upon his. He also knew that such smug and arbitrary divisions as "fair" and "foul" cannot be made of the word "fight," nor are they properly applicable as adjectives. The word stands all by itself and complete in its meaning, not to be tampered with, increased or diminished, like "love" or "red." You either do or you don't. It either is or it isn't. And either it was a fight or it wasn't. He had no advantage of protective armor that was denied his opponent. He was equally vulnerable. He was not a deliberately low puncher, though sometimes, with a touch of macabre humor, he liked to test out the courage and disposition of his opponent with a few low ones, but he was simply unconcerned with such niceties and obvious decadencies as a belt line. After all, wasn't it sufficient that when he got his man down he refrained from putting the boots to him?

In a way these probings of Dempsey's were frequently interesting tests and two men reacted quite differently to them. He hit Sharkey low. Sharkey immediately looked to the referee for help and made the error, during the rendering of his complaint to authority, of turning his head for a moment and taking his eyes from his opponent. Dempsey immediately hit him on the chin with a left hook while his head was turned and knocked him out. In Dempsey's school if you didn't keep your eye on your opponent you paid for it. He hit Gene Tunney low in both of their fights and Tunney took it without a murmur, kept his head and his temper, and beat Dempsey both times. In later years, as a referee, Dempsey would always say when instructing two boys before a bout: "All right now, fellas, let's both get in here and have a nice little fight." And he meant just that. The kids knew that with Dempsey as third man in the ring there was no use squawking or complaining about accidental low blows or roughness or any of the little extra-legal tendernesses that fighters sometimes visit upon one another. The best they could get out of him would be a "Never mind that, son. Come on, let's fight."

Perhaps the essential difference between two such champions as Dempsey and Tunney is best noticed when you listen to them discuss past contests. Dempsey will say: "When I fought Tommy Gibbons . . ." Tunney will invariably say: "Ah—when I boxed Carpentier . . ." Dempsey never boxed anybody, which is one reason why he was so worshipped and became such a glamorous figure. When the bell rang he ran out and began to attack his opponent, and he never stopped attacking him, trying to batter him to the floor, until the bell ended the round.

After all, in our dramatization of ourselves we rarely see ourselves indulging in fancy stuff except to toy with the victim for a moment before letting him have it and laying him away among the sweetpeas. Your hero, whether on the stage, in motion pictures, or in fiction, when the time comes for action lets the right go, and that's that. He is always a one-punch knocker-outer even though it is very hard to put a man away for keeps (ten seconds or more) with one punch, and Dempsey himself rarely did it. But his first punch that landed flush would be in the nature of an anæsthetic, stunning the victim, and stupefying him beyond the ability to defend himself, whereupon Dempsey would slug him into oblivion with a series of left and right hooks as he did Tunney in the seventh round of their famous second fight for the championship in Chicago in 1927 —except that Tunney got five extra seconds of count and was able to get up and come back.

In that round and that fight, incidentally, occurred an incident that to me will always be the complete characterization of Dempsey. About a minute of the round had passed when Dempsey caught Tunney with a right hook that knocked him towards the ropes and numbed him so that he couldn't get his guard up. Immediately Dempsey slugged him to the floor with rights and lefts, the last of which caught Tunney on the jaw even as he was collapsing slowly to the canvas. Then happened the historic long count, for which only Dempsey was to blame, and Tunney finally got up, glassy-eyed and still badly stricken, but recuperating quickly because he was in magnificent condition, and retaining sufficient of his stunned and badly scrambled intelligence to tell him what to do—which was to retreat.

Those were dramatic seconds. Tunney retreated. Dempsey pursued with his precious title (it hurt his pride terribly to lose it) almost in his hands. Round and round the ring they went, Tunney backwards with that peculiar limping gait of a back-pedaling fighter, Dempsey forwards after him with lust on his face. But Dempsey was then pugilistically an old man. He was then thirty-two and his tired legs could not stand the strain of that pursuit. He was not a smart enough boxer to sidestep and change his direction and herd Tunney into a corner or to the ropes where he could slug him again. He was a fighter with his kill in front of him. He could feel it slipping away from him and he knew but one direction in pursuit—forward.

Finally his legs failed him altogether. He stopped. And over his swarthy, blue-jowled fighter's face there spread a look the memory of which will never leave me as long as I live. First it was the expression of self-realization of one who knows that his race is run, that he is old and that he is finished. And then through it and replacing it there appeared such a glance of bitter, biting contempt for his opponent that for the moment I felt ashamed for the man who was running away. With his gloves Dempsey made little coaxing pawing motions to Tunney to come in and fight. That was it. Don't run. Come in and fight. This is a fight.

For that is what Dempsey would have done. Staggering blind, punch-drunk, head swimming, sick and reeling as he was when he was pushed back into the ring after Firpo knocked him out of it, and again after his terrible first-round beating at the hands of Sharkey, his instincts were yet to move forward, close with the enemy, and fight.

It would have been foolhardy had Tunney accepted this desperate battle gage, but as our hearts and not our heads reckon those things, it would have been glorious. In his place Dempsey would have done it and would have been knocked out as Tunney would have been. Tunney continued to run backwards, recovered, won the fight and retained his championship. And from his second losing encounter with the ex-Marine Dempsey emerged the greatest and most beloved popular sports hero the country has ever known—a title that, curiously, his greatest victories never won for him.

And after all, who can say that it was not deserved, because at least, unlike many other heroes, he had for those ringing, dramatic fourteen seconds justified the legends that had grown up around him, satisfied the picture of him that so many people had in their minds? He did hit Tunney, and hit him hard enough to keep him on the canvas for the officially required ten seconds and four more for good measure. That fate was against him and robbed him of his victory and his title was something that we could all understand. That made him human and one of us. And that he never once railed or complained against the luck of that fate or claimed the victory or sulked or was bitter brought him closer to divinity than many of us may come. Ah yes, there we were again, looking at ourselves in that satisfying hero's mold, smiling calmly and saying as Dempsey did: "It was just one of the breaks. Tunney fought a smart fight."

The old Dempsey training camps were probably the most colorful, exciting, picturesque gatherings ever. I was too young in the sports-writing game to see the one outside of Shelby, Montana, where he was preparing to meet Tom Gibbons, or the earlier one at Toledo when he was a tough young challenger training for the task (then thought impossible) of beating the enormous Willard.

But I remember the grand, exciting, bawdy atmosphere of the camp at Saratoga Springs at Uncle Crying Tom Luther's Hotel on the shore of the lake. There were sparring partners with bent noses and twisted ears, Negroes and white fighters, boxing-writers, handsome state troopers in their gray and purple uniforms; doubtful blondes who wandered in and out of the lay-out of wooden hotel and lake-front bungalows, and blondes about whom there was no doubt at all; a lady prizefighter; old semi-bald Uncle Tom, always crying and complaining over the Gargantuan pranks of the sports-writers; and Jack Kearns, smart, breezy, wise-cracking, scented, who virtually tore the hotel apart. The old, tough Dempsey was there, slim, dark-haired, still crinkle-nosed (you have probably forgotten that Dempsey once had a typical pug's bashed-in nose and had it lifted), dressed in trousers and an old gray sweater, playing checkers on the porch of his bungalow with a sparring partner. And wandering about the grounds was all the rag, tag, and bob-tail of the fight game, broken-down pugilists looking for a hand-out, visiting managers, the always dirty and down-at-the-heels One-Eye Connolly, and a fine assortment of bums and dames. There was nothing either high-hat or sinister about the plant. It was gay, low, vulgar, Rabelaisian, and rather marvelous.

This was of course before the days when clusters of million-aires and socialites of one kind or another patronized fighters and fight camps, and, too, just shortly before the time when the dangerous hot-eyed gangsters took over the fight business and brazenly visited the training camps to look over their prop-erties, mingling with the elite, or sat in smoldering groups in corners and weighed and speculated upon every arrival and talked out of the sides of their mouths.

But times were changing and so was Dempsey. This was the last of those merry, carefree, colorful camps. The next one was at Atlantic City at the dog-track, where the champion prepared for his first encounter with Gene Tunney. By that time Dempsey was rich. Kearns was a mortal enemy—they had quarrelled over the girl who was then his wife, the darkly glamorous Estelle Taylor, who had one trait which marred her chances for success as a prizefighter's wife, a devastating sense of humor. Detectives were already guarding Dempsey night and day, and one Tommy Loughran, a fast, brilliant, cream-puff, punching light heavyweight got a job with Dempsey as a sparring partner and wrote Dempsey's finish in letters large enough for all of us to see, except that we, too, were blinded by our own ballyhoo and the great Dempsey legend that we had helped to create. We refused to believe what we saw, a Dempsey unable to land a solid punch on Loughran, and Tommy stabbing and jabbing Dempsey as he pleased.

I remember that we made apologies for him. He was going easy on Tommy, because, after all, Tommy was of championship caliber in his own class and no ordinary sparring partner, and Dempsey didn't want to hurt him. That was a laugh; Dempsey, who never went easy on anybody, who would have broken Loughran in two if he could have caught him. Here again was an example of the strange grip that this man had even on the minds of the hard-boiled and unbelieving sportswriters trained to look for and detect weaknesses in a fighter.

His last camp for his final fight against Tunney, in Chicago, at the Lincoln Park racetrack, was probably the quietest and dullest of all. He had engaged old Leo Flynn to act as his manager, and Joe Benjamin was the camp jester, but he missed Kearns and the old life. His marriage with Estelle Taylor was beginning to break up. He was still too much the prizefighter for any sensitive woman. He lived alone near the track. But he was then no longer the ignorant, hungry, inarticulate, half-savage fighter. He had grown into a man.

I am not attempting in this short chapter to write either a life or a history of Jack Dempsey, but rather to give an impression of him as I remember him. But somehow I feel as though

I could go on and on, writing about him, and never exhaust the colorful, incredibly fascinating story of a strange man and a full life.

Because he began as a rough, tough nobody, a hard, mean, life-battered hobo, a kid with little or no education, truculent, bitter, disillusioned, restless, and vicious, digging food and living out of an equally hard rough world in which there was never any softness or any decency, a tramp, a bum, and a misfit at heart. I can see him as a surly, dangerous inhabitant of that spiteful nether world, just on the borderline of the criminal, a world of steely toughness, foul language, greasy food, dirty linen, gray clapboard shacks and unpainted frame houses, smells and stinks and curses, and nowhere any peace, comfort, or beauty.

And yet this boy who must have escaped only narrowly from being sucked into the underworld became a champion who eventually married a Hollywood moving-picture star who actually for a time caged him in a silken boudoir with stuffed taffeta and lace pillows and big, simpering painted dolls with bisque heads and nothing but voluminous satin skirts for bodies, squatting on his bed—Dempsey's bed. He learned to wear silk next to his skin and to eat with proper manners. He moved in those days through those absurd frills like a tiger in the circus, dressed up for the show in strange and humiliating clothes.

He had his nose remodeled, made a motion picture, took a triumphant tour through Europe, talked to the Prince of Wales in England. His lovely wife left him. He loved her terribly, too. Too terribly. Can you picture the old, hard Dempsey in a jealous rage? Had he met and married Estelle in his last phase, after he had quit the ring, when his restless, rising gorge was crushed deeper and deeper within him through experience, through living, and, above all, through disuse, this love-match might have lasted. But in those days he was still too close to the disgusting things that every prizefighter needs in his trade.

Curiously, I have never seen it written or commented upon

that nothing ever went to Dempsey's head—not his money, not his title, and not the amazing change in his social position. He is one of the three famous international sports characters and celebrities to remain unspoiled, natural and himself. The others are Bob Jones and Babe Ruth. The same bums, now a little older and frowsier, who used to put the bee or the arm, as the fight slang goes, on their more successful pal see him today and get the same hand-outs. His touch list must be staggering. Probably a fifth of the money he has made he has given away in touches, hand-outs, and loans that were never repaid.

The Dempsey of today is still a fascinating figure. As part owner and host at the loud, blatant, garish chophouse that bears his name on the corner of Eighth Avenue and Fiftieth Street, opposite Madison Square Garden, he has slipped into the Broadway post-crash scene and has become one of the landmarks of the city.

His restaurant is always jammed to the doors. You will see very few of the Broadway regulars there except on fight nights at the Garden after the show is over, when the fight-writers and some of the Broadway mob drop across the street for a glass of beer and to find out what Jack thought of the outcome of the match. The clientele consists mostly of out-of-towners who have come to see in the flesh the man whose breath-taking and fiction-like career they have been living for the past eighteen years. They are calling, in short, upon a beloved alter ego. They shake his hand, pat his broad back, and take home one of the red and gold menus with his picture and his autograph on it.

That restaurant, too, somehow seems indelibly imprinted upon my memory. You enter from a little door on Fiftieth Street and come into the foyer, where three skinny blondes, dressed in riding costumes, tan, ill-fitting jodhpurs, red coats, and white stocks, snatch your hat and top coat. To the right is the entrance to the long public bar. Remember, old John L. Sullivan once kept a saloon too. There is a green rope stretched across that entrance to the bar. The bums, the thugs, the panhandlers, and the drunks do not cross that deadline.

Off from the center of the foyer is a little glass and silver cocktail bar. Nobody ever seems to be in it. And to the left is a high desk with an enormous guestbook reposing on it and then the entrance to the restaurant is hard by. The restaurant proper is a huge, barn-like, cheerless place in red and gold, jammed and noisy, with a head waiter or two standing guard at the rope that bars ingress. There too, if he is not in the main room, you will find Dempsey. He will be dressed in a dark blue suit. He is not fat, but heavier, and his face is older and more settled. His hair is still blue-black, his chin faintly blue, and his movements still quick, restless, catlike.

If he knows you it will be: "Hello, pally" (in that high-pitched voice). "Glad to see you. Glad to see you. How's my old pardner? Sure, I can find room for you."

He sweeps the rope aside, taking you by the arm. He grips the shoulder of the head waiter. No matter how crowded it is, he will say: "Find a nice table for my friend from Portland, Oregon, here, and see that he gets taken care of. I'll be over later and have a chat with you, pardner. Hope you enjoy yourself."

And you march in, proudly, under escort. It feels like being presented at court. Or if he knows you very well he might take you down to a table himself and sit down with you for a moment. But only for a moment. He still cannot remain sitting in one spot for more than two or three minutes at a time. Like all men who have knocked about and been knocked about, he has a miraculous memory for names and faces. I have stood and listened to him rattle off greetings to one group after another: "Sure, sure, hello. How are you? Sure, sure, I remember you. Met you in Cleveland at the Athletic Club about five years ago. . . . Well, well, well, how's my old pardner from Toledo? How's the missus? She come with you? Remember me to her and the little girl—guess she's a big girl now. . . . Shake, pally. Sure, I remember your name. It's Bill Slotwell. How long's it been since I've seen you? Eleven years. Kansas

City, wasn't it?" This can go on indefinitely.

Probably sitting in the first booth, just inside the door, you will see Hannah Williams, the "Cheerful Little Earful" of the pre-crash days, his present wife, and mother of his two children, whom he adores as only hard, primitive men seem to love children. From six o'clock in the evening until closing time he works at his job, greeting, autographing, glad-handing, answering stale questions about his fights, suave, smooth, cordial, even-tempered, tactful.

This, then, is the haven in which this storm-driven ship is resting. I often wonder how deeply the old, cruel, snarling Dempsey is buried, and *does* character change? He wheels his daughter Joan, his first-born, in her carriage, and this is genuine, because now that his ring days are long over, there is no longer any need for the pretense of being a kindly soul and a "perfect gentleman" outside the ring. He is actually more the gentleman than most that come into his dining-hall. And it must be true that as men age the lust for fighting grows less, and that if there is no need or use for truculence and cruelty, these traits can become submerged. He loves his pert, bright little wife who has borne him children, and if the old, wild rages that tore his marriage to Estelle Taylor to bitter shreds ever boil and bubble over any more, no one knows of it, because there has been no hint or no sign of this lately.

It has been many years since he fought for his championship for the last time. There have been new heroes and new fighters and new champions, supermen, super-champions. But the name of Dempsey is still synonymous with the ability to lay a man low with a punch. The kids on the street still scuffle together and brawl and hit, and say: "Aw, who do you think you are—Jack Dempsey?"

III

HIS MAJESTY

THE KING

ONE OF the great characters of my time was George Herman (Babe) Ruth, the baseball-player. I do not mean to write like an old man reminiscing, but of course Babe Ruth is through as a ball-player. His legs went back on him (it is the legs that go first with practically all athletes), and my adjectives were beginning to look a trifle shopworn. A great many of them I managed to wear thin in over twelve years of writing about Ruth. For the Babe was and still is a wonderful person and a great human being. I do not write this as a pop-eyed cub or even as an exponent of the "Gee whiz, ain't he grand?" school of sportswriting, but in sober retrospection over the career of a man I genuinely love and admire.

The last time I saw Babe Ruth was at Jones Beach State Park on Long Island, where I was putting on a water circus for my paper. Ruth, finished as an active ball-player, had been brutally discarded by the game and its operators, for whom he did so much. It made me angry to see this glamorous figure suddenly completely neglected and out of the picture. I invited him to come down to the beach as guest star of the day's shows.

It was a warm, bright sunshiny seashore afternoon in August, a Saturday, and there were some seventy-five thousand people

30

jammed around the flat, sandy area of Zach's Bay, many of them standing waist-deep in the water to see the fun. Midway during the program Ruth was led out from the show control station, down the aisle bordering the bay, and out across the catwalk that led to our big water stage. No announcement had been made or was to be made until he reached the stage and the act then going on was concluded.

But as we walked, a murmur began in the vast crowd as they recognized the big, burly man with the ugly face, blob nose, curly black hair, cigar stuck out of the side of his mouth. There were individual cries of "Hi, Babe! Oh you Babe! Hey, Babe, look up here!" The name passed from lip to lip. The crowd caught fire like a blaze running over a dry meadow, and the murmur swelled and rose, gained and grew and took on volume, until by the time he reached the stage it was one thundering, booming roar drowning out the pounding of the surf on the beach a few hundred yards away. It shook the stands and the glassy surface of the water. It shook Ruth a little too, the man who had heard so many of these crowd roars. He stood facing into this gale of sound, grinning, his little eyes shining. The ringmaster had a stroke of genius. He dispensed with his microphone and simply swept his arm in Ruth's direction. The greeting redoubled.

And this was not a baseball crowd. Many of the people there had never seen a major-league baseball game. They were simply Mr. and Mrs. Average Citizen out for a day's fun at the beach. But they all knew Ruth and somehow loved him.

A few minutes later Babe began to hit fungo flies out into the bay. "Hitting fungo flies" is the baseball term for the act of throwing the ball up and out in front of you a little way and then hitting it up into the air with a specially constructed bat. It is used to knock flies out to the outfielders to give them practice. Ruth, incidentally, holds the world's record for distance in fungo-hitting. A most curious sight followed.

The first three baseballs had hardly splashed into the bay, the fourth was still in its arching flight, when the shore line—a half-mile or so of it—suddenly became frothed with white. The line of foam extended around the U of the bay and grew in width, white splashings in which dark heads bobbed, the beginning of one of the strangest and most exciting races I have ever witnessed. More than a thousand youngsters, girls as well as boys, with one sudden, simultaneous impulse, had taken to the water and were threshing out towards those tiny white baseballs bobbing on the blue surface of Zach's Bay. Many of them were competitors who had been waiting for their swimming races to be called and who should have been resting and husbanding their strength. They didn't care. There was but one immediate goal for that army of splashing, water-churning youngsters. It seems that there was magic on those baseballs.

There has always been a magic about that gross, ugly, coarse, Gargantuan figure of a man and everything he did. It is all the more remarkable because George Herman Ruth is not sculptured after the model of the hero. He is one of the ugliest men I have ever known. He was kneaded, rough-thumbed out of earth, a golem, a figurine that might have been made by a savage.

He is six feet in height, or close to it, with an unshapely body that features a tremendous, barrel-shaped torso that tapers down into too small legs and an amazingly fragile and delicate pair of ankles. But his head is even more remarkable. It is enormous, too large even for his big, bulky frame. His eyes are brown, small, and deep sunk, but clear and bright. His nose is flat and pushed in. Nobody did it for him; it grew that way. It gives him a quaintly appealing porcine look, emphasized by the little, glittering eyes. His mouth is large and thick-lipped and featured by fine white teeth. His hair is a dark brown, almost black, and crisp and curling.

His voice rumbles from the deep caverns of his massive chest, a great, deep, masculine voice, and his speech is coarse, salty, and completely man's talk, peppered with strong ribald oaths. It is the talk I used to hear in the Navy, with "son of a bitch" used so frequently, genially, and pleasantly that it loses all of its antisocial qualities and becomes merely another word that does not particularly disturb the ears any more than "guy" or "I'm blessed"—a peculiarity one often notices about strong speech. Habitual use of what is technically termed an oath eventually robs it of its sting. When Babe Ruth used to say casually: "I'm a bastard if that feller ain't hitten' 'em to left field now," he was merely using an accepted colloquialism of his early youth and stratum to indicate surprise, and therefore the word meant no more than if he had said: "I'm a wood nymph." Less.

Like all people who spring from what we like to call low origins, Ruth never had any inhibitions. The polite evasions of civilized speech and their interdictions, until recent years, were never for him, and sometimes he said shocking things. That is, they would have been shocking coming from an arch-bishop or a Princeton graduate or a virgin, but to me they never were because he was always so completely natural and never said them with the purpose of startling or shocking, but merely for the more utilitarian purpose of expressing himself and his meaning. His language for many years remained the robust, expressive, if thoroughly gutter speech of the asphalt and gut-ter world.

He was, after all, when first noticed, a tough kid in a Balti-more Catholic semi-correction school. His true antecedents— that is, his father and mother—apparently will always remain misty and unexplored. After all, Ruth was an orphan. What he remembers about his parents is hardly pleasant, and he will not talk of it. Suffice it to say that they, too, were made of gray clay, and that Ruth's youth was hard and bitter as was Dempsey's, but the rancid bitterness and hardness of cobble-stones and back-yard city slums, a drabness differing from those sections in the small country towns known as "across the rail-road tracks" only by its components.

That, of course, is one of the never dimming miracles of this inexplicable country, that half-brutes like Dempsey or Ruth can and do emerge from the filth and ashes to shine more brightly than any phoenix as the beloved heroes of the nation, rich beyond maddest fantasies, and, above all, looked up to and worshipped by children. And I marvel, too, how, as they age, these men who were toughies and hard nuts in their early years begin to take on a patina of civilization and gentleness. True, the layer never waxed very thick over Ruth's uncouth exterior, but he acquired it nevertheless. He can talk refined and gentle as long as you please now. It nearly kills him, but he can.

I am not equipped to tamper with the question of Ruth's mental age, because he was always a boyish, direct fellow who spent most of his time playing a game, but he is possessed of plenty of shrewdness and intelligence. Of his psychic age, however, I am prepared to suggest that it never grew beyond that of a nine-year-old.

I get a little tired when I read of prizefighters, ball-players, football heroes, and the like who are just "big, playful boys who never grew up." Ruth grew up, very slowly, it is true, but his spirit, or whatever it is that inhabits and animates his gross body, never did and never will. He merely has learned to discipline his appetites and desires. He never got over having them.

His reasoning and behavior were always engagingly childlike and wholly understandable. When he was poor and an orphan boy he had nothing and must have wanted everything. There was a time when he was undernourished and sometimes starving. No man who has ever gone hungry ever quite forgets it. Now, consider that in the years between 1914 and 1934 Babe Ruth in salary and prize money alone earned the sum of $1,000,000. With the perquisites that fall to every successful athlete in the United States, the endorsings, the syndicated articles, the sporting-goods material and candy bar bearing his name, the moving pictures, the radio, and the royalties, he must have made that sum over again. In 1914 his salary with the Baltimore team was $600 a year, in five years with Boston it was $5,000, and in ten years with New York it was $52,000 and eventually rose to $70,000.

Is any man who has starved and lived meanly, geared to accept and handle sudden wealth? And yet the most harmful thing that Ruth in all his life ever did with his money was one time nearly to kill himself through overeating. Whether or not it grew out of his early unsatisfied hungers, he was a glutton. One hot afternoon in some dreadful little Southern whistle stop on the training swing up through the cotton states on the way north, he was hungry and thirsty. Therefore he bought as many greasy, railroad-station hot dogs and bottles of arsenic green and jaundice-yellow soda pop as he could eat and drink. Eyewitnesses say he ate twelve frankfurters washed down with eight bottles of pop.

The result was the stomach-ache heard and felt around the world. Ruth never did anything in a small way. The biggest-pain-ever griped his middle. His training trip was interrupted. In New York he was carted from the train on a stretcher and taken to the hospital, where he very nearly died. Few if any American citizens have ever had such a death watch or caused so much public concern while lying on a sick-bed.

There was an inside story current at the time that actually, the dogs and the soda pop were successfully digested and that Ruth was suffering from something a little more sinister. Actually, which story was true I do not know. Both were easily applicable to Ruth. But in this instance the cause was far less important than the effect. A baseball-player lay close to death, and an entire nation held its breath, worried and fretted, and bought every edition of the newspapers to read the bulletins as though the life of a personal friend or a member of the family were at stake.

There was published at the time one of the most touching news pictures of the day. It was a shot of a couple of grimy street Arabs standing on the sidewalk beneath the hospital, looking up at the curtained window behind which lay the Babe. In their hands they clasped little bunches of flowers for their hero.

When you have worked on a great newspaper for many years

you come to regard such touching pictures with more than a faint tinge of suspicion. You can almost hear the photographers saying: "Hey! Wouldn't it make a swell shot to get a couple of dirty-faced kids looking up at the Babe's window? Let's grab a couple and pose 'em. Hey, Jack, run down to the corner—there's a florist there—and get a couple of cheap bunches of flowers. We'll get 'em to hold 'em and look up at his window, sad. Boy, that'll be a knockout." Photographers are that way—good ones.

But the point is that, whether or not the pictures were on the level, there was behind them a sound basis of fact. Ruth was loved and admired by children the country over. He had a magic about him; he was a character out of a fairy story, that drew youngsters to his side as well as grown-ups. Success and wealth had been showered upon him as it is in the stories and there he was in the flesh, to be looked at, touched, spoken to.

He was perhaps the most accessible of all our heroes. From April 14 through the first week in October he was in some ball park every day, a familiar and easily distinguished figure with his funny little mincing run, but there was nothing mincing about the cut he took at the ball, or the speed and amazing accuracy of his throw to home plate from deep right field. And if you could get down onto the field before a game, and youngsters with a little nerve usually could, he would pat you on top of the head and say: "Hullo, son. Shake hands"; or autograph a program or a baseball. Sometimes he did not do this with utter good grace, but always until the later years, when autograph-hunters had become a nerve-racking public menace, he did it. And sometimes when there was time out or a delay on the diamond he would back up to the right-field screen behind which were the bleachers and chat with the youngsters there.

One of the penalties of too close association with heroes and daily sports-reporting is the suspicion and cynicism already indicated. You learn eventually that, while there are no villains, there are no heroes either. And until you make the final discovery that there are only human beings, who are therefore all the more fascinating, you are liable to miss something.

One of the most beautiful of the Ruth stories is this one: There was a handsome kid aged around twelve or thirteen, son of a pleasant, middle-class suburban family, who had undergone an operation. The operation had been successful, but the boy failed to improve. He had slipped too far downhill. Something tremendous was needed to bring him back. The boy's idol was Babe Ruth. A baseball autographed by the Babe might prove the right stimulus to quicken that nearly extinct flame. A newspaperman went to Ruth and told him the story and asked him to autograph a baseball for the boy.

The next morning the nurse came into the room and said: "Johnny! Johnny! You must open your eyes and sit up for a moment. Someone is here to see you."

The door opened and it was God Himself who walked into the room, straight from His glittering throne, God dressed in a camel's hair polo coat and a flat, camel's hair cap, God with a flat nose and little piggy eyes, a big grin, and a fat black cigar sticking out of the side of it.

God gave His alias as Babe Ruth and sat at the foot of the bed and talked baseball as man to man for a little while with the earth child and then promised him a personal and private miracle all for himself. He said: "Ya know what I'm going to do this afternoon? I'm gonna hit a home run just for you. You watch. It's gonna be your home run. Now you hurry up and get well so you can come out and see me play."

When he left, the boy knew that God had been there, because He left a shiny white American League baseball with the familiar "Babe Ruth" traced on the horsehide in ink as evidence of His presence. And what is more, he performed the miracle. He hit that home run that afternoon. How did he know that he would be able to do it? Ruth always seemed to know. The boy could not die after that; not after he had thus been held close to the august breast of divinity and been a party to a genuine grade-A special Number One miracle.

Did Babe Ruth think up and execute that wonderful, simple

visit to a sick child? Or was it cooked up by his wise, hard-boiled syndicate manager or some smart newspaperman scenting a heart story that would thrill the country? I don't know. I never really wanted to know, but I remember that at the time I had my suspicions. There were too many photographers and reporters present.

But does it really matter? He went. He sat and talked to the boy as long as the doctors would permit him to stay. And he did hit that home run in the afternoon, the boy's private, personal home run, promised and dedicated to him, the sweetest and most thrilling gift a child could want. The pictures and the story covered the county. People looked, read, gulped, and felt an emotion and said in effect: "You gotta love a guy like that, don't you?" And so they loved him.

I learned to love him because he was all man. In his early days before the great reformation he drank, he smoked, he cursed, he wenched, he indulged himself, he brawled and sulked, and got the swelled head and got over it. He was discovering, living and enjoying this wonderful thing called life with all of his senses, enjoying it more than anyone I have ever known. God, life was swell! All the food he could eat, beer and whisky, girls with red or black or yellow hair and soft lips, baseball every day, nice warm places to sleep, silk underwear, fine warm clothing, plenty of pals, money in the pants pocket, more where that came from, name and pictures in the papers, a big shiny automobile to ride around in—wow!

And yet it never made him mean. He never forgot his early days. For that matter, he didn't want to forget them, because thinking of them sharpened his enjoyment of the new ones so much more. And he always had a tremendous earnestness and sincerity and, above all, something that only a great and really simple man could have: a sense of responsibility to the millions of people, young and old, who loved him and thought that he was a hero and a fine man.

This is perhaps the greatest truth about the Babe—that no matter how phony or drippingly sentimental the situation in

which he found himself might be, whether it was the outcome
of natural instincts on his part to be kind or whether it was as
carefully stage-managed as the first visit of a cub columnist to
the home of a particularly vicious prizefighter, Ruth was always
the honest and sincere element in the situation. He, if no one
else, believed in it and played it up to the hilt, not ever for his
own personal gain or glory or to build up an elaborate false
character to be sold to his public, but because he believed that
that was the kind of person he was. His generosity and his
affections were just as Gargantuan as his appetites.

Consider for instance the brilliantly phony plea to Babe
Ruth made by his friend Senator Jimmy Walker at a baseball-
writers' banquet at the close of a season during which Ruth had
been a particularly bad boy, had broken training, had quarreled with Miller Huggins, his manager, had been fined and
suspended and sent home, had, in short, acted the part of a
spoiled, willful, naughty brat.

The Senator rose to speak in a banquet hall filled with tough,
hard-boiled, worldly-wise baseball-writers whose daily job it is
to peddle treacle about the baseball heroes and soft-pedal the
sour stuff, baseball managers, perhaps as tough and hard a
group of men as there is in sports, celebrities of every kind; and
he made a personal plea to Babe Ruth to reform himself and
behave because he owed it to the dirty-faced kids in the streets
who worshipped him; the Babe, he said, had a great responsibility to the youth of the country and he must not shirk it.

It was maudlin; it was in some ways cheap and tear-jerking.
But, as I have suggested, it was likewise brilliant, and the brittly
hard, cynical Senator of the State of New York knew what he
was doing. Because Ruth robbed it of all cheapness, of all sen-
sationalism, or everything that was vulgarly maudlin, by getting
to his feet and, with tears streaming down his big, ugly face,
promising the dirty-faced kids of the nation to behave—for
their sake. And then he kept his promise. He was never in
trouble again. From that time on he began to learn a little
about moderation and restraint. Nor did it make him any

the less a picturesque character, because he never went sissy or holy on the boys. He retained all of his appetites and gusto for living. He merely toned them down. He learned what every celebrity in the United States eventually must learn—to perform his peccadillos in strict privacy if possible. Formerly Ruth had perpetrated his right out in public.

Ruth's baseball record is a remarkable one and deserves inclusion even in such an informal estimate of him as this. He has an all-time total of 708 home runs and 723 homers, adding those he hit in World Series. He holds the record for the most home runs hit in one season: namely, 60, scored in 1927 in a season of 151 league games. He likewise holds the world's record for the total number of bases on balls during a playing career, 2,036, an indication of what the opposing pitchers thought of him. For twelve years he led his American League in home runs hit, and for eleven years hit forty or more out of the park each season. There are dozens of other minor records that one could dig out of the files and the record-books, all connected with his prodigious hitting, such as runs batted in, runs scored, extra base hits, and so on; but they still remain dusty figures and reveal nothing of the manner of his making these numbers—numbers which in two or three generations will be all that will remain of George Herman Ruth, except legend.

For he played ball on the same enormous scale on which he lived his life, intensely, fervently, and with tremendous sincerity and passion. It was impossible to watch him at bat without experiencing an emotion. I have seen hundreds of ballplayers at the plate, and none of them managed to convey the message of impending doom to a pitcher that Babe Ruth did with the cock of his head, the position of his legs, and the little, gentle waving of the bat, feathered in his two big paws.

And, curiously, no home run that Ruth ever hit managed to hint at the energy, power, effort, and sincerity of purpose that went into a swing as much as one strike-out. Just as when he connected the result was the most perfect thing of its kind, a ball whacked so high, wide, and handsome that no stadium in the entire country could contain it, so was his strike-out the absolute acme of frustration. He would swing himself twice around until his legs were braided. Often he would twist himself clear off his feet. If he had ever connected with that one . . .

Every move that Ruth made brought some kind of answering sound from the crowd in the stands. Each swung strike left a trail of laughter, but backed by a chorus of respectful and awed "Oooooooooohs" as the audience realized the power that had gone to waste and the narrow escape the pitcher had had. Ruth's throws to home plate from the outfield, or to a base, so accurate that the receiver never had to move a step from his position to receive them, always brought ripples of incredulous laughter, the "I'm seeing it, but I don't believe it" kind.

And of course his home runs brought forth pandemonium, a curious double rejoicing in which the spectator celebrated not only Babe's feat and its effect upon the outcome of the game, but also his excellent luck in being present and with his own eyes beholding the great happening. There must be an enormous amount of fetishism in our hero-worship of successful athletes, and seeing Ruth hit a home run always seemed to have definitely a stimulating effect upon people, almost as though by having been there when it happened, some of his magic stuck to them. Behind the autograph craze which sends the crowd clamoring around Ruth and other celebrities for signatures there is pure fetishism, with the touch of the signature of the great one desired for a talisman.

Because Ruth will always be one of the great success stories, the fairy tale come true—From Rags to Riches, or the Orphan Who Made Good. It is one of the favorite fables of our democracy, and when it comes to life as it sometimes does in startling places, we are inclined to regard the lucky character as more royal than royalty.

We apply the titles of Kings and Queens to our successful athletes, as expressions of a belief in their fortunate birth, anointed and under a lucky star. Thus Ruth was always and always will be the King of Swat, a distinct and royal personage to whom the ordinary rules of life do not seem to apply. For among the other blessings with which he was apparently showered when he entered this world—blessings which, it is true, were not apparent at the time—was the gift of being able to deliver where there was something important at stake, when it meant the most, when the greatest number of eyes were upon him. We admire this trait greatly, and all our fictional heroes are endowed with it. They always come through at the right time, just as Ruth hit his home run for the sick boy the day he promised to do so.

And so when I think back over the great deeds of sport that I have witnessed and think particularly of the ones that have warmed my heart and made it glow beyond all cynicism, I remember with most pleasure the last world series in which Ruth played, back in 1932, and which involved the New York Yankees and the Chicago Cubs. The game took place in Chicago, and Root was pitching for the Western team. The Cubs were giving Ruth an unmerciful riding down on the field, and the sallies were deliberately vicious and foul, having chiefly to do with his origin, upon which, as I have indicated, there may be considerable speculation. He had already hit one home run, and when he came to bat in the latter part of the game, the entire Cub bench came out to the edge of the dugout and began to shout filth and abuse at him.

Root put over the first pitch and Ruth swung at it and missed. There was a great roar of delight from the partisan crowd, which hated everything that came from New York, and the players redoubled their insults. Ruth held up one finger so that everyone could see it. He was indicating that that was just one strike. The crowd hooted him. Root pitched again and Ruth missed for the second time, and the park rocked with laughter. The Cub players grew louder and more raucous. The Babe held up two fingers. The crowd razzed him, and there was nothing good-natured about it, because his magnificent effrontery was goading them badly.

Two balls, wide pitches, intervened. And at this point, Ruth made the most marvelous and impudent gesture I have ever seen. With his forefinger extended he pointed to the flagpole in center field, the farthest point removed from the plate. There was no mistaking his meaning. He was advising crowd, pitcher, and jeering Cubs that that was the exact spot where Root's next pitch would leave the park.

The incensed crowd gave forth a long-drawn-out and lusty "Booooooo!" Ruth made them choke on it by slugging the ball out of the premises at exactly that point, the center-field flagpole, for his second home run of the day and probably the only home run in the entire history of baseball that was ever called in advance, as to both time and place.

Ruth could do those things, take those chances and get away with them, because he was The Babe and because his imagination told him that it was a fine, heroic, and Ruthian thing to do. And he had the ability to deliver. I suppose in fifty or sixty years the legend will be that Ruth could call his shots any time.

But once is sufficient for me, and I saw him do that.

IV

MITT THE

QUEEN TOO

OF ALL the well-known women players of my time, which included Suzanne Lenglen, Molla Mallory, Mary K. Browne, Helen Hull Jacobs, and others, the most famous of all was Mrs. Helen Wills Moody, the former Helen Wills of Berkeley, California, better known as "Our Helen," and still better known as "Queen Helen." Lenglen, the Frenchwoman, was a better tennis-player than Helen. English girls of the type of Betty Nutl.all and Kay Stammers have been a lot cuter-looking on the courts. But when the great woman athletic performer of these past years is named, it will be Helen Wills who is remembered first.

"What are little girls made of? Sugar and spice and everything nice," runs the old nursery rhyme. What was Helen Wills made of? A strong, sound, well-learned tennis game backed by great concentration, will-power, and stamina and powerful legs and shoulders, a cool, calm, finely chiseled Grecian beauty with the perfect profile of an Athenian statue, a white eyeshade (that became a national fad), a nickname ("Little Miss Poker-Face"), enormous ambition, a socially aspiring mother, courage, tenacity, a good disposition buried beneath a coldly and carefully acquired snobbishness, and eventually a well-trained husband who remained completely

44

in the background as all well-trained husbands of lady celebrities should until he was recently divorced.

It is not the ideal description of the perfect heroine of the perfect American story. Our Helen was not exactly a faultless or always heroic little girl. But Our Helen she became and so remained, because when she first arrived in the East to play in the Women's National Tennis Championships in 1922, she was a breathless, pretty, pink-cheeked, leggy thing with two long brown braids down her back, with bows on them, that bounced and jiggled when she ran from side to side of the tennis court. She was young and girlish and everybody loved her immediately and spoiled her. She was no more than a child prodigy at that stage, and children are not particularly fair game for baiting under any conditions. In addition reports of tennis matches were always softer and more gentlemanly than other sports-writing.

It was part and parcel of the bitter and rugged style of sports-writing of that period, initiated by the best of them all, W. O. McGeehan, to print, if you felt like it: "Joe Doakes, the light-welterweight champion, has been drunk for his last three fights. That bum hand he complained of in the fourth round he didn't get in training; he got it socking his old lady for pinching his bottle." But tennis was always strictly a sissy sport, no matter how many gallons of perspiration were shed, or pounds burned away during its play, and you never, especially if you were a tennis-writer by profession and wished to return to write tennis another day, printed: "Mary Jones, the tennis-player, is a discourteous, bad-mannered, ill-tempered little snob who ought to be kept at home until someone whales some manners into her," even if it were true.

And probably to some extent we had guilty consciences anyway, realizing how much we were contributing to the making of complete egoists out of normal young men and women by writing too much about them. Helen Wills, at first a shy, normally sweet young girl, did not become really difficult until after she had been a champion for a few years, developed into an unbeatable player, was sought after by the society-conscious tennis crowd, and had been presented at the court of St. James's. And by that time it was too late. She had already, on our sports pages and in our headlines, become "Our Helen," America's own little girl. You may, if you like, attack an American hero or heroine in the columns of the press, but it is not generally considered good business. Your circulation begins to fall off if you destroy too many illusions, especially if you yourself have created them. It is a curious tenet of the American press that you must only boot a lady or a gentleman when she or he is down. But of that, more later.

Actually, Helen Wills never really harmed anybody or anything beyond the feelings of certain of her friends who liked her and helped her to get to what is known as the top, and some of whom she then snubbed or cut off the list, a not unusual performance in our great democracy. Her manners towards members of the press and photographers were sometimes appalling and if any natural sweetness and instincts to be kind were sometimes smothered beneath the proper tennis front that she copied—in fact, traced—from the tennis set, it was not particularly important, because she was strictly in the unessential luxury class, as were all tennis-players.

But we certainly all went on a fine, and strictly phony, emotional bender the year that Helen Wills went to France to meet and play the then champion of the world, Suzanne Lenglen. I remember definitely swallowing or conveniently forgetting all I knew about the girl being a spoiled and somewhat calculating little lady and contributing my bit to the general press hysteria with a meandering and touching column or sports editorial to the effect that tomorrow a little American girl beloved by all Americans was going to her greatest test in a foreign country, far from home, and that she must win because she was a fine American girl that everybody loved, and so give a thought to Helen Wills, folks, the highest type of American girl, and our very own, in this her hour of trial, etc., etc., etc. . . . Apparently it was what the customers wanted to read,

because it netted a slew of letters from people signing themselves Mrs. J. Basutio, or G. Carmichael, saying in effect: "Last
night I said a prayer for Our Helen to win her victory over there
in France the way our boys did."

It was still just a tennis match, but we were whooping it up
in those days and it was ballyhooed into the battle of the ages,
with the cool, peaches-and-cream-skinned, clear-eyed, beautiful
Helen fighting for the forces of youth and light, democracy and
right, against the unattractive Suzanne, a foreigner, representing the menace that is always met with and defeated by our
fine American manhood and womanhood. Only on this particular day something went askew with right and virtue. Lenglen gave Our Helen a trimming in three sets while the nation
practically went into full mourning. The pair never met on
a tennis court again.

There hangs over my desk, as I write this, a curious memento
of that great occasion, an amateurish pencil drawing of Suzanne
Lenglen, sketched and signed by Helen Wills. At the time it
was made, my paper paid the lush sum of five hundred dollars
for it under the impression that it was purchasing an exclusive
drawing by Helen Wills of her famous opponent-to-be. Technically it was, but ethically it was a sell. Realizing that Miss
Wills was an art student and that a drawing of Lenglen by her
would have tremendous news value and fit magnificently into
the big ballyhoo without disturbing her amateur status under
our conveniently elastic interpretations, we cabled to our cor-
respondent in France to sound the little lady out on price.
She accepted the commission, money in advance, price five
hundred dollars. But she never told us that the morning
World had had the same idea, only sooner, and that she had
already closed with them for a full page of original drawings
having to do with tennis in France. She sent the *World* its
page, and a week later our single drawing was mailed to us.
When it arrived it wasn't worth the postage it took to carry it
overseas, because the *World's* page had already appeared. It
had lost all value as news, and it certainly had very little as art.

The girl had caught us very neatly because theoretically we weren't buying it as news, but strictly as drawing. If we chose to be suckers and pay five hundred dollars for something worth fifty cents, that was our look-out.

This unimportant incident serves as an indication which way the wind was blowing. Ruthlessness is more or less an essential in any social climb, and the girl climbed high and traveled far from a position of no particular importance as the daughter of a San Francisco doctor to the world's champion tennis-player and everything that went with it.

Ah, but she was a grand champion, and she could pat that tennis ball. She would gallop through a tournament at Forest Hills without the loss of a single set, and very few games. She never in all her life lost a Wightman Cup match to England. She won seven world's championships at Wimbledon and lost but two sets in the seven final matches. And all that really mattered to the sporting public was that she was handsome to look at and that she kept on winning. Helen Wills became as much a part of daily life through the medium of the newspapers as Ruth, Dempsey, Rickard, Jones, and other sports celebrities whose records, habits, and personalities we knew as well as those of our own families.

The routine was nearly always the same. Come spring, and Helen Wills, later Mrs. Moody, would pack her trunk and her racquets and head east, passing through New York Wimbledon-bound. After Wimbledon would come the Wightman Cup matches, alternately in England and Forest Hills, Long Island, and then the Women's Championships at Forest Hills, through which she would move, dropping a game here and there, but rarely a set. No one could extend her. She hit too hard, ran too fast, placed her shots too well, didn't get tired, was too smart. There was practically a standing head in every composing-room: "Helen Wins Again." The only time there was a new national champion was when she remained on the Coast for one reason or another and did not compete.

And curiously, and dramatically enough, before the thing

that happened in 1934 and made her previously inviolate person the target for a thorough and brutal newspaper attack, she had changed again and from a spoiled and selfish girl had become rather a pleasant human being, as all great athletes seem to do. But where Ruth and Dempsey had to be brought from rough to smooth, Helen Wills needed to tear away a false, unnatural front that she wore like a cold gray veil. The girl behind it shone through rarely, but when she did she was so bright, gay, sunny, and lovable that one wondered how she ever managed to keep it hidden for so long.

I remember one time while there was a tournament going on at Forest Hills that Miss Wills had played a practice match with a boy by the name of Fritz Mercur, a sixth or seventh ranking player. Helen beat him. It got into the newspapers but without the extenuating information that Mercur by agreement had remained on the baseline without coming up to the net. Mercur took an unmerciful kidding from the other men at having been beaten by a girl, even though it was Helen Wills, because among the athletes at least there has never been any illusion about the comparative strength of a man and a woman at the same game. Mercur begged Helen to play him again. Somehow, the word circulated among the reporters and tenniswriters that there was going to be some fun on the No. 1 court of the West Side Tennis Club in the early afternoon when an unscheduled match was to be played.

There was. Promptly at one o'clock Fritz Mercur and Helen Wills trotted onto the championship court just in front of the marquee. No match had been advertised for that time. The stadium was empty and bare except for those of us who had heard the rumors—a handful of writers and a few officials. There was no umpire or cluster of linesmen. Two ball boys shagged balls for them and the best amateur woman player in the world and a high-ranking male player went at it hammer and tongs, all restrictions off, a couple of kids testing out which was the better tennis-player.

It was a grand, heart-warming show and the girl apparently

had the time of her young life. For the first time I was aware of the fact that she loved to play tennis. She let her hair down for this one. Gone was the so-called poker-face, the grim, impassive expression, from her face. She grinned. She laughed. She even giggled. The Queen giggled! Mercur, rushing the net of course, beat her in straight sets and regained his tarnished honor. But the girl gave him a fine battle, beat him on base-line shots, made him run, ran herself ragged chasing his half-volleys and smashes at the net, tried storming the net herself, and for that off-guard hour showed herself to be a gay, sprightly, pleasing young girl who could enjoy herself and be gracious in the process, instead of the cold, superior, emotionless sphinx that evidently was her idea of how a famous lady athlete should comport herself.

Perhaps the stuffy, social-climbing tennis officials are to blame for the solemn pall and funereal hush that always characterize an important tennis tournament, and perhaps a naturally gay and vital girl eventually succumbed to that atmosphere. It is the oldsters after all who set the pace, and the youngsters merely copy them. For many years Helen Wills was a perfect mirror of the collection of stuffed shirts, male and female, to be found running any big tennis tournament.

But nothing, to date, has ever explained what she did in the finals of the National Championships at Forest Hills in 1934 when, having lost the first set to her bitterest and perpetual rival, Helen Hull Jacobs, and far behind in the second set, Helen Wills Moody suddenly claimed an injury to her back, forfeited the set, match, and championship, and walked off the court beaten for the American championship for the first time in her long career. And yet Helen Jacobs didn't have the satisfaction of whipping her the full two sets.

Practically unanimously the press of the country landed on Queen Helen with both feet and called her a coward, a quitter and a poor sport who could not face defeat, but who instead took a shameful advantage of a gallant opponent who had played second fiddle to her for so many years, by casting the shade of doubt upon what might have been her final day of triumph. It was the feeling of press and public that, spine or no spine, Mrs. Moody might have managed to stick out those last few games, take her licking like a sportsman, shake hands with her conqueror as Helen Jacobs had so many times shaken hands with her, and then gone off to bed. Of course no one but Mrs. Moody actually knew how much her spine was hurting her at the moment when she defaulted. The facts were that shortly afterwards she went to the hospital for an operation, was in bed for a month and out of competition for over a year.

But to this day no one knows whether during that match the pain became suddenly so acute that, frightened, she stopped before she should do herself some permanent harm, or whether she simply quit rather than give her rival the satisfaction of a clean-cut victory over her. But the howl that went up in the press over her sudden and dramatic default struck me as being strictly revenge on the part of the boys. For the first time since Our Helen had appeared upon the scene, the handcuffs were off. It was now woman against woman. Helen Jacobs had suddenly become the appealing figure and the cold, queenly Mrs. Moody looked very much like a jealous woman and the villain of the piece. Some ten thousand people had seen her walk off that court, apparently without so much as a limp. Every newspaper reported it, and for the first time America's inviolable sports heroine could be attacked and scolded without danger of reprisals on the papers. She paid back, with interest, for the years when she had been a spoiled and insufferable little snob. And of course, as suggested before, the ridiculous thing was that by that time she had become rather a decent little person.

But the gentlemen of the press never forget. I do not know whether Helen Wills Moody ever considered her position in the newspapers as impregnable, or whether she ever considered it at all. But if she read the papers after the debacle at Forest Hills she must have been surprised, to say the least. The lovely, appealing figure of Our Helen had quite vanished and in its place was just another girl athlete who couldn't take it. They were remembering that, years before, Suzanne Lenglen had done the same thing to Molla Mallory, and on the same courts. La Mallory was beating the supposedly unbeatable French-woman. Suzanne complained of a cough—and quit. The girls after all were all alike, athletes and good enough sports while they were winning, but when they lost, reverting to type and becoming—women.

But if Helen Wills quit like a whipped pup on the Forest Hills courts, she licked her wounds at home rather magnifi-cently like a hurt lioness. My personal opinion of the incident is that the girl was probably in such agony from a sacroiliac dis-placement, than which there is nothing more painful, that she did not particularly care how it would look if she defaulted or what anyone thought or might say. She simply wanted to find surcease. She retired to the Coast after the match, refused to be interviewed, refused to answer the critics, refused to offer any further alibis. She simply had nothing to say. It was quite the smartest thing she ever did. Her siege in the hospital did more for her than talk ever could have done. But, hospital or no hospital, she was in disgrace with the public.

It may now be noticed that the career of Helen Wills Moody might be said to take on the aspect of a well-knit three-act play. Act One, introduction and arrival in the East, rise to heights as champion and public darling who conquers Europe as well as America. First-act curtain falls on indications of the contrast between the Helen Wills pictured in the public prints and the Helen Wills that actually was.

Act Two, the downfall. The girl hailed for years as the finest example of all that is sweet, brave, honest, and true in Ameri-can womanhood is caught out in a snide, cheap, and unsports-manlike act. Disgrace followed by oblivion and the triumph of a quietly gloating rival. But wait! Was our heroine perhaps unjustly accused?

Act Three? Why, any dramatist will tell you. Vindication! Queen Helen lives again. Long live the Queen! But what a last act that girl put on! . . .

One day in the spring of 1935, with no previous announcements, Mrs. Helen Wills Moody suddenly packed her trunks and her favorite tennis bats and left San Francisco for the East. New York was just a stopover again. She was Wimbledon-bound. Yes, she felt better. Her old injury was quite healed and the doctors had told her it was safe to play. Yes, she had been playing considerable tennis and felt that she was back on her game again. No, she wasn't making the trip especially to play Miss Jacobs. One could never tell whom one would meet finally in a tennis tournament. So many things might happen. Yes, she would go to Paris to do some shopping. . . . The usual platitudes, the usual nothings for the usual nuisances of the press. Only this time she didn't fool anyone. Helen Wills Moody was on the war-path for Helen Hull Jacobs. And how.

She was a repressed and self-contained girl, that Helen Wills. But the winter before, I had visited her in San Francisco for a little chat. Never by word or gesture did she ever hint that she cared about what had happened at Forest Hills or that she ever intended doing anything about it. And yet I came away strangely convinced that beneath that cool, well tailored, exterior crust, there burned hot fires. She must have thought of that scene and of Helen Jacobs a million times, and a million times must have said to herself: "I'll beat you! I'll beat you! I'll beat you! I'll come back." Snob or no snob, climber or no climber, a pure flame burned in that girl, and I loved her for it because she was a fighter. Yes, she was. When she left California on that casual trip to Wimbledon it raised the short hairs at the back of my neck because she had left her lair like a jungle cat on the prowl. If I had been Jacobs I should have shaken in my shoes. If ever one woman stalked another, that was it.

That the two ever should have met again on that famous center court at Wimbledon in the most hard-fought and dramatic match ever played between two women was one of those strange miracles of matching that sport sometimes provides, a situation that only a dramatist well versed in the art of hokum would dare to reproduce. Jacobs might never have reached the final round, or Moody might have been eliminated on the way up to the finals, because the English girls are playing perhaps the best women's tennis in the world today. As a matter of fact, Mrs. Moody was defeated in England in a small preliminary tournament that year.

How she must have wanted that match! Can one imagine the tension under which she played? Championship, hell! She wanted Jacobs back again so that she could prove whether or not she was afraid of her, whether or not she had quit that day at Forest Hills. It was a double burden that Mrs. Moody carried all through that tournament at Wimbledon. She had to keep herself in the running and at the same time worry over whether Miss Jacobs would survive into the final round in the opposite bracket.

In all the history of sport there has never been such a complete and dramatic vindication in trial by combat. There came a moment in the final match when Mrs. Moody was within one point of defeat. The score was 6–3, 3–6, 5–2 in games and match point, 40–30, advantage Miss Jacobs. Mrs. Moody didn't quit. Off a hard shot she made a desperate get, raised an easy lob to the net and watched Miss Jacobs come in to kill it and kill her hopes along with it too. She looked the end squarely and gallantly in the face, and it was not the end she must have dreamed of so many, many days and nights when she opened those secret places of her self and read what was written there. There, then, was the finish, a little white ball floating not high enough, not hard enough over a cord net, a cripple that any week-end tennis duffer could put away. Well, at least she had been able to prove that she was capable of accepting an honorable defeat at the hands of her bitter rival. At that point the bitter rival succumbed to an inexplicable attack of nerves; with the victory won, she smashed the easy kill into the net and it was deuce again.

Helen Wills Moody then took that game, and the next four along with it, to beat Miss Jacobs 7–5 in the last set to win the

match and the Wimbledon championship, which is the world
title. If you tried to write that story as fiction nobody would
believe it and no editor would publish it. It seems incredible
that a situation should arise which would permit the heroine
thereof to score a double triumph and satisfy every dramatic
angle. And yet it did. Mrs. Moody was within a point of defeat and proved that she could take it like a sportswoman. And
then when Fate intervened and gave her a reprieve she went on
to show that she was still the better tennis-player, had more
nerve, courage, and stamina, was, in short, a champion.

And thereafter she made the smartest move ever. She passed
up the National Championships at Forest Hills, which Miss
Jacobs then went on to win, and serenely and quietly retired
to San Francisco again. I can close my eyes again and see that
fine lioness licking her chops. It had been a good hunt. There
never was a better one. There was some gossip of her returning to Wimbledon in the spring of 1936, but I was glad when
I read a note in a paper saying that she was through with the
big tournaments and had decided to devote herself to some
kind of dress-designing. I was glad to know that she, too, had
somehow felt the dramatic sequence of those three acts and
the magnificent, unsurpassable climax at Wimbledon. She
knew when to ring down the curtain.

V

PITY THE

POOR GIANT

THERE IS probably no more scandalous, pitiful, incredible story in all the record of these last mad sports years than the tale of the living giant, a creature out of the legends of antiquity, who was made into a prizefighter. He was taught and trained by a wise, scheming little French boxing manager who had an Oxford University degree, and he was later acquired and developed into the heavyweight champion of the world by a group of American gangsters and mob men; then finally, when his usefulness as a meal ticket was outlived, he was discarded in the most shameful chapter in all boxing.

This unfortunate pituitary case, who might have been Angoulaffre, or Balan, or Fierabras, Gogmagog, or Gargantua himself, was a poor simple-minded peasant by the name of Primo Carnera, the first son of a stone-cutter of Sequals, Italy. He stood six feet seven inches in height, and weighed two hundred and sixty-eight pounds. He became the heavyweight champion, yet never in all his life was he ever anything more than a freak and a fourth-rater at prizefighting. He must have grossed more than two millions of dollars during the years that he was being exhibited, and he hasn't a cent to show for it today.

There is no room here for more than a brief and hasty glance back over the implications of the tragedy of Primo Carnera. And yet I could not seem to take my leave from sports without it. The scene and the story still fascinate me, the sheer impudence of the men who handled the giant, their conscienceless cruelty, their complete depravity towards another human being, the sure, cool manner in which they hoaxed hundreds of thousands of people. Poor Primo! A giant in stature and strength, a terrible figure of a man, with the might of ten men, he was a helpless lamb among wolves who used him until there was nothing more left to use, until the last possible penny had been squeezed from his big carcass, and then abandoned him. His last days in the United States were spent alone in a hospital. One leg was paralyzed, the result of beatings taken around the head. None of the carrion birds who had picked him clean ever came back to see him or to help him.

No one who was present in Madison Square Garden the night that Primo Carnera was first introduced to American audiences will ever forget him as he came bounding down the aisle from the dressing-room and climbed into the ring. It was a masterpiece of stage management.

He wore black fighting trunks on the side of which was embroidered the head of a wild boar in red silk. He disdained the usual fighter's bathrobe and instead wore a sleeveless vest of a particularly hideous shade of green, and on his head a cap of the same shade, several sizes too large for him and with an enormous visor that made him look even larger than he was. Leon See, the Frenchman, then his manager, was a small man. The bucket-carriers and sponge-wielders were chosen for size too—diminutive men; everything was done to increase the impression of Primo's size.

Carnera was the only giant I have ever seen who was well proportioned throughout his body for his height. His legs were massive and he was truly thewed like an oak. His waist was comparatively small and clean, but from it rose a torso like a Spanish hogshead from which sprouted two tremendous arms, the biceps of which stood out like grapefruit. His hands were like Virginia hams, and his fingers were ten thick red sausages.

His head was large, even for the size of his body, and looking at him you were immediately struck with his dreadful gummy mouth and sharp, irregular, snaggle teeth. His lips were inclined to be loose and flabby. He had a good nose and fine, kind brown eyes. But his legs looked even more enormous and tree-like than they were, owing to the great blue bulging varicose veins that wandered down them on both sides and stuck out far enough so that you could have knocked them off with a baseball bat. His skin was brown and glistening and he invariably smelled of garlic.

This was the horror that came into the Madison Square Garden ring and sent a sincere shudder through the packed house. That is to say, he was horrible until he commenced to fight, when he became merely pitiful and an object demanding sympathy. Behind what passed for the wild battle blaze in his eyes and the dreadful gummy leer, emphasized by the size of the red rubber mouthpiece (tooth-protector) with which they provided him, there was nothing but bewilderment and complete helplessness. The truth was that, handicapped by rules and regulations, a sport he did not understand and was not temperamentally fitted for, and those silly brown leather bags laced to his fingers, never at any time could he fight a lick. His entire record, with a few exceptions, must be thrown out as one gigantic falsehood, staged and engineered, planned and executed by the men who had him in tow and who were building him up for the public as a man-killer and an invincible fighter.

But I think the most dreadful part of the story is that the poor floundering giant was duped along with the spectators. He was permitted, in fact encouraged, to believe that his silly pawings and pushings, when they connected, sent men staggering into unconsciousness and defeat. It was not until late in his career, when in spite of himself he learned something through sheer experience and number of fights, that he ever knocked anyone out on the level. But he never could fight, and never will. In spite of his great size and strength and his well-proportioned body, he remained nothing but a glandular freak who should have remained with the small French traveling circus from which Leon See took him.

This big, good-natured, docile man was exhibiting himself in a small wandering cirque in the south of France as a strong man and Greco-Roman wrestler, engaging all comers and local talent in the nightly show, having found that it paid him more and offered a better life than that of his chosen profession of mosaic-worker. Here he was discovered by a former French boxing champion who signed him up and apprenticed him to one Monsieur Leon See to be taught the rudiments of *la boxe*. It is highly probable that the time spent as a wrestler set his muscles and prevented him from ever becoming a knockout puncher. But Monsieur Leon See was taking no chances. He taught and trained Carnera strictly as a defensive boxer.

Now, it must be understood that Leon See was one of the most intelligent, smart and wily men that ever turned a fighter loose from his corner. He was not much more scrupulous than the bevy of public enemies who eventually took Carnera away from him simply by muscling him, but he was much more far-seeing and he had certain well-thought-out notions and theories about the ridiculous game of boxing. Among them was the excellent and sensible thought that the human head was never intended by nature to be punched, and that secondly, from the manner of its construction out of hundreds of tiny, delicately articulated bones, the closed fist was never meant to be one of man's most effective weapons. In this last idea, Monsieur See was not alone. The coterie of tough guys and mobsters who eventually relieved him of his interest in Carnera rarely used the fist, reckoning it, as did See, an inefficient weapon. The boys always favored the pistol or Roscoe, also known as the Difference, the Equalizer, the Rod, and the Heat.

See was a keen student of the human body—for a prizefight manager—and he knew something about men. He was aware that abnormalities of size were usually compensated for by weaknesses elsewhere. He found out—exactly how is not known—that Primo Carnera would never be able to absorb a hard punch to the chin. He may have had some secret rehearsal in a gymnasium somewhere in Paris and, having ordered some workaday heavyweight to clout Primo one just to see what would happen, saw that the giant came all undone, wobbled and collapsed. Be that as it may, Monsieur See knew. And never at any time while he was connected with Carnera would he permit anyone to punch Primo in the head—neither his sparring partners nor his opponents. Since both received their pay from practically the same source, this was not so difficult to arrange as might be imagined. But See also had something else. He was a Frenchman and so he had a heart. He loved big Carnera.

Years later See proved to be right. When Carnera through exigent circumstances was forced to fight without benefit of prearrangement, and the heavyweights began to sight along that big, protruding jaw of his and nail him for direct hits, he was slaughtered. He was brave and game and apparently could take punches to the body all the night long. But one hard, true tap on the chin and he fell down goggle-eyed. For a long time during the early years, however, nobody was permitted to hit him there, and Carnera himself began to think he was invincible.

Primo's first trip to the United States was arranged through an American contact man and importer of foreign fighting talent, a character from Tin-Ear Alley named Walter Friedman or, as Damon Runyon nicknamed him, Walter (Good-Time Charley) Friedman. See was smart enough to know that without an American "in," without cutting in an American manager, he would not get very far in America. What he was not quite smart enough to know was how deep his "in" took him, that the ramifications of Friedman's business and other connections were to lead through some very tough and rapacious parties.

Carnera's first fight in New York involved him with a lanky Swede named Big Boy Peterson. In this fight poor Carnera was hardly able to get out of his own way and caused his opponent the most frightful embarrassment through not being able to strike a blow that looked sufficiently hard to enable him to keep his end of the bargain, if there was one. Eventually Peterson succumbed to a push as Carnera lumbered and floundered past him, and to make assurance doubly sure, the Swede hit himself a punch on the jaw as he went down. Someone had to hit him.

Now, this was a shameless swindle from start to finish, one way or another. If Peterson was making an honest effort to fight he never should have been permitted to enter the ring. The press unanimously announced beforehand that it would probably be a sell and a fake, and when it was over, suggested strongly that it had been. But it said so in a gay and light-hearted manner as though the whole thing were pretty funny (as indeed it was), and there was no one on the New York State Athletic Commission either sufficiently intelligent or courageous enough to throw Primo and his handlers and fixers right out of the ring and thence out of the country. The Peterson fight in Madison Square Garden, the stronghold of professional boxing, was a sort of a test case by the Carnera crowd to see how much they could get away with. On that score it was a clean-cut success. They found out that they could get away with anything. And so they proceeded to do just that. Primo's first American tour was organized, a tour that grossed something like $700,000, of which handsome piece of money Carnera received practically nothing. He was barnstormed across the country in the most cold-blooded, graceless, shameful series of fixed, bought, coerced, or plain out-and-out tank acts ever. If one of them was contested on its merits it was only because the opponent by no possible stretch of the imagination, or his own efforts could harm Carnera or even hit him.

Where the fight could not be bought—that is to say, where the fighter was unwilling to succumb to a tap on the elbow for a price—guns were produced by sinister strangers to threaten him, and where neither threats nor money were sufficient to bag the fight, he was crossed or tricked, as in the case of Bombo

Chevalier, a big California Negro who was fascinated by the size of Carnera's chin, and nothing would do but he was going to hit it, just to see what would happen. Between rounds one of Chevalier's own attendants rubbed red pepper or some other inflammatory substance into his eyes so that he lost all interest in tapping anybody's chin.

In Newark, New Jersey, a Negro was visited in his dressing-room before the bout by an unknown party not necessarily connected with Carnera's management, and was asked to inspect shooting irons, and in Philadelphia another Negro, Ace Clark, was amusing himself readying up Carnera for a knockout—he had already completely closed one of Primo's eyes—when somebody suggested he look down and see what the stranger beneath his corner was holding under his coat, and what caliber it was.

Every known build-up fighter was lined up for this tour, including faithful old hands like K. O. Christner, Chuck Wiggens, and poor Farmer Lodge. Political and gangster friends in the cities visited volunteered with their private heavyweights for quick splashes that might look well on the record-books. It was all for the cause. The more money Carnera made, the more the boys would have to cut up amongst themselves. It was all just one big happy family. It seemed almost as though every scamp in the boxing game contributed his bit somehow to that Carnera build-up.

Friedman, as has been indicated, was the go-between, and although Leon See was quite capable of all the planning necessary to keep Carnera in the victory columns, nevertheless it would have been considered bad form, and downright dangerous, if See had not cut the local boys in. And, at that, I suspect the said local boys showed the amiable and gifted Frog a few things about building up a potential heavyweight champion that made the two Stribling fights arranged by Monsieur See, one in Paris and the other in London and both ending in fouls, look like Holy Gospel.

As adviser and co-director of this tour, Broadway Bill Duffy was cut in. Bill was then in the night-club and fight-managing business, but in his youth he had been convicted of a little alfresco burgling and had been sent away for a spell. He was still to achieve the highest pinnacle of fame that can come to an American—to be named a Public Enemy. It is a curious commentary upon the conduct of boxing around New York that Duffy was allowed to operate as a manager and a second when there was a rule on the books of the State Athletic Commission, if indeed it was not written directly into the boxing law, that no one ever convicted of a felony was to be eligible for any kind of a license.

Duffy usually split even on things with his dearest friend, Owen Madden, better known as Owney, who had also been away for a time in connection with the demise of a policeman. Owney was out on parole at the time—he was sent back later —making beer (and very good beer it was, too) and acting as silent partner in the operation of a number of prizefighters. Also in this crowd was a charming but tough individual known as Big Frenchy De Mange who made news one evening by getting himself snatched and held for ransom by Mad-Dog Vincent Coll. The Mad Dog was subsequently rubbed out in an East Side drug-store telephone booth. But the subject, after all, is Primo Carnera and not gangsters and racket men, though pretty soon it was all one subject and all one sweet and fragrant mess. The boys had their connections in every town. The Philadelphia underworld collaborated through the medium of the always friendly and helpful Maximilian Boo-Boo Hoff, and the same courtesies were extended all the way through to the Pacific Coast, where occurred the Bombo Chevalier incident, which was too nauseous even for the local commission there to stomach. There was an investigation resulting in the suspension of a few unimportant people. But Carnera and his swindle went merrily onwards.

And it continued until he won the heavyweight championship of the world by ostensibly knocking out Jack Sharkey, then world's champion, in the sixth round, with a right uppercut. I say ostensibly because nothing will ever convince me that that was an honest prizefight, contested on its merits.

Sharkey's reputation and the reputation of Fat John Buckley, his manager, were bad. Both had been involved in some curious ring encounters. The reputation of the Carnera entourage by the time the Sharkey fight came along, in 1933, was notorious, and the training camps of both gladiators were simply festering with mobsters and tough guys. Duffy, Madden, et Cie., were spread out all over Carnera's training quarters at Dr. Bier's Health Farm at Pompton Lakes, New Jersey. A traveling chapter of Detroit's famous Purple Gang hung out at Gus Wilson's for a while during Sharkey's rehearsals. Part of their business there was to muscle in on the concession of the fight pictures.

If that fight was on the level, it wasn't like either of the companies operating the two pugs. If it was honest, the only explanation was that the boys were going sissy. As far as Primo knew, the right uppercut with which he tagged Sharkey in the sixth round was enough to kill a steer. He had knocked out many men with the same punch. Now he was the heavyweight champion of the world, and even if he didn't have any money to show for it, Italy and Mussolini were going to be very pleased. I have often wondered how long he remained innocent, how long it was before he began to catch on.

For instance, it must have been a terrible surprise and considerable of an eye-opener to Carnera the night he fought Tommy Loughran in Miami as heavyweight champion of the world. It was a no-decision match and a bad one for the gang to make, but they had to do something because they were desperate for money at the time. If the Sharkey fight was crooked, it is probable that the entire end of Primo's purse had to be paid over for the fix.

The Loughran fight had to go on the level because no one had ever managed to tamper with Loughran, and neither he nor his manager was afraid of guns. And Tommy had another curious and valuable protection. He was a good Catholic, and many priests were his friends. The gunmen were a little shy of those padres, who might usually be found in twos and threes at Tommy's home or his training camps. But the mob figured that with a hundred-pound advantage in weight Carnera could take care of Loughran, who was little more than a light heavy-weight and never was a hard hitter. During the fight Carnera hit Loughran more than a dozen of the same uppercuts that had stretched Sharkey twitching on the canvas, and never even reddened Tommy's face. Loughran was a cream-puff puncher and yet he staggered Carnera several times with right hands and was himself never in any kind of danger from a punch. He merely got tired from having Carnera leaning on him for half an hour. If nothing else, that fight beneath the Miami moon exposed how incompetent Carnera was as a bruiser, and how utterly false were the stories about his invincibility, be-sides casting fresh suspicion upon his knockout of Sharkey. We had all seen Loughran put on the floor by a 175-pounder. If a man weighing around 280 pounds, as Primo did for that fight, hit him flush on the jaw and couldn't drop him, and yet had knocked out one of the cleverest heavyweights in the busi-ness, it wasn't hard to arrive at a conclusion. It was obvious that he was a phony and the first stiff-punching heavyweight who was leveling would knock him out.

Max Baer did it the very next summer. The following sum-mer Joe Louis did it again, and then an almost unknown Negro heavyweight by the name of Leroy Haynes accomplished the feat for the third time. And that was the beginning of the end of Primo.

His lucrative campaigns and the winning of the heavyweight championship had enriched everyone connected with him ex-cept poor Primo, who saw very little of the money he earned. There were too many silent partners and "boys" who had little pieces of him. Monsieur See had long since been dispensed with and shipped back to France for his health; he had served his purpose. But it was an evil day for Carnera when they chased Leon back to Paris, for Leon never would have permitted anyone to belt Carnera on his vulnerable chin. As suggested, the little Frenchman had a love for the big fellow whom he had taught and trained and watched over so carefully. The Duffy crowd had no love for anything. Fighters' chins were made to be smacked and they might just as well get used to taking the punches there.

It seemed as though their power was beginning to lose some of its effectiveness, exhausted perhaps by its own virus and viciousness, shortly after they had made Carnera champion. Primo escaped to Italy with his title and nothing else and later returned here for the disastrous fight with Loughran under the guidance of a little Italian banker by the name of Luigi Soresi, who appeared to be genuinely trying to get and keep for poor Carnera some of the money he was making.

The by-products of the Miami affair were typical and pathetic. Duffy and company were living over a Miami night club in style and spending money like water—Primo's money. Carnera was relegated to a cheap cottage back of the town with a trainer. No one really looked after him. No one cared particularly whether he trained or not. He came into the ring against Loughran twenty pounds overweight. Shortly after that, Duffy was clapped into the jug for a spell for some boyish pranks with his income tax, and from the cooler he wrote pleading letters at the time that Carnera was preparing to defend his title against Baer, maintaining that he was needed to guide, advise, and teach Primo, to prime him for the first serious defense of his title, and that he should be given furlough from quod to attend to this matter. Carnera vigorously denied that he needed him. He was only too delighted to have Duffy held in durance vile. Of course what was really killing Uncle Will was that he was where for the first time he couldn't get his fingers on a nice big slice of the sugar that big, stupid Wop would make for boxing Baer.

It is difficult to bag or fix a heavyweight championship prizefight, though it has been done. But in the post-war sports renaissance there was so much money at stake in a heavyweight championship fight that it took more cash than most could produce to purchase either champion or challenger. It stood to reason that if the champion figured to make a million dollars or more out of his title he wasn't going to sell out for any less. Too, the power of the gangs was weakening. Repeal dealt them a terrible blow and took away their chief source of revenue. Three or four years before, Carnera's title would have been safe because his handlers would not have accepted any challenger for the title unless he agreed to preserve the state of the champion's health throughout the encounter. And there were always ways and means of keeping a challenger from double-crossing.

But Duffy was in the sneezer, as the boys sometimes quaintly called the jailhouse, Carnera was broke and needed money. He could only get it by fighting Baer. And the Baer fight could not be fixed. Baer's reputation was good; at least, he had not been caught out in any shady fights. He was a powerful hitter and it was apparent that now at last the rest of us were going to be made privy to what it was that happened when Carnera was struck forcefully on the chin. We didn't have to wait long. He was knocked down three times in the first round, and lost his championship in the eleventh round on a technical knockout when he was helpless, having been knocked down a total of thirteen times during the ten and a half rounds.

Not, however, until he fought and was knocked out by Joe Louis was it apparent what a dreadful thing had been done to this great hulk of a man. Strange to feel pity and sympathy excited for one so gross and enormous and strong. But the out sizes of the world are not the happy men, and their bulk is often of little use or help to them. If anything, it is a handicap when up against the speed and timing and balance of a normal man. Carnera's great strength was practically useless to him in the ring. The hardest blow he could strike was little more than a push. True, if he caught you in a corner he could club you insensible, but no smart fighter is caught in corners, and the big man was never fast enough anyway to catch anyone but out-and-out tramps.

When he fought Joe Louis he was defensively but little better than he was the first time I saw him, which, as it happened, was not in Madison Square Garden, but in the smoky, stuffy, subterranean Salle Wagram, a little fight club in Paris where I happened to be one evening when Jeff Dickson was promoting a fight between Primo Carnera, who had then been fighting a little less than a year, and one Moise Bouquillon, a light heavyweight who weighed 174 pounds. Monsieur See was experimenting a little with his giant. It was obvious that Bouquillon was going to be unable to hurt him very much, but what I noted that evening and never forgot was that the giant was likewise unable to hurt the little Frenchman. Curiously, that fight was almost an exact duplicate of the one that Carnera as champion later fought with Loughran. Walter (Good-Time Charley) Friedman was there too. Many years later he told me quite frankly: "Boy, was that a lousy break for us that you come walking into that Salle Wagram that night and see that the big guy can't punch! Just that night you hadda be there. Leon wanted to see if he could go ten rounds without falling down. And you hadda be there. We coulda got away with a lot more if you don't walk in there and write stories about how he can't punch."

Joe Louis slugged Carnera into bleating submission, cruelly and brutally. Handsome Uncle Will Duffy was back in his corner again, jawing angrily at him when he was led trembling and quivering back to his chair after the referee had saved him again, one side of his mouth smashed in, dazed and dripping blood. The very first right-hand punch Louis hit him broke Carnera's mouth and hurt him dreadfully.

Here, then, was the complete sell. He had nothing. His title was gone, his money squandered by the gang. And the one thing he thought he had, an unbeatable skill in defense and an irresistible crushing power in attack that no man living could withstand, never existed. It was a fable as legendary as the great giants of mythology that he resembled. The carrion birds that had fed upon this poor, big, dumb man had picked him clean. They had left him nothing, not even his pride and his self-respect, and that probably was the cruelest thing of all.

In his last fight, the one with Haynes, he was again severely beaten about the head. One of his legs refused to function. The fight was stopped. While he lay in the hospital in New York for treatment, as I have said, he lay alone.

I often wonder what that hulk of a man thinks today as he looks back over the manner in which he was swindled, tricked and cheated at every turn, as he recalls the great sums of money that he earned, all of it gone beyond recall. The world has no place for him, not even as a freak in a circus, from whence he emerged and where he might happily have spent his life and become prosperous. Because as a giant, a terror and a horror, he stands exposed as a poor, unwilling fraud who was no man-killer at all, but a rather helpless, sad creature who, when slugged by a 185-pound mortal, either toppled stricken to the floor or staggered about or bled or had to be saved from annihilation by a third man who obligingly stepped between him and his tormentors.

He was born far, far too late. He belonged to the twelfth or thirteenth century, when he would have been a man-at-arms and a famous fellow with mace and halberd, pike or bill. At least he would have fought nobly and to the limit of his great strength, properly armed, because Carnera was a courageous fellow to the limit of his endurance, game and a willing fighter when aroused. In those days he would have won honor afield and would have got himself decently killed, or, surviving, would have been retired by his feudal lord to round out his days and talk over the old brave fights.

Today there is nothing left for this man but reflection upon his humiliations. He was just a big sucker whom the wise guys took and trimmed. What an epitaph for one who came from the ancient and noble race of giants.

All this took place in our country, Anno Domini 1930–1935.

VI

ONE HERO

THE SPORTS-WRITER has few if any heroes. We create many because it is our business to do so, but we do not believe in them. We know them too well. We are concerned as often, sometimes, with keeping them and their weaknesses and pecca-dillos out of the paper as we are with putting them in. We see them with their hair down in the locker-rooms, dressing-rooms, or their homes. Frequently we come quite unawares upon little meannesses. When they fall from grace we are usually the first to know it, and when their patience is tried, it is generally to us that they are rude and ill-tempered. We sing of their mus-cles, their courage, their gameness, and their skill because it seems to amuse readers and sells papers, but we rarely consider them as people and, strictly speaking, leave their characters alone because that is dangerous ground.

Also, we grow up with them and see them change from pleas-ant and sometimes unspoiled youngsters into grievous public pets, boors, snobs, and false figures. I am, by nature, a hero-worshipper, as, I guess, most of us are, but in all the years of contact with the famous ones of sport I have found only one that would stand up in every way as a gentleman as well as a celebrity, a fine, decent, human being as well as a newsprint personage, and who never once, since I have known him, has let me down in my estimate of him. That one is Robert Tyre Jones, Jr., the golf-player from Atlanta, Georgia. And Jones in his day was considered the champion of champions—in other words, better and more perfect at playing his game than any of the other champions were at theirs. He was the best golf-player the world has ever known, and still is, because no one has yet appeared capable of challenging his record.

Probably no celebrity in sport ever attracted quite so much attention or was so dominating a figure and yet remained completely unspoiled. Jones even had his own personal Boswell, Mr. O. B. Keeler of the Atlanta *Journal*, one of the better sports-writers. For a great many years Keeler reported on Jones almost exclusively. Jones was hero-worshipped by Atlantans and the golf public generally nearly *ad nauseam*, and yet he never lost his head or permitted it to swell. In Scotland and England, where he played in tournaments, the natives practically made a god out of him. He remained unaffected. He was exposed to the attacks of the most ill-bred and ruthless pests in the world, the curiosity-seeking golf nuts and autograph-hunters, and his privacy was assailed from morning until night. He never in all his career could engage in a friendly golf match (except on his home course) without being followed and swamped with attention and, more often, annoyance. Yet I never heard of his being deliberately rude. The only thing I think he ever permitted himself to do when chivvied and harassed beyond human endurance, particularly during an important tournament, was quietly to turn and walk away.

He has a record of some ten years' contact with press and public and the golf world, in which, to my knowledge, he never once said the wrong thing in any public utterance or interview, never insulted anyone or hurt the feelings of any sect, organization, or people. I have never known him deliberately to lie to the press, the common fault of every newspaper celebrity. He had a gorgeous instinct for doing the right thing—such as asking to be permitted to leave the trophy representing the British Open Championship in the keeping of the Royal and Ancient Golf Club at St. Andrews, Scotland, where he won it. He made the Scotch love him as one of their own.

He was a good loser, but even a better winner. And he had

the almost unbelievable intelligence and grace to quit after his greatest accomplishment, his grand slam of 1930, when he won the amateur and open championships of Great Britain and the United States, the four major tournaments of the golf world.

Withal, he was no prig or goody-goody. He was wholly a real man. He could enjoy a good, clean, dirty story, if you know what I mean. He smoked. He swore when the occasion demanded it, and he didn't offer a polite substitute, but talked straight and salty without the prissy apologies and sly looks with which certain types of celebrities usually accompany cussing, looks that are intended to mean: "I am a famous personage known all over the country, but just a plain fellow at bottom. Look, I said 'damn.'" A golf ball from the time it is hit until it comes to earth again remains in the air just a fraction over six seconds. I have heard Jones (when playing privately, of course) crowd an amazing number of descriptive adjectives pertaining to the shot, the ball, and himself into that comparatively brief space of time.

I have seen Jones sit in the locker-room with his gang after a hard round or match, and get pleasantly tiddled on corn whisky, his favorite drink. But he drank as he did everything else, like a gentleman of breeding. I doubt whether anyone ever saw him drunk. But he knew as does everybody else that the real delight of golf occurs after the game, when the hot shower with the ice-cold finish has cooled and refreshed, and the gang gathers in the locker-room and sits around drinking highballs, bragging, moaning over lost shots, and telling lies. This was the part of the game that Jones loved best, and he was always to be found in a corner of the locker-room after the play, surrounded by a few friends, relaxing from the high nerve-tension of tournament golf, with a highball and a cigarette.

Few people realize that Jones played golf under a very curious handicap. Nobody hated him, outside of the few who were jealous of his success and his bearing. He was probably one of the best-loved athletes who ever went into competition. Every step that he took on a golf course from the time he first came to fame, back in 1923, was dogged by worshipping and well-meaning friends who played every stroke with him, moaned and sympathized when he went into traps or trouble, cheered every success, and clung to him as though he was their prophet. Well, he was, too. It must be remembered that he was a living example and proof that this very cranky and cantankerous game can be played. Some of these friends, especially the oldest ones from Atlanta, he loved very much. They were like family to him. Many of them used to place large wagers on him to win. And from the time he discovered how much his winning meant to them, mainly in affection and pride—ever so much more than it meant to him—he was a miserable man.

An atmosphere of sweetness and light throughout is of no particular value to a competitor at anything. The blade is whetted to a much keener edge if there is a little snarling opposition in the crowd, something to fight, something to whip. Jones's galleries were practically one hundred per cent for Jones. And his friends, unwittingly, but just as effectively, nevertheless, piled up the tension on his nerves. Somehow, they fed their own egos upon his triumphs, where Jones fed his not at all. There was a Jones cult that was truly amazing. It went about maintaining that Jones was the greatest player that ever lived, the most perfect stylist, the finest shot-maker, etc., etc. All this was very close to the truth, but it was tough on Jones. A great deal of the time he played under a strain that turned him sick to the stomach out on the course, owing to his desire not to let his friends down. He never took anything but a cup of soup between rounds because he couldn't keep it down. He used to play with what looked like a very sulky and ill-tempered expression around his mouth. He was neither sulky nor ill-tempered. He was concentrated on getting the ball down the hole and fighting off nausea.

He went on playing big-time golf long after tournaments must have ceased to be any joy or pleasure to him whatsoever, purely for the sake of his friends, because they would have been so disappointed had he not entered. Any time he played, it was Jones against the field, and the field was liable to run second in the betting, which of course was all wrong. The field was out over the hills by itself, playing in comparative quiet, while Jones more often than not had from five to eight thousand semi-lunatics trampling at his heels and swarming over the right of way, or running up and trying to pat his shoulder, or shouting encouragement to him on the walk between divot and ball. Bless them, they all loved him and brought him nothing but worship. He couldn't very well have been cross with them even if he had been the type that is cross with anybody. They only wished him well—and therefore came close to making a nervous wreck out of him.

He was born Robert Tyre Jones, Jr., but millions of people knew him merely as Bobby—Bobby Jones. And he hated the name Bobby. If he knew you well, he would sometimes dryly request that you call him Bob, and not Bobby. From the crowd he accepted the Bobby as it was meant, a diminutive of affection. This is a trivial and unimportant item until you try to picture yourself going through life eternally being hailed by a name that you thoroughly detest. And it is the same with signing autographs.

The average man is not requested for his autograph, except on a check, more than once or twice in his life, and those few times it is heady and tasty wine. But no one who has not been through the mill has even the faintest notion of how wearing on the nerves and exasperating the constant and unremitting request for autographs becomes. Most of the time they are no requests at all, but a command. Paper and pencil are merely shoved under the nose of the celebrity, no matter what he is doing or how he may be engaged. If he refuses to sign, he is a snob and stuck up and his popularity suffers. If he signs the first few to be agreeable, he is lost. As fast as he scribbles his name, fresh pieces of paper are thrust at him, filthy scraps picked up from the floor, backs of envelopes, ticket stubs, old visiting-cards, menus, programs, match-covers, anything that is handy. They come from the front and the side, and from around his neck. It is a sort of fever that runs through a crowd. Not one in ten is a real autograph-collector. It is more as though they were seeking a talisman or fetish. Jones's patience always amazed me. He was the only celebrity I ever knew who was prepared to accept as gracefully as possible every penalty there is to be paid for fame and publicity in the United States.

This patience extended likewise to golf pests, nuts, casual acquaintances, and crashers of every kind. Nobody in my hearing ever talked to Jones about anything but golf. Have you any conception of how thoroughly maddening this might come to be? Ever since he won his first championship he has listened to either pleas for advice, or dull, long-winded stories about what Whosis (the narrator, of course) did at a certain hole on the tough Whatsis course, where his ball lay, with a full description of the hazards and horrors that surrounded it, where the green was situated, where the big tree was, what club Whosis selected, how he stood, what he thought, what the situation of the game was, how he swung, and what were the results. And the cadging for advice usually followed on top of that, beginning with the detested "Bobby," and going on interminably with "Do you think if I held my hands like this" (business of holding hands like that) "and got my hip around this way" (contortion of getting hip around) "that I could straighten myself out?"

Every visitor of any prominence who ever came through Atlanta immediately pulled every wire possible to get an invitation to play a round of golf with Jones, and here again Jones hated to refuse the requests for such games made by friends. And so he would be yanked away from business (he was at one time a practicing lawyer) or his pleasure, to play around the course with some impossible and execrable dub who scuffed and sclaffed and shanked and hacked his way around. Patiently Jones would play around with him, always waiting and hoping for the one good shot that would enable him to bestow the accolade: "Fine shot, partner!" Oh yes, they were always Jones's partners. ·And that remark was more treasured than a citation from the President would have been. The dubs went home in an ecstasy and rehearsed the story: "So we come up to the sixteenth. Bobby and I are partners—you know Bobby Jones, of course—and he hooked his drive into the rough, but I laid my third, stiff, and he called out: 'Fine shot, partner,' just like that. Of course he got his four too, but he said I took the pressure off him. Yeah, we won."

But Jones wasn't even a golf snob. Actually he never cared how badly a man played or how insufferable a duffer he was, provided that he was good fun, a pleasant companion, could tell merry stories, and didn't take the game or himself too seriously. Several of his favorite golfing companions play in the nineties and hundreds. It didn't matter if it wasn't golf as long as it was fun.

But most of the visitors who wangled a game with Jones were so anxious to make a showing that what little game they had immediately fell apart and the harder they tried, the worse they got and the more embarrassed and flustered. Jones was never anything but kind. I would give much to know from what limitless wells he drew patience, courtesy, and restraint. A 105 player would no more have thought of approaching his low-handicap club foursome and asking to be taken around than he would of calling up Lindbergh and asking for a hop. But Jones was fair game all his golfing life (and still is, for that matter) for every duffer with sufficient social or business standing to make a match with Jones possible.

Before I knew Jones well, early in my sports-writing career, I was sent down to Atlanta by a national magazine, assigned to play a round of golf with him and report what it was like to play with the great one. Bob agreed to a game. (I was still a cub then and quite unknown as either a writer or columnist, but it made no difference to Jones. Later, on a similar assignment, Helen Wills refused to play with me.) He invited two of his friends and we went out to East Lake, his home course. Nervous, self-conscious, and badly frightened, I blew up on the first tee and stayed blown for the entire eighteen holes except that

I went higher each hole. I doubt whether I ever suffered so acutely in all my life. But I learned something about Jones in that round. Towards the end, after taking nine to get close to the green, I botched my niblick approach, cutting the legs out from under the ball instead of hitting it properly, but with astonishing results, because the ball rose into the air, dropped two feet from the pin, and stayed there. Jones sneaked a great sigh of relief and said: "Fine shot, partner. Well played." And then we looked at each other. His face was all properly regulated respect and mingled admiration and serious pleasure at having been permitted to witness such a miraculous demonstration of a difficult game, but there was something funny going on at the corners of his mouth. I guess I must have had a strange expression too, because suddenly we both fell down on the green and howled with laughter, and after that everything was all right.

I do not remember ever knowing a happier and more warming relationship to exist between father and son than there is between Bob and Dad Jones, or, as he is better known, "The Colonel." "Dad Jones," somehow, on paper sounds sticky, sentimental and made-to-order, but it isn't, the way Jones says it. They are always hugely amused at each other. They are golfing companions and drinking companions. His father's golf and golfing troubles are a constant delight to Jones. He would probably rather play with his father in a foursome than with anyone else because the Colonel gets so mad. Having shared in the creation of the perfect golfing machine, Jones Senior is always a little at a loss to understand his own shortcomings and blames them on the game or the clubs or the wind. Bob loves to stand and listen to his father talk to a ball in flight. The Colonel plays around in the eighties, but is always having trouble with his game in one department or another and comes plaintively and grudgingly to his son for readjustment. After a few highballs in the locker-room he likes to sing quartets, and if in the post-tournament clink, hubbub, and clatter of the locker-rooms the slightly off-key strains of "Oh honey, honey, bless yo' ha'ht," arise at the far end of the room, it is as likely as not to be the two Joneses, arms around one another, with two pals, bent over close, brows almost touching, doing swipes.

One ought not, I suppose, to write about Jones without mentioning his record and his golf game. He played in thirteen amateur championships in the United States, won five of them, and twice finished second. The closest approach to that performance was turned in by Jerry Travers, who won the event four times, but in an era when competition was not nearly as keen. Playing as an amateur against the best golf professionals in the world, Jones won four U. S. Open Golf Championships and four times finished second out of eleven trials. There is no record in modern high-pressure golf to equal this, although back in the early nineteen-hundreds one Willie Anderson won the championship five times. But in those days 314 for seventy-two holes was good enough. In Jones's day nothing over three hundred had a chance. The British Amateur was the hardest title for Jones to win, and he succeeded in winning it only once out of three times, but he took three out of the four British Open Championships in which he competed. And finally there was of course the grand slam of the four major championships in one year. The odds against his completing the slam when he started out were almost incalculable, because instead of decreasing each time he won one, they increased.

But I find the story going dead at this point when I quote figures of play or try to explain Jones's swing or the simple, efficient mechanics he employed to lace a golf ball far and accurately. It has always seemed to me that as a golf-player Jones was something of a physical freak. In his physical make-up he quite accidentally combined all the necessary qualities of perfect co-ordination, sense of rhythm, balance, and timing that are needed to play the exasperating and elusive game of golf with anything approaching perfection. If such perfection could be acquired solely by study and practice, all of the professional players who earn their living by golf would have it. Of course Jones also had the mental equipment, a fine competitive temperament, and great powers of concentration.

But I find the personality and character of the man far more fascinating than his golf. While I enjoy playing, if I can find three companionable lunatics, I think that golf is essentially a silly game, especially in the light of the fuss and bother that are made over it, and the "Whosis came thundering down the fairway, his mashie flashing like a gleaming sword, his shots cannonading into the cup," type of golf-reporting always made me a little ill. I remember following Jones around many a golf course, admiring the power of his drives, the startling precision of his approaches, and the uncanny line and speed of his putts, and thrilling, likewise, to some of his sub-par bursts such as his five threes in a row at Winged Foot one year, one of them an eagle on a par-five hole, but I think I was much more excited at discovering that in Jones I had at last found a crack performer and a real champion who had a genuine sense of humor and gift of laughter.

Of the famous sportsmen or women, top-flight athletes or champions, of whom that could be said, there were very few. Somehow, laughter does not seem to lie close to the surface of champions. They are for the most part dull and solemn dodos. Probably if they had any humor or sense of the ridiculous whatsoever they could never go on to become champions and live the life and do some of the things that are required of such people. Most athletes take themselves dead seriously. You generally find the laughing ones in the second flight. There have been many athletes with a sense of fun, or who were pranksters or, at worst, out and out practical jokers. (Vinnie Richards had a good sense of humor and I suspect it didn't help him any. He was never national singles champion.) But the only one I can ever remember who had a deep, bubbling, impish, joyous, creative sense of humor was the quiet little golfer from Atlanta. And it probably accounted for most of his virtues.

He is a small man and would be inclined to be chunky if he let himself go. He is good-looking in a pleasant, square-jawed way. He is not heavily muscled. His speech is slow and pleas-

antly but not affectedly Southern. His wit is quick, sharp, darting, typically and characteristically American, and, as with all
men of real, sound humor, directed mostly at himself. Also it
is without malice except where a little malice occasionally is
needed.

I suspect that the Jones humor has been what has really got
him through all these trying years—and if you don't think it is
trying to be a celebrity in our country, wait until you manage to
chin yourself four hundred times or outsit everyone else on a
flagpole—when at times the assaults on his nerves, good nature,
and good manners would otherwise have been unbearable. It
would not be fair to say that Jones never took himself seriously.
When he entered a tournament he entered to win. He was
quite willing to admit that he did not like to lose. But his sense
of the eternal ridiculous lay very close to the surface and I think
he often saw himself as a slightly comic figure that did things
that amused him vastly. People who are able successfully to
laugh at themselves are able to take a great amount more of
punishment and abuse than the humorless crew. It takes much
more to snap the temper of a man who can read something
funny into any and every situation. Well, what more can I say
for my hero? He was a gentleman and there was laughter in his
heart and on his lips, and he loved his friends.

VII

BY HORATIO

ALGER, JR.

JAMES JOSEPH TUNNEY was once an unknown, no-account clerk in a Greenwich Village office in New York City, a quiet, undistinguished, good-looking Irish boy who might barely be listed as living on the fringe of the white-collar class. He belonged to the great unidentified mass, and his importance except to himself was nil.

James Joseph became Gene Tunney, heavyweight boxing champion of the world, who was paid one million dollars for a single performance, married a wealthy society girl, and retired from the ring as undefeated heavyweight champion. No fictional story ever based on the beloved from-rags-to-riches theme was ever more unbelievably fantastic or more characteristic of the cockeyed post-war sports period that made it possible. Twenty-five years ago it could not have happened. It took war, post-war inflation, an unprecedented sports mania, the weirdest assortment of characters ever gathered beneath one tent—and Gene Tunney, himself probably the most remarkable of all the people who were featured in the success story to end all success stories.

The dramatis personæ of this goofy comedy are themselves sufficiently astonishing, but they all figured in the final happy ending and contributed in one way or another to it.

First there was the hero, Gene Tunney, one of the handsomest men who ever laced on a boxing glove, the Leyendecker Arrow Collar man of the advertisements come to life. The heroine was Polly Lauder, Greenwich, Connecticut, society girl, social registerite, allied to the Carnegie millions. The heavy was Jack Dempsey, heavyweight champion of the world, the most feared and colorful character of the modern prize-ring. The deus ex machina was Tex Rickard, former faro dealer and far-West gambling-house proprietor become the world's greatest promoter of prizefights, and included in the cast were the United States Marines; Georges Carpentier, boulevardier, manufacturer of boxes designed to hold Camembert cheese, ex-soldier of France, and light-heavyweight prizefighter; Maxie Boo-Boo Hoff, Philadelphia underworld boss, dabbler in prizefight promotions, and alleged proprietor of an imposing string of maisons de joie; William L. Muldoon, a reformed wrestler turned anti-tobacco crusader, health-farm proprietor, and member of the New York State Athletic Commission; James J. Farley, a small-time state politician from Haverstraw, New York, a whistle stop along the Hudson, a member of the boxing commission, and eventually Postmaster General of the United States of America; Al Capone, America's greatest gangster and robber baron, now a guest in the nation's most impregnable cooler, Alcatraz; Estelle Taylor, a glamorous motion-picture queen; Sam Pryor, a hero-worshipping semi-social American business man from Greenwich, Connecticut, who went abroad with the A.E.F.; Bill McCabe, a connoisseur of prizefighters, likewise a soldier; Billy Gibson, an old-time fight manager, once manager of Benny Leonard, lightweight champion of the world; Dave Barry, a referee with a poor sense of time; Italian Jack Herman, a mediocre prizefighter with a spotty record; Harry Wills, a Negro prizefighter and perpetual heavyweight-championship contender; and a chorus and assortment of walk-ons consisting of millionaires, socialites, bums, gangsters, promoters, fighters, and fight managers, not ever forgetting John Q. Public, who paid the freight.

The plot in itself was simple. Young American boy, who has done a little boxing with no particular success, enlists in the Marine Corps when war comes, and goes to France, where he wins the light heavyweight championship of the American Expeditionary Force and makes admiring friends who upon his return continue acquaintance and one of whom, a wealthy business man, introduces him to a fine girl with whom he falls in love, but who is out of his reach because of position and wealth. Decides he can hurdle the social barrier, but must be a millionaire in his own right before he can ask her to marry him. Self-educates himself, wins heavyweight championship of the world, makes a million dollars, weds the girl.

But the incredible feature of the tale is that where the amassing of a million dollars for a man who starts with nothing may be considered a lifetime job, Gene Tunney did it in forty minutes by the clock. The times, the age, the situation, the strange characters who wandered in and out of his story, made it possible for him to earn that amount in a single ten-round contest, win the contest, and retire from the ring undefeated and wealthy.

There are those who believe that the time, the place, the era, and the accidental components of any situation are unimportant, that it is the man that counts and that he would triumph or gain his end under any set of circumstances. The story of Tunney makes out a hard case for this philosophy. There were disquiet, ambition, and courage in his soul, but he needed the war, Tex Rickard, Jack Dempsey, the million-dollar gates and the wildest spendingest era in the history of the country to help him. Without them he might still be totting up columns of figures on his high stool, or at best have become one of the many minor pugilists who clutter up the record-books for a time and then vanish into the limbo whence they came.

So many extraneous events influenced his plot. It was Muldoon and Farley, the New York boxing commissioners, who first insisted that Dempsey fight Harry Wills, the Negro, before any other contender, and then outlawed the match in New

York State. This gave rise to the circumstances that made Rickard sign Tunney as challenger, giving him his chance, and taking the match to Philadelphia, where it was fought in a pouring rain, a circumstance that certainly was no aid to Dempsey or his style. Or suppose that Dempsey had not met and married Estelle Taylor, with the result that he became estranged from his manager, Jack Kearns. There are many who believe that had Kearns trained Dempsey and been in his corner that soaking night in Philadelphia, events might have turned out differently. But would they, at that? There is documentary evidence that Tunney signed a pact with Maxie Hoff, boss of the Philadelphia nether regions, in which Hoff was to give Tunney what is known as "protection."

Had Tunney not fought in the A.E.F., he never would have made the contacts that eventually led him to his love-affair and his bride. And had Dempsey not allied himself with Al Capone in Chicago at the time of their second fight, Dave Barry, who gave Tunney the long count, never would have been in the ring that night. Davey Miller was the number-one referee around Chicago in those days. But Davey was Capone's man, and too blatantly so. The situation outraged the Chicago boxing commission sufficiently to give it courage to buck Capone, keep Miller out of the ring, and substitute Barry, with the results that are history. Miller would have counted Tunney out.

Scandal fogged Tunney at every turn on his way to the top, because boxing is a scandalous game, but somehow it never managed to hurt him and he always stepped clear of it. Hoff sued him and produced the agreement bearing Tunney's signature. After Tunney knocked out Italian Jack Herman, a newspaper charged that Herman had succumbed to the good old push to the shoulder-blade, a libelous statement if untrue, especially since it was intimated that the Tunney management had engineered the deal. Nothing ever came of that, and nobody ever knew whether it was true or false. I once asked Tunney point-blank about it and he replied with considerable logic:

"Why bother to fix that one? If I can't knock out all the Italian Jack Hermans there are, one after the other, I'd never put on another glove."

Just what "protection" Hoff was to have given him, or did give him, never developed because when the bell rang for the first fight with Dempsey to begin, it turned out that it was Dempsey and not Tunney who needed protection. There was nothing particularly remarkable about the fact that a prizefighter should have made a deal for assistance in a strange town. The help that gangsters could give to prizefighters was always problematical, but most fighters preferred not to take chances. The remarkable thing is that the same young man could contract two alliances separated by a distance greater than that between the two poles—Boo-Boo Hoff and the Lauder family— and get away with both. The qualities of Gene Tunney I suspect have never been fully appreciated. Coming from the middle stratum, he was neither gangster nor hoodlum nor blueblood, but apparently he was able to use the one connection as a stepping-stone to the other. Only an Irishman could try that. And only an exceptionally strong character could get away with it. There was never any weakness in Tunney. He always knew what he wanted and how to play the game to get it. But it takes an unusual man to play a dirty game to attain clean ends and not suffer damage from it. Not that Tunney played a deliberately dirty game during his fighting career, but no one ever got to the top of a game as essentially foul and unprincipled as prizefighting with absolutely clean hands. Tunney was always very badly misjudged, and by those of us who were closest to him and to boxing. From where we sat, it looked as though he were a prizefighter, a common pug with a decidedly snobbish and unpuglike desire to mingle with his betters. The truth was that Tunney was far from common. He was in many ways an idealist. He was always ambitious and preferred the company of pleasant people to toughs. But he had the great strength of character to take that little stroll through the sewer when there was no other way. His end always justified the means, to him. His curious associations were made not from choice, but from necessity.

The story-book hero goes through life resisting every temptation and preferring to sacrifice himself rather than abandon his ideals, and we like to read about him because it is such a pretty picture; but we know that in life it doesn't work that way and that all strong men and great men, with few exceptions, have had, at one time or another in their careers, the strength to do something to attain an end that they would prefer to forget once the end is reached. And it is only when they fail to attain that end that they are not forgiven. I maintain that it takes extraordinary strength for a man constitutionally decent and essentially idealistic temporarily to abandon those ideals for eventual better service to them. It is more Machiavellian than Christian, but disciples of Messer Niccolò's recipe rule the earth today. We may not admire it, but we recognize it. Tunney apparently had that strength when he needed it. When it was possible to ply his trade decently, he did.

Probably no athlete ever has had to take the public beating that fell to Tunney on his way to realizing his ambitions. He was caught groping for light, serenity, and education and ridiculed for it. He probably never knew it, but he was paying the penalty for violating a popular concept—that of the pugilist. The only serious mistake he ever made in his career was when he let his managers, for publicity, trade on his genuine appetite for education and beauty. Again we all mistook the real Tunney for the false, and the false for the real. We kidded him nearly to oblivion about Shakspere and books because we thought it was a phony pose. But that wasn't the part that was phony. That was real. It was the pugilist that was false. Tunney was always an artificial fighter. He never in all his career in the ring made a natural movement. For that very reason he was one of the most correct fighters the ring has ever known and one of the best boxers. He only lost one fight in his entire career, and that, properly enough, to unorthodoxy. He was soundly thrashed by the wholly unpredictable Harry Greb. But it is an indication of Tunney's mental capacity and powers of study that he demanded a return fight with Greb and reversed the decision.

Certainly Tunney overplayed his rapidly acquired learning, but no more than any college sophomore. He was so avid for education that he never bothered with selection. He took it all in, in great gulps. He took so much in that some of it had to spill over. This phase would have been unnoticed had he been on a campus. But he was by choice and profession a prizefighter, and the effect against that background was comic and sometimes even a little pathetic, had any of us been attuned to pathos.

When the typical denizen of the fight world said bitterly: "That Tunney! Thinks we're not good enough for him . . ." he was quite right. It was exactly what Tunney thought. And they weren't good enough, either, but I don't believe Tunney ever lost much time brooding over it, because it doesn't take much to be better than the average citizen of Cauliflower Alley. He was accused of base ingratitude to the fine game that had made him, because he had the intelligence and strength of character to escape from it before boxing had a chance to exhibit its usual form of gratitude to the men who participate in it—jiggly legs, stuttering tongue, failing sight, and an empty purse.

Tunney was thoroughly unspectacular in the ring, but he was workmanlike and efficient. Boxing actually is a science, and Tunney studied it from that angle. If there was any truth in the scientific angle, it could, with study, application, and practice, be made to serve his purpose. Fighters like Dempsey and Joe Louis and others too numerous to list are natural battlers. Their styles are developed from within themselves and suited to their physical abilities and temperaments, and all of them have weaknesses which eventually prove their undoing. It is safe to say that in the ring Tunney had no weaknesses. He made occasional mistakes—*vide* the time Dempsey put him down in that historical eighth round in Chicago; but no one is ever perfect. His style was correct by the book. When he knocked men out as he did Carpentier and Tom Gibbons and Tom Heeney, it was because he hit them so often compared to the number of times they were able to hit him that eventually they collapsed from the accumulative and numbing effect of steady punishment. He would have knocked Dempsey out both times, in Philadelphia as well as Chicago, had the fights gone fifteen rounds instead of ten. Dempsey was on the verge of collapse at the end of each fight.

Before he was ever matched with Dempsey for the title, Tunney once said to Ned Brown, a newspaperman: "I've seen Dempsey fight and I was impressed with his lack of knowledge of boxing. He knows so little about the science of boxing that I'll surely knock him out if I ever get the opportunity to fight him. I'm not saying that Dempsey is not a great fighter. He is just that, a great natural fighter, but I'm certain that I can outbox him. He's got to hit you to beat you, and he won't hit me —that is, not with any of the pile-driver punches that he has landed on the others. He couldn't do much with Tom Gibbons. I knocked out Gibbons, and Dempsey couldn't. I know I'm a faster and straighter hitter than Dempsey. Jack never was much of a stayer. By that I mean he fights so fast in the early part of the bout that he tires quickly. Generally by the time he tires he has the other fellow all in too. Witness the Willard and Dempsey fight. Jack was almost as all in at the finish as Willard was. When he fights me he'll not be hitting me, and I will be hitting him—and hitting him hard, too. That is, of course, if I'm ever lucky enough to meet him in the ring."

That sort of talk drew loud and raucous laughter from the cognoscenti and experts, most of whom were as far off in their predictions of the outcome of the first Dempsey-Tunney fight as they were when they prophesied that Joe Louis, a natural fighter, would annihilate Max Schmeling, another chap who knew more than a little about boxing. But the interview was an exact description of what actually happened when Tunney and Dempsey *did* meet—barring the knockout. And the bout was too short for that. Dempsey could not have gone two more rounds in Philadelphia.

Tunney left nothing to chance. His style was orthodox and correct, straight left-hand leads and straight right-hand crosses delivered from the shoulder, the fastest punch there is and one that will always beat a hooker. Schmeling used it to beat hooker Louis. Tunney worked for years hardening his hands, chopping trees, doing manual labor, strengthening the bones, pickling them in brine to harden the skin, because they were the weapons of his trade. Three fourths of the fighters in the business know nothing about taking care of their hands and as the result lose thousands of dollars annually through being laid up with injuries to their knuckles, thumbs, or wrists. Tunney was the only fighter I ever knew who spent hours on the road, practicing *running backwards*, because when a fighter goes into retreat in the ring, he moves in that direction and that direction only. His famous retreat from Dempsey and a certain knockout after he got up off the floor in Chicago may have been unromantic, but it was effective and masterly. He was prepared for it.

His care of his body was as efficient as his study of the art of self-defense. He knew that without condition and perfect training he could not carry out the maneuvers demanded by the science for survival and victory. He also knew that he must always be in shape to withstand punishment, as the boxer has not yet been born who can go into a fifteen-round fight, carry any kind of an attack, and not have to take a certain amount of punches. Tunney took as few as was humanly possible.

The night before he broke his camp at Stroudsburg, Pennsylvania, in the Pocono Mountains, where he trained for his first fight with Dempsey, he did a thing that was characteristic. And he did it practically in privacy. Only one or two of the boxing-writers were there. What was the use of too much coverage? He was going to be knocked out by Dempsey anyway.

Tunney in his final workout took on three of his best sparring partners for a round each and never let a punch go the entire time, but contented himself merely with blocking, slipping, and ducking punches. I had a little boxing-writer on the job down there by the name of Jackie Farrell. Farrell reported to me that it was the most marvelous exhibition he had ever seen anywhere, any time. Tunney boxed the entire nine minutes, consecutively and without a rest, one man after the other, each spar-mate attacking him for three minutes, and in that time not one solid punch was landed on him. It didn't seem possible, but it happened. I wish I had listened to Farrell. I picked Dempsey.

Tunney's faults were all those of youth, tactlessness, a devastating frankness, and inability to conceal his dislikes. If he was a social climber as he was always accused of being, at least he was consistent at it, and he got there. I have thought lately that Tunney was always smart enough to know that many of the crew of socially prominent and wealthy millionaires, as they were called in the fight racket, were patronizing him because he was a famous personage and the heavyweight champion of the world, and it was at the time fashionable to consort with prizefighters, but he was also smart enough to get his back out of them. He used them as much as they used him. Someone had told him or he found out for himself that if you can manage to consort with money long enough some of it will eventually rub off onto you. But many fine people genuinely liked Gene because he was a likable personality.

Eventually the public that once despised him caught on to the fact that by and large, as men are in this far from perfect world, he was a pretty good specimen. Two years ago I got him to make one of his rare public appearances. We had invited a team of English amateur boxers to come to the United States and meet our Golden Gloves team in an international match at the Yankee Stadium. I wanted a referee who understood boxing and who could be trusted to be scrupulously impartial to a guest as well as home boy, who would know what he was looking at and call them as he saw them. I went to Gene Tunney and asked him to take on the job. He was a little diffident as to what his reception might be. But I had a hunch, and it was the right one. When Tunney was announced as the referee and climbed through the ropes, the fifty thousand odd people in the stadium rose and cheered him for ten minutes. He had never received an ovation like that before. It came a little late, but must have been a great satisfaction nevertheless.

VIII

SHOOT THE

MILLION

THERE HAVE been in the past years just five prizefight gates that ran to a million dollars or over, and William Harrison Dempsey figured in all of them. When he departed from the sports stage a great many in the audience got up and left too, because the million-dollar gates came to an end when he stopped prizefighting in public. The next act was Tunney versus Tom Heeney of Australia for the heavyweight championship of the world, and it drew only $691,014. The year was 1928, the time midsummer, still a year before the crash. That fight, as well as the previous ones, the million-dollar gates, were all of them promoted by George L. (Tex) Rickard, the former faro dealer from Texas, via Nome, who became the world's greatest prizefight promoter.

Rickard and Dempsey are inseparably knit together in the American phenomenon of the million-dollar gate. The story of what lay behind these fantastic receipts has to me always been a fascinating one. I have never seen it written.

Which took the lead, star or showman? Did Rickard affix himself to Dempsey's kite, or vice versa? Neither. Each complemented the other perfectly. There was the era, the time, the money—and the two men, and the luck of a host of contributory circumstances.

In five fights promoted by Tex Rickard, Dempsey, with the collaboration of Georges Carpentier of France, Luis Angel Firpo of the Argentine, Gene Tunney of New York, twice, and Jack Sharkey of Boston, drew a total of $8,600,000. The first million-dollar fight on record was the strange brawl between Dempsey and Carpentier in Jersey City on July 2, 1921, two years after the end of the war. It furnishes us with many of the clues to the secret of the million-dollar gates. High water mark for this manner of squandering money was reached on the 22nd of September 1927 when the second Dempsey-Tunney fight drew $2,658,000 cash money, out of which, to the everlasting pride or shame of the era, depending upon how you look at it, for a performance lasting thirty minutes by delicately balanced stop watches, Gene Tunney was paid a cool million dollars, the highest wage ever earned by a professional athlete in modern times.

If in the telling of this story Rickard appears to overshadow Dempsey in his contributions to this great social achievement, it must be remembered that Dempsey was always the constant in any situation, the vital, animating, unchangeable factor. Rickard played the cards, but the ace of spades was, as it always is, the highest card in the deck. Dempsey was it.

The million-dollar gate may be explained rather simply. It came quite naturally when Rickard made prizefighting not only respectable, but universally interesting and essentially dramatic. He did this in many ways, but chiefly by either a lucky accident or an astute piece of reasoning. Rickard was a crude, self-made man, a gambler and showman. He was not particularly well educated and probably never looked into a book of psychology in all his life. But he was definitely the first prizefight promoter to recognize that the essential features of every dramatic conflict are a hero and a villain, black and white, good and evil, the white roses and the red. Whether or not he stumbled upon this by accident or was sufficiently astute to think it out for himself no one will ever know, because Rickard never talked very much—another of his valuable assets. But from the time that he drew his first big gate, $452,522, close to half a million dollars, with Dempsey and Willard at Toledo, the bland, thin-lipped Texan was never without a hero and a villain in his fights with but one exception. And, strangest of all, his star, Dempsey, played both roles equally well. Dempsey was the villain in the Carpentier fight and the hero in the Firpo match, the villain in the first defense of his title against Gene Tunney, and a hero in their second fight, and again a hero the night he fought Sharkey.

By making boxing attractive to all classes of people Rickard immediately increased the percentage of potential ticket-buyers in any given community, and by giving the public someone to root for or against he sent them trooping to the selling booths in numbers never before recorded. But contained in the phrase "making boxing attractive to all classes of people," may be found Rickard's greatest stroke, one that is overlooked generally in any estimate of his successes. He broke down the barriers that up to his time had kept women away from prize-fights. He made it possible for them to attend his performances in comfort and without fear of annoyance or molestation. And then he made them want to go.

The professional prizefights of the pre-Rickard days were rough, rowdy, haphazard affairs, usually interdicted by the law or the police and patronized chiefly by bloods and sports, roughnecks and toughs, the men of what we are satisfied to call the lower classes. You bought a ticket of admission to some stuffy, stinking, airless arena, often no more than a large cellar or back-room assembly hall, but had no guarantee of a seat with it, unless you could rough-and-tumble a little yourself. It was ten to one that when you got to your chair someone would be sitting in it. The ushers, if there were any, were few and far between and were all petty grafters and chiselers. What police there were looked out for their own interests. A woman attending had no protection beyond what might be offered by her escort. Ladies of that period were never seen at prizefights any more than they were ever seen standing up and drinking at bars. There would be long unexplained delays between fights, brawls in the audience, substitution of fighters without notice, raids by police. The whole thing from beginning to end was thoroughly disreputable.

With his Dempsey-Carpentier fight Rickard made his first point-blank appeal to women. For the first time he presented a pugilist with definite sex and woman appeal. The frail, handsome, blond Frenchman with the gay smile, the debonair manner, and the gallant war record was a different type altogether from the black-visaged, frowning Dempsey, the ponderous, ugly Willard, the freckled Fitzsimmons, the squat, shapeless Tom Sharkey, the big, bruising Jim Jeffries. Carpentier had everything that appealed to women. He was good-looking, a boulevardier, a Frenchman, and a war hero. He danced beautifully, could sing French chansonnettes, had a dimple in his cheek. Ike Dorgan, Rickard's brilliant ballyhoo man nicknamed him the Orchid Man, and planted his training camp on Long Island close to Port Washington, which is next door to Syosset, which is not far from Meadowbrook, which is only a short distance from Oyster Bay, smack in the middle of the social crowd.

Gorgeous Georges, then, was the bait. But Rickard was also smart enough to see that conditions were right for the girls if and when they rose to it. His portals, aisles, and seats were carefully numbered. He hired a huge staff of ushers, directors, and special policemen and drilled and rehearsed them for weeks. Each usher had a small enough section to enable him to handle it. The patrons arriving were immediately directed to their proper aisles and promptly and courteously led to empty seats waiting for them. They then witnessed a boxing show that ran off like clockwork. Promptly at the hour announced for the start, two preliminary boys were in the ring, and as fast as two boxers quit the platform, two more were waiting at the steps below to take their places. There were police and firemen in profusion to maintain order and safety. Rickard had made it no more difficult or unpleasant to attend one of his performances than it was to go to the theater, a ball game, or a football match. And this service extended from the highest-priced seat right down to the bottom of the scale.

It is impossible to overestimate the importance of Rickard's stroke as a prizefight promoter when he broke down the barriers that had previously existed and made it possible for women to attend the prizefights he promoted without losing face or caste. Of course the post-war change in morals and mores had a good deal to do with this too, but Rickard helped it along and was the first to take advantage of it. The baseball clubs are still trying to attract women to the big-league games with their periodic "Ladies' Days" on which women with escorts (who must buy a ticket) are admitted free to the ball parks, in an effort to develop their taste for the game.

The logic of the thing is so simple and striking that it is a wonder that no one thought of it before. When the women attend, one sells two tickets where previously but one was sold. And likewise the show immediately gains class and tone, especially in such an absolute matriarchy as the United States.

But there was another important bit of accurate psychology to which Rickard was privy and it was quite naturally a hangover from his gambling days. He knew that money breeds money. He knew how to exhibit it, use it, ballyhoo it, spend it, make it work for him. From the time that he piled twenty thousand dollars in gold in a store window in Goldfields, Nevada, the purse for the Gans-Nelson fight, to the climax when he handed Tunney that much-photographed check for a million dollars, Rickard used money to make money. If he paid his boxers what seemed like utterly fantastic and immoral sums, it had its effect; the money poured right back again through the box office. He surrounded all of his promotions with the glitter of gold, because he had learned its power and its attraction in Alaska and in the West, where only gold was money. It was Rickard who printed the first embossed gold-backed fight ticket that looked like a treasury certificate and was infinitely more precious. The gambler that he was knew that pikers never won.

The racetrack men have another expression for it: "You can't win with scared money." Rickard's money was never scared, because he always had wealthy backers, chief among them John Ringling, the circus man. And so he spent. He spent on the construction of arenas, on publicity and ballyhoo, on ushers and police, but mostly on his fighters.

By rewarding prizefighters for their services with small fortunes ranging from a hundred thousand to a million dollars, he took them out of the class of common pugs and bruisers and made them people of consequence. A lightweight champion could make $150,000 in one night. A light heavyweight could earn $250,000, and a heavyweight who was not even a champion, half a million. Here were no grubby, uncouth roughnecks slogging one another bloody for ham-and-beans money, cheap pugs who lived in the underworld from whence they sprang, but a true aristocracy of the ring, men who drove high-priced cars, owned beautiful country homes, had fat bank-accounts, and dressed like millionaires. Whether they fought well or not, it was worth while going to see men with such a fantastic earning capacity, one that became simply stupendous when broken down into dollars earned per minute of competition. For the Firpo fight Dempsey was actually paid close to $120,000 per fighting minute, $20,000 a second. The fight lasted exactly three minutes and fifty-eight seconds, and Dempsey's purse was $470,000.

True, the times had to be right, with money to burn and money to squander, plus the worst of all war hangovers, the lust and craving for stimulation and excitement to replace and resolve the terrible nervous pitch at which people had lived from 1914 to 1919. But times were right. All of these things were a part of the nation, and from them Rickard distilled the elements which resulted in the staggering figures appearing at the beginning of this chapter.

What is it that makes people leave their homes of a night and fight their way through traffic, subway, elevated, and surface car and bus crowds to an outdoor stadium seating anywhere from 70,000 to 130,000, to battle even worse crushes and jams to get inside to attend a prizefight? Ordinarily the answer might be: "To see two evenly matched men fight it out with their hands; to be present to see the thrills when they settle the question of supremacy." This is true enough and there will always be spectators who will come to see two well-matched fighters who have reached the top in different brackets, so to speak, colliding in a final match to decide the undisputed champion.

But arrange a match, let us say, between a big man and a smaller man and hint that there is every possibility that the little man will knock the big man right out of his shoes, and if the public believes you, prepare to print more tickets.

Now, let on that the little man is not only a boxer, but was also a soldier who fought for his country as well and had his hide punctured by enemy shot and shell, while the bigger man has narrowly escaped charges of being a slacker by rushing to the shipyards, donning a pair of phony overalls, and posing for pictures with a riveting machine in his hands, and you find that you will have to call out the reserves. Because you are selling admission not only to a fight, but at one and the same time to living drama, the oldest and most time-tried hokum—virtue agin scallawaggery.

It was that primarily that sold the Dempsey-Carpentier fight in such quantities, with Dempsey figuring as the villain and Carpentier as the lily-white hero. It had to be something like that, because on the face of it, it was no match at all. Carpentier never in his life was more than a light heavyweight who could make 173 pounds, but who usually weighed in around 170 or even less and who for the Dempsey fight, for which his weight during the training period was kept a secret, was hardly more than a heavy middleweight.

Carpentier, too, was invaluable to Rickard in cracking the social surface. Tex's promotional venture at Toledo back in 1919 when some twenty thousand people had contributed half a million dollars for the privilege of viewing his version of Jack the Giant-killer, with Dempsey spreading the superior sneer that rested on Willard's features as the bout started all over his face in a bloody pulp, must have given him some idea of what could be done if one only had a larger audience from which to draw one's customers. The crowd that baked in the Toledo sun as Dempsey battered Willard was with few exceptions strictly a male audience and not a high-class one. Women were exceptional and the social element was strictly absent.

Rickard always had a great yearning for what he called "the finest class of people." And I never knew whether it was this yearning and the means he took to satisfy it that led to his success or whether he acquired his passion for them after he discovered what they meant to his promotional adventures. But I remember him the year before he died in Miami following an operation for a gangrenous appendix, standing just inside the front lobby gates of Madison Square Garden as the crowd came in for some prizefight or other. There was a plentiful sprinkling of men in silk hats, white ties, and tails, and lovely women enshrouded in fine evening-wraps. Tex beamed and seized me by the arm. "Look at all those fine people coming to patronize my shows," he said. "Finest class of people I ever seed. Imagine all them high-class people patronizing Tex Rickard." It was more than coincidence that the arrival of the high-class people and the million-dollar gates was simultaneous. When Carpentier made his appeal to the upper crust, the barriers were down.

The rhythm of Rickard's promotions remains constant and the amazing thing is that the public in the space of some six or seven years was made to switch its appraisal and opinion of Dempsey so completely as to make him either the hero or the villain of the play.

Dempsey gained no stature by knocking out Carpentier, the show in which he was definitely cast as the heavy or menace. Some seventy-five thousand people came solely to see the smaller man whip him and they were none too pleased over the unhappy ending. And yet two years later when Rickard cast him this time as the hero to enter the lists against another wild, dark-visaged giant, one Luis Angel Firpo who had come up from the Argentine to take the heavyweight championship of the world (America's most precious possession, to hear Rickard's ballyhoo men tell it) out of the country, the public accepted him immediately. To arms! Who would prevent this monstrous thing? Why, America's own Jack Dempsey, of course, Dempsey the hundred-per-cent American boy, Dempsey the Giant-killer, Dempsey who had kept that damned frog (by this time) from taking the title back to France.

The ball was rolling. The ice had been well broken. Prizefighting had become respectable, and, what is more, it was fun. Eighty-two thousand people attended that one.

In the third million-dollar fight there was another aboutface. Dempsey was villain again to many people, and the boyish, fair-haired, studious Gene Tunney was installed as hero and underdog. Tunney had been overseas with the U. S. Marines. Tunney loved good books. Tunney, above all, had friends among the "finest people I ever seed." Tunney was practically an unknown who dared to challenge the most terrible hitter that ever lived—by that time, 1926, the Dempsey legend was in full swing. As a matter of fact, Rickard cashed in double on that one, because the nice people came to see Tunney, and the tough guys reported at the turnstiles to see Dempsey knock the book-reading dude right back to Shakspere.

One year later Dempsey was hero again—and what a hero, in two fights that within sixty days of one another drew a total of $3,733,529! His fight with Jack Sharkey in New York grossed $1,083,529 on July 21. And in Chicago on the evening of September 22 he and Gene Tunney, in their famous return match, drew $2,650,000, an all-time money record for a single prizefight gate.

Against Sharkey, Dempsey was pictured as the old iron-fisted mauler, greater and better loved in defeat than ever he had been in victory, struggling along the grim and thorny come-back trail and having to dispose of Sharkey, the big windbag and blabbermouth.

And when Rickard put Dempsey and Tunney back into the ring again two months later, it was Tunney who was the villain, and Dempsey, for the last time, had the appealing leading role. It was the old master making a come-back against the slick dude who had wangled his title from him with a lot of smart boxing tricks. By that time the tables had been turned on Tunney, who suddenly found himself pictured a priggish, snobbish, bookish fellow, too proud to associate with common prizefighters. There were comparatively few in that crowd of 105,000 people at Soldiers Field, Chicago, that night who were rooting for Tunney.

And that ended the cycle. Justice again failed to triumph. Tunney won, Dempsey retired, and the next heavyweight championship ended in the first promotional loss that was ever charged against Tex Rickard. It is just as interesting to examine the causes of this failure. The match was between Gene Tunney and Tom Heeney. Tunney himself picked Heeney, not Rickard, and there was just nothing that could be done with Heeney. He was a squat, stodgy, unimpressive New Zealander, with a pleasing smile and an unimpressive record. He had no particular punch and certainly no showmanship or color. He fitted into the part of neither hero nor villain. There was no great dramatic story connected with his fight against Tunney, except that he was trying to make a couple of dollars for himself and his manager.

Not much could be done plugging the international angle (New Zealand was so far off) and stressing the necessity of keeping the title in America, since unfortunately it leaked out that Tunney himself had selected Heeney as an opponent because he was jolly well certain that he could whip him. The sympathy, if any, was with Heeney, who was named the Hard Rock from Down Under, stressing his durability; but that very durability and ability to take punishment made him a difficult object for sympathy, and he had no sex appeal whatsoever. Tunney was still unpopular because of his long-count victory over Dempsey. Everybody knew that Heeney wasn't going to do anything to Tunney. The publicity died aborning, as it were.

It was, I remember, almost pitiful when in an attempt to save the affair from being an utter flop Rickard sent for the man who for years had been such a magic talisman, whose name had caused such a flood of gold to flow from the pockets of the public to the strong-boxes of the Rickard promotions, in the last desperate hope that Dempsey might stimulate sales.

Jack came down to Red Bank, New Jersey, one hot afternoon to watch Heeney train, and after trying not to see three spar-mates cuffing Heeney around most unmercifully (one of them was James J. Braddock, probably the first heavyweight ever to rise from spar boy to heavyweight champion), arose at the ringside and spoke a little memorized speech about the challenger being a good man and having a fine chance against Tunney. Somebody laughed, and the fight turned up its toes then and there. At that, it grossed close to $700,000 which was not exactly straw, but by the time the fighters were paid off and expenses reckoned, Rickard had lost $200,000. The glamour was beginning to wear off the heavyweights. The stock-market collapse finished them.

There were certain other elements besides the main one of the dramatic set-ups that led to these million-dollar hauls out of prizefights. For one thing, there was Dempsey's durability. He won his championship in 1919, and he was fighting to win it back again eight years later, having held it for seven. And for another there was Rickard's luck in being able to procure such marvelous foils for Dempsey each time he presented him to the public. There was always the Dempsey punch, too, which never changed. It was simply the problem that altered. Was Dempsey's punch sufficiently dangerous and lethal to extinguish Whosis? Or could our hero, Whatsis, sample Dempsey's punch and survive? These questions were always answered in dollars and cents at the box office.

There was another important factor, and that was the open-ing up of the columns of the newspapers to a type of publicity and ballyhoo that differed entirely from any that had ever be-fore featured prizefighters or ball-players or six-day bicycle-riders. It was the beginning of the era of personal publicity.

By personal publicity is meant the close watch kept by the sports pages—and the news side, as well—upon every single phase of the life of an athlete. He was no longer news only when he was fighting or preparing to fight. He was always news. He was news in his friendships, in his courtship, his love-affairs, and his marriage, his home life, his hobbies, his lawsuits and ac-cidents, his trips and travels, his troubles and his quarrels, the birth of his children, the death of a relative. The fight-writer discussed his body and his professional career, the sob sister went into his home and the columnist explored his mental processes and his mind—if he had any.

The result was that the prizefighters of the million-dollar era were better known to the readers of newspapers than members of the reader's own family. They knew all there was to know about them. If they had not seen them personally, they had seen them in moving pictures or newsreels or in still pictures. These men had become a part of the daily life, literally, of mil-lions upon millions of people.

Thus, when they were signed for a fight, it was just as though a personal friend or a close relative were suddenly to become involved in an unavoidable brawl with a neighbor down the block. By Jove, you knew *him* too, and all about him; and you certainly wouldn't want to miss being around for the squabble.

These prizefights, too, always managed somehow to point up the individual life-dramas of the men who were engaging in them, and climax situations in their careers that were better than any stage play. There was always some great human story connected with them, it seemed. For instance, when Dempsey went to Philadelphia to train for his first fight with Gene Tun-ney, it was his first match without the man who made him—

Jack Kearns. Their great Damon and Pythias friendship had broken up over a woman, and a glamorous one at that, a motion-picture star who was Dempsey's wife. Why, it was all more dramatic and gripping than any screen story. And by paying Mr. Rickard the modest sum of twenty-five or fifty dollars and taking a little trip to Philadelphia you could actually be present and see what happened when this man Dempsey went into action for the first time without his alter ego at his elbow.

Or you read that Gene Tunney was trying to make a million dollars so that he could ask a wealthy society girl to marry him, a fiction story right out of the *Saturday Evening Post*. By purchasing a seat for the Chicago fight you could with your own eyes see the young man earn the million dollars that was to make it possible for him to pop the question. Or this fighter or that one was broke and his home crumbling. He needed to win his next fight to save all. The public was privy to all of these affairs. The newspapers let them in on everything they could find out. From time to time life histories of the celebrities were printed. Well, each fight was such history in the making. And if you were lucky and had a good seat, you might even hear a wife or sweetheart (when Max Baer fought, it was pretty nearly the female population of the entire first three rows) scream in pain and terror as her man went down.

And, curiously, the crowds themselves drew crowds. There was no hope of sitting in a front seat unless you were a celebrity, bootlegger, gangster, politician, or friend of the favored last-named, but the crowd itself, lying like a great black monster in the shadows back of the center patch of bright white ring lights, was a spectacle, and coming to see and admire itself, this monster fattened and grew larger and larger. If a fight promised to draw the largest crowd in the history of pugilism it was considered sufficient reason for rushing out to purchase a ticket, because whether the fight was any good or not, the gathering of one hundred and twenty thousand persons in one arena would be worth the trouble. And it was, too. Those million-dollar crowds were something to see.

Too, it meant something to have been present. It was definitely a badge of opulency and indicated that you belonged to the smart and moneyed set. Here again were Rickard's brilliant publicity and his unerring instinct in getting the right people to go to his fights, because if the right people went and the newspapers printed pictures of them sitting on their eight inches of pine bench, or listed their names, and you were not among them or at least couldn't produce a ticket stub to show that you had been in the same inclosure with them, even though it wasn't in the same county, owing to the size of the arena, then you were not a right person.

Money? There was always fresh money. We were rolling in wealth in those days. Rickard's fight headquarters were like the bonanza days in the rich mining camps. In Philadelphia and Chicago, where took place his greatest money promotions, he rented an entire floor of the most gaudy and glittering hotels and set up his offices there. His tickets were always large, six inches long and three inches wide, so that when you handed over a hundred-dollar bill for two, you felt that you had received something, gold-backed and handsomely engraved.

In and out the doors of those old-fashioned, perfumed, glittering hotel suites, wandered men with money in their fists, gold-currency yellow-backs, thousand-dollar bills, or certified checks for two and three thousand dollars for blocks of seats for a "little party for some of the boys." Firms in addition to paying bonuses used to make it a practice of purchasing a block of seats for their entire sales or office staffs, and giving a party the same night to boot.

There was money crammed into safes, stuffed into desk drawers, lying around loose in wire baskets. As fast as the girls could hand them out, sometimes, these cardboard slabs turned into money. Men would plead for twenty tickets, worth a thousand dollars or so, inside the first twenty rows ". . . and here's a couple of C's for you, girlie, if you can fix it up." Plainclothesmen and coppers with guns and cartridge bandoliers worn outside stood guard at the doors and watched the never thinning crowd of thugs, politicians, fight managers, society men, plain and fancy whores, gang leaders, bootleggers, actors, newspapermen, bankers and brokers, mingling in the corridors waiting to get into the sacred chambers to explain to Rickard, or whomever they could get to nearest him, just why it was imperative that they be permitted to present him with cash or certified checks running into thousands upon thousands of dollars for seats.

Tex was always around, bland, smooth, grinning under his wide-brimmed fedora hat with the front turned down, carrying his gold-headed cane and a cigar. When he had to read a letter he affixed gold-rimmed glasses to his nose. He was always accessible to the right people, and it was startling sometimes to note the range of people who were right.

They were scandalous, gaudy, exciting, incredible days. The voices of the homeless and the starving were weak, faint, and distant in those times, and nobody heard them over the clamor of the ballyhoo, anyway. "What's that? Mike has a pair in the third row he'll let you have for five hundred? Grab 'em! It's a bargain." For sheer, naked immorality, it was hard to beat.

I always have to think of those days, somehow, in comparison with the last performance in which Rickard figured, when his painted corpse lay in state in Madison Square Garden, the great steel and concrete sports arena in New York, of which he was president and director. His last audience, come to patronize him, thousands upon thousands of people, filed past his bier in a never ending line.

I remember choosing to view the scene from the topmost gallery at the east end of the Garden. There was an entrance to this gallery from the offices of the Garden concessionaire, the hot-dog and soda-pop man, and I sat for an hour or more watching, surrounded by white-coated candy and soft-drink butchers.

The west end of the Garden had been turned into an altar of flowers, in the center of which was Rickard's expensive coffin, of the type and design which in those days we called the

"Gangster's Special." It was massive and of bronze, fluted, scrolled, and ornamented with glass covering half the top, so that one could peer down through at the mummy within. There was no light in the Garden except for a row of slanting shafts of late sun that cut down through the narrow clerestory windows just beneath the roof of the building. Two of these fell athwart the bier.

There was no noise in the Garden that day except for the ceaseless slurp-scrape, slurp-scrape, slurp-scrape of feet shuffing over the terrazzo floor, and coughs and clearings of throats that echoed through the arena. In from the right they came, down and around they filed and out to the left. Ushers and frock-coated undertaker's staff men and uniformed Garden special police kept the crowd moving. Up to the coffin, a brief look, on and out.

Rickard's lips and cheeks were tinted with paint to compensate for the changes made in his appearance by the rigors of dying of a gangrenous appendix. He did not in the least resemble the Rickard that I had known. Apparently the best that the modern mortician can deliver is a caricature.

There were two or three sports-writers sitting up on the top shelf with us watching the procession. One of them said: "Boy, I'll bet they've got him lashed down so's he can't spin. Would he be revolving in that box if he saw this mob all coming in here on the cuff!"

The last show of the man who had turned prizefighting into a million-dollar industry was free.

IX

AMATEURS?

THERE AIN'T

NONE

IN DEPARTING this happy and more or less carefree world where nothing is ever more important than one young man in shirt and drawers and spiked shoes chasing another young man similarly attired, or seventy thousand people sitting tense and semi-hysterical, wondering whether one big loogan who has been hit on the chin by another big loogan is going to get up so that he can be hit again, or the same number of people waiting breathless to see whether a man with a big leather glove is going to catch a little white ball descending upon him from the sky, I realize that I have left the amateur question still unsolved. I have been yipping and yapping at the boys to turn square for the last ten or twelve years. If they are not tired of it, I am. And besides, time is growing short. There is nothing left for me to do but have myself one more big yell and then slam the door.

If you try to arrive at a proper and watertight definition of exactly what an amateur is, you will wind up considerably confused. The dictionary says that an amateur is one who is not rated as a professional, and that a professional is one, generally, who has competed in sport for a stake or purse, or gate money, or with a professional for a prize, or who has taught or trained in sports or athletics for pay. To this, modern amateur governing bodies have added that a professional is also anyone who capitalizes his athletic skill or name, directly or indirectly, for pay. But the exigencies of modern sports still leave considerable room for doubt and argument. The American sportswriter comes much closer to it. He defines an amateur as a guy who won't take a check.

But it seems to me, from my experience in watching and dealing with amateurs over a long period of years, that too much latitude is permitted even in the last critical definition. In my book, an amateur golfer is one who goes out to his club on a Sunday morning and dubs around between eighty and a hundred and ten. An amateur tennis-player is a gentleman or a lady who appears on the courts week-ends and hopes he or she won't get too many shots on the backhand, which is always weak. And an amateur runner is a commuter running for the 8.13 out of Larchmont, or Port Washington, and catching it. Otherwise I do not know of any genuine amateurs in the United States of America.

We are, by dint of long practice, the greatest nation of hypocrites on the face of the globe. If we have any conception of the real meaning of the word "amateur," we never let it disturb us. We ask only one thing of an amateur, and that is that he doesn't let us catch him taking the dough. So long as his ten, fifty, or a hundred dollars is slipped to him in private and doesn't get into the newspapers, we are satisfied. So long as the football-player working his way through college will make the pretense of dropping into the boiler-room of the dormitory or gymnasium once a week and waving his hand at the furnace, he may accept whatever stipend the prominent alumnus or the graduate manager of athletics is willing to pay him. And just so long as the track athlete is photographed fondling his tuppenny gold medal or near-silver loving cup, nobody cares or inquires into the expense accounts he has turned in.

Typically, we have only one way of smelling out a cheating amateur, whenever a hunt is on. Is or isn't there the taint of ready cash in the air? But I have known amateurs who never took a cent of money, or a free trip, or a new pair of shoes, who in my estimation have been out-and-out professionals. And I have known a few professionals that I would class as amateurs. It is simply that as soon as boys or girls devote their entire time to a sport, they are no longer amateurs. It is much less a case of venality than proficiency. The entire subversive scandal of amateur athletics would be ended if certain standards of proficiency and the amount of time devoted to a game were made the basis of determining an amateur or a professional status. It would also be a considerable help if the various amateur protective and regulating bodies would get out of the racket of promoting amateur sports for gate receipts.

The U. S. Lawn Tennis Association, for instance, has no use for a real amateur tennis-player on the Davis Cup team, because a real amateur cannot maintain the standard of play demanded by big-time tennis. Week-end tennis or occasional tournament play won't do. The candidate for a berth on the Davis Cup team must play *all* the time. He must make the swing of the winter real-estate and chamber-of-commerce tournaments in the South to keep his edge for the spring and summer competitions. He must live the life of a tennis professional, but accept (openly) none of the benefits. The tennis association, while professionalizing him to the extent of preempting all of his time, yet insists upon maintaining the fiction of his so-called amateur standing.

The amateur (*sic*) football-player must give every second of his free time to football practice and blackboard lectures, and more and more demands upon his time are being made by the high-pressure football college teams which have now included and lengthened spring practice as a vital part of the training necessary. It would be interesting to compare the time spent in practice by the professional teams with that demanded by certain college elevens.

AMATEURS? THERE AIN'T NONE   111

And consider the hypothetical cases of Jones and Smith universities. Jones University schedules an hour or two of football practice a day, after classes and late laboratory, after which the players return to their studies or their entertainment. Smith University, on the other hand, practices from six to eight weeks in the spring—giving the boys the fundamentals, it is called. Three weeks before the opening of the fall term the candidates are taken away to a camp in the country, where they practice both morning and afternoons. During the school term, practice starts at three o'clock in the afternoon and continues on until well after dark under floodlights. After supper two or three times a week the players repair to the gymnasium for blackboard talks and lectures. Neither university—for the sake of argument—pays its players a cent. But would you call them both strictly amateurs? I wouldn't.

Top-flight golf-players find it necessary to work from two to three hours in the morning on the practice tee and then play the course in the afternoon, to maintain tournament edge, besides playing in every available tournament. Only a rich boy or a loafer can devote all of his time to play. And as soon as he devotes all of his time and does nothing else, he has in my opinion become a professional, whether he gets any money out of it or not. It is obvious that the amateur who can compete on even terms with the professional golfers, unless like Bob Jones he is an exception, is no amateur at all. And even in a sport where an amateur is generally not supposed to be able to defeat a professional, the standard of amateur excellence and the championship is usually set by a chap who has nothing else to do but practice and participate in his sport. Many of our amateur golfers are business men or college kids. But you don't see them stepping out and cleaning up the professionals.

There are amateur boxers who have had from two hundred and fifty to three hundred fights as amateurs, and professional boxers who have fought no more than thirty or forty bouts. Which is the amateur and which the professional? And, cash

considerations excluded, wherein lies the fairness and sportsmanship of matching an amateur boxer who has had fifteen or
twenty fights with one who for reasons of his own has decided
to remain technically an amateur over a period of three or four
years with a couple of hundred fights? This boy may have his
A.A.U. registration card as an amateur certified to, but he is
a professional nevertheless from the point of view of experience, and the twenty-fight amateur might just as well be fighting a professional. The licking doesn't feel any better because
his opponent has an A.A.U. card.

The old money standard for amateurs won't do any more,
because with very few exceptions everyone takes money for
sport, in one form or another, and chiefly in the engraved or
minted form. Why, then, if they all take it, don't they turn
professional? For one thing, because from a business point of
view, both before and after the crash, the boys and girls found
it much more profitable to compete as amateurs than as professionals. There was more money in it. As soon as someone
came along and showed them that there was more money as
an out-and-out professional, many of them turned.

Track athletics and boxing furnish us with two perfect examples. For years there has been no market for professional
foot-runners and jumpers. But the amateur runner who is
colorful, who can break records and draw crowds, will fill arenas
night after night. He can make plenty for himself, and does.
And it is no secret how he does it. Therein lies the scandal.
The Amateur Athletic Union must know what is going on,
but if it stops it, it also stops a chief source of revenue—gate
receipts. One famous runner was such a financial success that
he had to have a manager to conduct his tour. Clubs wanting
to book him for track meets did business with the manager,
not with the runner. He was responsible for drawing thousands
of dollars in gate receipts. As a professional he wouldn't have
been worth a dime, but as an amateur he was putting foot-
running on a big-business basis and coining money—for someone. The public was perfectly well satisfied to have him pry

his share loose from the people who made the money—if he could. And the A.A.U. had neither the courage nor the inclination to brand him a professional and throw him out. Or maybe they didn't have the evidence. One of the easiest things in the world is not to have evidence when evidence is liable to prove embarrassing.

Public opinion, anyway, is usually with the athlete. Somehow, it grates on what we fondly believe is our sense of fair play to see a runner who has spent a lifetime developing his muscles, his wind and his competitive brain turn into a drawing card good for twenty or thirty thousand dollars every time he appears, and then get paid off with a die-cut medal that cost thirty-five or forty dollars, but on which your Uncle Ike, for his own mother should it kill him, couldn't allow more than ten or fifteen dollars.

Amateur boxing is the greatest professional racket in all sport—unless it is amateur hockey that is worse—and the reason why a boy today finds it more profitable to box as an amateur than to turn professional is purely economic. Amateur boxing was always something of a petty professional racket, but never to the extent that it has become in recent years.

In the palmy days of professional boxing, amateur boxing was mostly a training ground for youngsters who intended to turn professional eventually. With professional boxing in the ascendancy, amateur bouts were not particularly well attended and there wasn't much money for the amateur boxers. They took it out in experience and publicity. As soon as they were able they turned professional and began to cash in.

But when the bottom fell out of boxing, as it did out of everything else, in 1929, most of the professional fight clubs folded up. The fight patron then turned to the amateur clubs for his entertainment. The amateur clubs had something to offer—rattling good fights at cheap prices—for a dollar or two-dollar top, at the highest, because they had cheap labor. Even the smallest professional club, putting on a star bout, a semi-final, and preliminaries, could not stage a show under

$1,500 or $2,000. But an amateur organization could and did stage boxing shows with no more expense than three or four hundred dollars, and undersell the professional outfits on admission price.

Professional boxers were a drug on the market, with no place to ply their trade. The smart amateur boxer with skill and a little color soon discovered that he could make better wages fighting often as an amateur than fighting infrequently or not at all as a professional. His price was low: a semi-gold watch, salable at circa twenty dollars, occasionally a fifty-dollar bill or a couple of suits of clothes. At that price a club could present an evening of fifteen amateur bouts, including two or three four-man classes in which two out of the four men in the class, the two losers, received nothing; and after the winners were paid off or rewarded, a small profit remained for the clubs, the public had seen a good card, and everybody was happy.

The boys, many of them, could and did box two and three times a week, made their little stakes, and were satisfied. Even had times been good, they could have boxed no more than once a month as professionals, or perhaps twice, with a manager cutting a third of their purses and taking a third more for expenses.

There was nothing particularly vicious about this system, except the fashion, perhaps, of calling it amateur sport. None of the amateur boxers became millionaires. Most of them had families which they helped to support by this means. The bouts were short—three rounds—they didn't get badly hurt, and the fifty or seventy-five dollars a week they were able to bring home during the hard times, with the father of the family mostly unemployed and many mouths to feed, was strictly money from heaven. But is there any interpretation under which these boys could be considered amateurs? Yet, registered under and controlled by the Amateur Athletic Union, they fought, ostensibly, what the newspapers liked to call "Simon-pure"; and not one in ten ever was a pure amateur, either in spirit or in fact. The kids learn quickly. The first prize won by a novice boxer usually finds its place on the family altar of important keepsakes. His first wrist-watch goes around his wrist, his second to his best friend, and thereafter the trinkets and jewelry are converted into cash. Unfortunately, in a futile attempt to protect its precious amateurism there is an A.A.U. ruling that all prizes must be engraved or inscribed. This is slightly damaging to the resale value. But the boys sell them anyway for what they can get.

The A.A.U. must close its eyes to this as it must to all the irregularities in all branches of amateur sport, in order to continue to exist. Occasionally a face-saving victim is found; some misguided youth, either in need of money or too greedy to keep up the necessary and prescribed appearances, goes outside his home territory and fights himself a four- or a six-round bout in Syracuse or Binghamton or Scranton for a hundred dollars, cash money, and is caught at it. With a great calling together of committees, pounding of gavels, and solemn statements to the press, he is found guilty of professionalism, his card as an amateur is taken up, he is read out of the party, and appearances have been satisfied.

In the same manner the Lawn Tennis Association, or the golf body, or the Intercollegiate Athletic Association will catch a young athlete in the act of selling a belt or a sports implement in a sporting-goods store, or indorsing a brand of yeast or nerve tonic or cigarette, or an automobile, or will apprehend a college player who during his summer vacation played semi-pro baseball under the name of Joe Doakes for fifty dollars a week, or who, perhaps, when the football season was over, slipped away for a week-end to a town a hundred or so miles away and collected a few dollars for playing halfback for the Four Corners Bulldogs under the name of Psmith.

Out they go, bag and baggage, branded as dirty professionals and a detriment to fine, clean amateur sport, never again to be permitted to compete under the pure and, worst blow of all, profitable banner of modern amateurism. The newspapers print the pictures of the tarnished athletes and also those of the expulsion committees sitting around a long table passing sentence with hurt looks on their faces. Thereupon for a time they have justified their existence as regulators of sport and whipped another coat of whitewash on their particular game. After which the chiseling, grafting, cheating, and petit larceny can resume with renewed vigor because everyone has just had a clear demonstration that sport is pure and clean and that dirty professionals are cast out into darkness.

If the various associations (all self-appointed) that govern amateur sport really wished to clean house of all athletes who were not amateurs under the strictest interpretation, there wouldn't be enough competitors left to hold a caucus race, let alone regular competition. They would have to throw them all out, boxers, runners, tennis- and golf-players, baseball, football, and hockey men, because in one form or another practically every athlete in the United States today is guilty of some breach of the amateur code, and the better known the athlete, the more certain the breach. Very few would escape. Under the present system the worst offenders are never caught and never will be, because they are too smart. It is only the dumb athlete who is found out and banished.

But the result of such a house-cleaning would be disastrous —to the associations. With no amateur athletes, there would be no need for amateur governing bodies. And these bodies are too fond of the prestige—in some cases social position, in others petty power to rule and regulate the lives of others and to wear pretty gilt badges—to legislate themselves out of business. It is much easier for them to regulate what they can, keep a coat of surface paint as bright as they can over their respective sports, and shutting their eyes to the rest, tell themselves that inasmuch as they cannot prove it, it isn't so.

Technically the athlete is supposed to be competing for the fun of it, because he loves the sport and enjoys playing. But once the game reaches the high-pressure, big-money level, as all our games do eventually, there is precious little fun left in it for the athlete. He is required to remain an amateur while his governing association functions strictly as a professional promotion organization, whether or not its members serve without pay.

Actually, once he has signed an entry blank to appear at and run in a certain track meet, he can no longer exercise any option as an amateur competing for the fun of the thing, and stay home on that night and listen to the radio because he does not happen to feel like running. That entry blank that he has signed is as rigid a contractual obligation as any legal form signed by a professional prizefighter or ball-player. It is true that no one can force him to keep to it and appear, but if he wishes to continue to enjoy the pleasures and profits of amateur competition he knows that he must, otherwise the A.A.U. or whatever the governing body happens to be will suspend or blacklist him for what technically amounts to a breach of contract. He can no longer then compete in any sanctioned A.A.U. meet until that suspension is lifted.

Here again we see the topsy-turvy character of amateur sport competition. The athlete is listed as an amateur competing without pay, but the governing body realizes and acknowledges his value as a drawing card at the gate and protects its member clubs—that is, the athletic organizations that form the body of the various associations, and that run the big track meets, boxing shows, golf and tennis tournaments—from incurring loss, and facing scandal because of false advertising.

Thus, if the New York Athletic Club receives a signed entry blank from Johnny Doe, the famous three-quarter-miler and world's record-holder, that he will compete in the feature event of the annual track meet conducted by that club, it is entitled to advertise that fact. The club is then selling Brother Doe for what he will bring at the gate. And the news usually is sufficient to sell out, let us say, Madison Square Garden, with thousands turned away. If Johnny Doe were to exercise his prerogative as an amateur, competing for the fun and love of the sport, by calling up three hours before the show and saying: "I do not love running tonight and have an idea that it would be no fun at all," the N.Y.A.C. would be in considerable hot water. The customers would demand their money back on the grounds that the tickets had been sold under false pretenses. And so the runner, should he suggest such a thing, would be advised that it is true, he need not run on that particular evening, but that he will also never run again thereafter.

For the Amateur Athletic Union has him bound by an amateur contract that is just as effective as the contract covering the services of a prizefighter; more effective, even. Because breach of contract on the part of a professional athlete must be aired in open court, before an impartial judge. The amateur body meets and passes sentence, and that is that. The most celebrated of such cases in recent times, was the suspension of Jesse Owens, the colored American one-man track team, who, after winning four gold medals at Berlin in the Olympic games, was suspended by the A.A.U. for failing to fill a contract to run in Sweden, where he had been booked by the A.A.U.

The athlete under our system has no rights and very little freedom. He is supposed to be satisfied with the cheers (and the boos, since a sports crowd has no manners and, having paid an admission, treats the amateur exactly like a professional) and the medal or loving cup for his end. Naturally, this system cannot work any more than any one-way racket can. He must then get what he can by subterfuge. If he comes to New York for a track meet, from San Francisco or Los Angeles, and remains there for two or three more meets and races, the promoters of each and every such track meet may be required to pay his entire traveling expenses from the west coast to New York. Or he dickers carefully through an intermediary for cash on the side, left somewhere in an envelope (no checks, please), or the club will arrange perhaps to buy back his prize from him at two or three times its value. True, the prizes won in the United States by an amateur athlete are subject at any time to a call for inspection by the local registration committee, but it never calls for them. It wouldn't dare.

It does not take much of an imagination to picture an athletic governing body as a monopolistic organization operating an air-tight racket of supplying cheap athletic labor. If the organizations promoting amateur sports events had to pay the athletes in proportion to their drawing power, they wouldn't make any money—or not as much. We will see later how perfectly this operates in the biggest racket of all—college football.

And in the meantime the chiseling, lying, cheating, petty grafting, and subterfuge goes on and weaves prettily into the pattern of the national blanket of hypocrisy. The law, you remember, said you mustn't drink, but you drank just the same. It says that you mustn't gamble, but you know a place where they will let you buck a wheel or a crap game. You mustn't speed, but you can get the ticket fixed. Lotteries are barred, but don't let that stop you from buying a sweepstake ticket. The regulations say that a college football-player shall be a bona-fide student with a certain scholastic standing, but don't let that bother you. Just you lug that football for touchdowns or open up those holes, and somebody will fix the rest for you. You are not supposed to take money for playing a game of golf or tennis, or boxing, or running, so just take it out in a couple of new suits of clothes or a merchandising certificate, which isn't money at all. There is nothing in our great territory that cannot be fixed or squared if you know the right people or have money or are a big shot in sports. They need you, buddy, not you them, so don't worry. They'll have to take care of you. Just keep up those appearances, don't take checks, never give a receipt, and you'll be all right. That's the way they do things around here.

What's that? Your conscience? What's the difference? Nobody will ever be the wiser. Hell, everybody's getting away with it. You might as well get yours too, brother. Don't be a sucker all your life. They tell me that Bjenks, the tennisplayer, gets plenty. When he goes to a tournament at the big Health Springs Hotel, they give him a car to drive around while he's down there, his room, board, and laundry free, and he can sign checks for anything he wants. No, they won't squawk if he draws a little dough on a voucher from the cashier now and then, as long as he doesn't draw too much. No use being a pig about it. All goes on his hotel bill, to be totaled up at the end of the tournament. What do they do with the hotel bill? Tear it up, of course. You don't think they give it to *him*, do you? Why, what would be the good of that? And, anyway, isn't he attracting hundreds of people to the hotel to see him play in the tournament? They're making plenty of jack out of him. It's only fair to take care of him in return.

What's your game? Golf? Can't afford to play, eh? Got just the thing for you. Fellow I know, J. G. Whoffenheimer, of the Whoffenheimer Dye and Chemical Works, Inc., has a place for you in his office. Nice job, good salary, easy hours. What's that—you don't know anything about dyes or chemistry? No, no, no, you don't get the idea at all. I told you this was just the thing for you. You don't have to know anything about the business. You just go down to the office every morning and check in, or call up on the telephone and see whether J. G. wants to play golf in the afternoon or wants you to take some of the out-of-town buyers or wholesale men out to the club and play around with them. Give them a thrill to say they played around with the North-Southeast amateur champion. Get it? J. G. is a lousy golfer, but he is trying to improve his game, see? You're not instructing him, because that's against the amateur rule and you want to be very careful about the amateur rule. But if he asks you any questions about golf or what makes him slice to hellangone, while you're playing a friendly game, you can tell him, can't you? Sure, you're just being hired to be his private golf teacher, but what's the difference as long as nobody finds out or can prove it? You're on the books as assistant sales supervisor or something, and it's okey doke.

Amateur hockey! Now, there's a real amateur sport for you. You just love to play hockey for the fun and excitement of it two or three times a week in scheduled games, taking the bumps and the bruises and shocks and cuts while ten thousand or so people cheer you on. Ten thousand people represent a gate of fifteen or eighteen thousand dollars that is going to someone, isn't it? Well, then, if you get an envelope stuck into your hotel mailbox on the road, or find one in your inside coat pocket when you change clothes in the locker-room to dress for the street, and there is fifty dollars in the envelope, why, just take it as a gift from the Brownies; ask no questions and you'll get along. That is, unless you are a sucker who really *likes* to play for nothing.

Basketball? Dozens of ways to make a little change. The pro and the semi-pro game is making money all over the country. You can be Smith in Paterson, New Jersey, on Monday, Jones in Passaic on Tuesday, Brown in Brooklyn Wednesday, and White in Bridgeport Thursday. Better rest up a night on Friday so that when you play under your own name for your dear old college on Saturday night, you won't have telltale circles under your eyes and go stale. Or, if you're really good and want a soft job with plenty of dough, you can get fixed up with the B. & Z. Crackerdust Co. Their team is leading the amateur basketball league of the Southwest. You get someone to punch the time clock for you and that's that. The only thing the company is fussy about is your showing up on time for the basketball games, putting on your jersey with "B. & Z. Crackerdust Co." on the back, and playing winning basketball.

I have often wondered what the boys and girls think of the business, as they begin to learn the racket, youngsters who have gone into sport for the thrill and excitement and pleasure of it at first, to wake up gradually to the fact that they were being played for suckers by their elders, who in return for this would frequently let them get away with murder. They learn all too quickly. The American amateur athlete who cannot capitalize in some tangible form upon his skill and publicity, and doesn't, is either too dumb to be successful at anything but patting a ball with a stick or running around a track or lugging a football, or else is nothing but a rank amateur and not deserving of the fair name.

X

INSIDE

THE

INSIDE

BASEBALL CAN be the most fascinating game in the world to watch and also the dullest, depending very often upon circumstances—that is to say, the quality of the play, the caliber and situation of the competing teams, and also what you yourself bring into the park. All games are alike in form and intent. One man tries to beat another man, or one group of men try to worst another group through skill, courage, and physical condition. It is merely the materials with which they are provided for this purpose, the rules, and the playing grounds that differ. The more intricate the game and tangled the rules and complicated the materials, the more difficult it is to understand, but the more fascinating it becomes when you do understand it.

When two men face each other in a boxing ring with gloves on their hands and begin to fight when the bell rings, and stop fighting when it rings again after three minutes, it is reasonably obvious to anyone what is going on and what they are trying to do to each other and the means they are employing. The struggle is a simple hand-to-hand trial for complete mastery within certain time limits, and because the struggle sometimes gets atavistic, abysmal, and terrifying, with show of blood, it is arresting and arousing. The novice spectator becomes an expert after witnessing his first prizefight or boxing match because everything is plain and simple and easy to see. It takes rather longer to know what is going on on a baseball field, what the trials and the problems of the various players are, what can be done and what cannot be done; and even so, many people who have been going to games for years do not know exactly what it is all about because they have never taken the trouble to find out. They love it, though, because they do realize that there is a fine balance struck between offense and defense and that, by a lucky accident in the laying out of the playing field and the development of the game, you may sit by and witness the development of real drama and the working of keen wits in fast bodies.

Baseball talk is a great bore, baseball-players are not exactly intellectual giants, and baseball figures, box scores and averages even duller. But the things that take place on the field in a tight game played to the hilt by a couple of major-league clubs can be completely captivating.

If games as a whole bore you, you will never like baseball. But if you can take pleasure in the story of conflict unfolded before your eyes, it is only necessary to become a little more familiar with the materials used by baseball-players and the rules under which they operate to find something that can be quite as fascinating, for instance, as the theater. In one afternoon at the ball yard you may, if you know where and how to look for it, come upon half a dozen split-second races between a running man and a thrown ball, in which the hundredth part of a second is all the difference between success and failure, dozens of examples of skill triumphant, skill defeated, traps baited and snapped shut upon victims, human courage, human folly, and human cowardice, narrow escapes, heroes, villains, individual deeds that verge upon the miraculous, bits of co-operation between two men or among three or four that are really beautiful to see in their rhythm and perfection, heroes turned suddenly into clowns and goats, clowns becoming heroes, speed, grace, and sometimes even a curious beauty, the beauty of the perfection of a well-pitched, well-defended game.

The patterns of the game are of themselves interesting and pleasing to the eye. The rich chocolate-brown or pale tan of the infield is contrasted with the fine soothing green of the outfield. The base paths are neatly geometrical, and the white foul lines on either side of the home plate start their diverging roads towards infinity. There is a place for everyone and every place is neatly marked off with white lime. There is a base at each corner of the square, and a player stationed at, or close to, each base. The outfield is divided into three sections, right, center, and left field, and each field has a patrolman stationed in his appointed place. Pitcher and catcher stand on a line that is the hypotenuse of the right-angle triangle made by the three bases, home, first, and second. And pleasingly anti-geometrical is the shortstop, who is placed with no heed to design at all, midway between second and third base, upsetting the whole scheme of regularity like a tiny beauty mark on the cheek of a pretty girl.

One team dresses in white, the other in gray. And the action is static rather than fluid, with sharp, refreshing changes from tension and immobility to quick, brilliant bursts of motion. You may see this curiously exaggerated in newsreel photographs of ball games, because the camera cuts in usually just a second before the flashes of action on the diamond. You catch a glimpse of them stock still first, and then suddenly men are streaking around the bases, heads down, legs twinkling, while fielders glide in to make their quick, graceful defensive moves.

But the plot behind the patterns is even more exciting. Let us take a simple example; the score is tied, there is one out, a runner is on first base, and a heavy hitter is at bat, crouched a little over the plate, waving his mace back and forth gently but menacingly. And, incidentally, he doesn't do this in hopes of frightening the pitcher. He is merely keeping his bat moving because the action he is to be called upon to meet is so fast that he will be hopelessly beaten if he hasn't begun to move a little in advance of it.

There they are, then, the eleven men involved at the moment in what from the point of view of the eventual outcome of the game may be definitely the crisis. The first baseman is dividing his attention between keeping the runner at his base from gaining too much of a lead, and still covering his territory defensively. If the ball is hit, the runner on first will come charging at full clip into second base. Depending upon where the ball is hit to, either the second baseman or the shortstop will have to get there to take the throw and the shock. Or he may not even wait for a hit, but try to steal in the little bit of time between the start of the pitcher's delivery and the passage of the ball to catcher and thence to second baseman. The shortstop is intent upon the delicate problem of starting a successful double play and retiring the side. The third baseman has moved in a little to speed up the fielding of a possible bunt or roller in the infield, and yet he must not leave the space around his base unprotected through which a sharply driven ball may scoot for two or three bases and disaster.

The outfielders have shifted their positions to suit the known batting habits of the hitter. The burly, powerful figure squatting behind the bat, the catcher, is the man in control of the entire situation, and the pitcher is his tool, obeying his brain and his strategy, telegraphed to him by means of finger signals. Or perhaps the catcher is merely an intermediary who transmits the signals and will of an even better strategic mind in the person of the manager sitting on the bench. And the batter is one lone man playing the other nine men, their speed and skill, the intelligence of the catcher in playing his weaknesses, and the control of the pitcher and his ability to obey the orders of the catcher, combined against him. Every move that follows will have a direct bearing upon the outcome of the game. Nothing is unimportant. A double play will badly hurt the morale of the side thus retired with victory in its grasp. A hit or an error or a stolen base may equally upset the equilibrium of the defending team. But still more fascinating and exciting is the fact that all of the men involved are playing a match against time and distance and dealing with the smallest fragments of seconds that can be split on the dial of a delicate stop watch.

The baseball diamond is no diamond at all, but actually a square set up on one of its points, and the bases, home to first, first to second, second to third, and third to home, are each exactly 90 feet apart. The pitcher's box is 60½ feet from home plate. The distance from home plate to second base, which is the line on which the catcher throws in the attempt to catch a man out who is stealing, is a fraction over 127 feet. And the entire science and thrill of the American game of baseball, developed from an old English game called rounders, lie tucked away in those measurements. They are very rarely examined, and still more rarely thought of, even by the players. Most of the men who play the game haven't the vaguest notion of the miracles of timing and precision that they perform.

The infielders, for instance, have a fraction under three seconds in which to field a batted ball and get it over to first base ahead of the runner, because the batter only has to run a distance of thirty yards to reach first. From a standing start a fast man can do it in three and two tenths seconds, and a left-handed batter perhaps one or two tenths of a second faster, because he is on the right-hand side of the plate and a yard closer to his goal. If the fielder can get that ball to first base in just under three seconds, the runner is out. A few tenths of a second over the three seconds and he is safe and a potential run is menacing the defense.

Now, look at the second hand of your watch and note the time it takes for three seconds to tick off—one . . . two . . . three and gone. In this time, the infielder judges the speed and direction of a ball hit with all the weight and force behind the body of a man, moves in to meet it, figuring the hop as he does so, and the number of steps he must take to reach it, catches it and throws it again all in one motion while still moving forward. There is nothing prettier for timing and rhythm in any sport than to watch a shortstop or third baseman (whose problems are greater because, of the infielders, they are farthest removed from first base and have a greater distance to throw) come in fast for a slow roller, and as he is moving, swoop on the ball like a gull dropping for a fish, and with a continuation of the same movement with which he picked it up, get it away on a line for first base with an underhand throw across his forward-bending body. So precious and vital are those tenths of seconds that if he tries to straighten up, or draw his arm back to gain more speed and accuracy, the play is over. The runner has crossed first base.

How much faster, then, and more beautiful in speed and execution is the double play when three men handle the ball in the same length of time and retire two runners on the one play, the man speeding to second (and he has a good head start) and the batter heading for first. Three seconds flat or better, and yet the shortstop fields the batted ball, or rather scoops it over to the second baseman, who sends it on to first. It would take a delicate timing instrument to measure the fraction of a second that the shortstop actually has possession of the ball. Crack! goes the bat. Step, and flip, goes the shortstop! The second baseman in that time has run from his position perhaps five or six yards from the bag as the ball is started towards him by the shortstop. Ball and man meet on the base, and likewise with the same motion, in which there is no check or hesitation, the second baseman whirls and lines the ball down to first. He can whip that ball the ninety feet from second to first in three fifths of a second. And he is lucky to have that much time left.

The catcher has a pretty problem to throw out a man who is trying to steal. A good base-runner will take a lead of from two to three or four yards from first base before he suddenly ducks his head and breaks for second with every ounce of speed he can muster. He can make it in something around three seconds flat, or even a tenth or two under. Unlike a force-out, where it is merely necessary to touch the bag once the ball is in the fielder's possession, the second baseman or shortstop, who receives the throw at second, must touch the runner with the ball before his spikes cut into the bag or he hooks it with his leg. Here is a fine, brisk bit of juggling with time. The runner starts his dash with the wind-up of the pitcher or, as he rarely winds up with a man on base, with his first move to pitch the ball to the batter, usually the first tension or drawing back of the arm. From that time on, the hurler is committed and must go through with the pitch.

The ball travels the sixty feet to the plate, and, just to be mother's little helping hand, the batter takes a cut at it to make it more difficult for the catcher and throw him off if he can. The catcher must receive the ball perfectly, straighten up, whip off his heavy mask, draw back his arm, and fire the ball on a line, not in the general direction of second base, but to the foot of the bag, about ankle-high, so that the receiver is spared that precious tenth of a second or more in getting it onto the sliding runner. If the maneuver is completed inside of three seconds and the throw is accurate, the runner is out. Anything over that and he is safe. It takes a ten-second man to steal a base successfully these days—that is, a man who can run a hundred yards in ten seconds. And every inch of ground that he can chisel by increasing his lead off first without getting caught at it and thrown out at first, is important and vital to the success of this maneuver and has a direct bearing upon the eventual outcome of the game. Those seemingly endless throws that the pitcher makes over to first base to hold the runner close to the bag are not made for exercise or to annoy the customers. The purpose is to reduce those inches. The inches otherwise will be translated into hundredths of a second around second base and spell the difference between safe and out. A man can score from second on a single. Runs depend upon those tiny measurements.

As a matter of fact, no game in the world is as tidy and dramatically neat as baseball, with cause and effect, crime and punishment, motive and result, so cleanly defined. The consequences of a single error or failure pyramid inexorably as the game goes on and finally prove to be the events that have won or lost the day, exactly as the minor, unnoticed incidents unfolded at the beginning of a well-constructed play suddenly loom up as prime and all-important to the climax.

Pretty, too, is the personal duel between pitcher and batter, or rather between the pitcher and his alter or commanding ego, the catcher, and the man who is trying to hit. The problem of the batter seems tremendously magnified when one considers what might be termed the ballistics and forces under which he operates.

The distance between the pitcher's box and home plate, as has been noted, is 60½ feet. And a fast ball will make the trip from the hand of the thrower to the mitt of the catcher somewhere between three and four tenths of a second. That doesn't exactly give a batter much time to turn the matter over in his head and make up his mind whether he will take a cut at it or let it pass for a ball, though it is true the average pitch is somewhat slower and the ball takes four to five tenths of a second for its flight. The average baseball bat is only about three feet long, and the batter's arm permits it to extend for another foot or so. Actually, out of that entire distance of 60½ feet that is traversed by the ball in less than half a second, it is in position to be hit safely by the batter for only three feet of the journey. This brings the time element in which a ball remains in a position where it may be met with the bat close to an absurdity, an impossibility; something around two one-hundredths of a second, which is cutting it rather fine. And still the batsmen manage, on an average, to hit safely one third of the baseballs thrown at them.

To assist the batter and to strike a better balance between him and the pitcher, the latter is forced, if he wishes to register a called strike, to throw the ball to the hitter down a groove a little more than a foot wide, the width of the home plate. And if the pitcher throws more than four of them outside this groove, the batter, as everyone knows, is entitled to the equivalent of a hit, a free passage to first base. The batter is further permitted two misses without penalty. If he misses the third time he is out.

Thus, the activity centered on home plate is really very simple to understand; three strikes out, four balls a walk. But the drama that is packed into that simple arrangement of figures, the swift changes of fortune and situation whereby first one and then the other finds himself in difficulties which with stunning suddenness are liable to mushroom into the loss of the game, explain a good deal of the fascination of the sport.

For instance, the so-called three strikes allotted the batter are a great snare and delusion. In point of fact it is only two strikes, for he is allowed to miss the ball only twice, but nobody but the batter ever thinks of that. The third time he misses it he is out. And yet there is magic in that number "three" and he strides to the plate with great confidence in his allotment of three strikes, a confidence that is only slightly dented upon the calling or taking of the first one, because, after all, there are still two more chances left. Two strikes and he is in for it. Now he must hit. The margin of possible failure has been wiped out. The pressure has suddenly become almost unbearable. And three chances had seemed such a safe margin when he first stepped up to the plate!

But note how the balance of power seesaws between pitcher and hitter. Batter up! The first one comes over—a ball. The batter smirks and pounds the plate with satisfaction. The advantage lies with him now. If the pitcher throws another wide one it means that three out of his next four pitches must be in that groove or the batter walks. Very nice. And so the next throw will bear looking at very closely, because the chances are it will be a strike. There is a little pressure on the pitcher and none whatsoever on the batter. He can afford to relax a little and let the pitcher commit himself on the next ball. He does. Ball two! Ha! Two balls and no strikes. Lovely. The batsman begins to preen himself a little and the pitcher to perspire. That man serving 'em up from the little mound is in for it now. Strike one! Oh, oh! Now the batter is doing a little more thinking. The next one will be more of a problem. Shall he let it pass and hope it will be a third ball, putting the pitcher definitely on the spot, or should he reason that the latter will try to burn it over and get *him* in the hole? Ugh! Strike two! Swung at it and missed it by a foot. Guessed wrong. The pitcher fooled him (or rather the catcher). He should have let it go. Outguessed. Now the batter begins to sweat. The advantage lies with the enemy now. Two balls and two strikes and the pitcher has another ball to waste and can tease him with a bad one, or take a chance of breaking a fast one over the corner of the plate and getting him out. Hardly a moment ago the batter had the situation well in hand. Now he is in a mess. That confounded pitcher is just playing with him. Look at him grinning up there on the mound. All the confidence has oozed out of the hitter and into the hurler. Here it comes —zip! Has the umpire's right arm flashed up? No! A ball! Three and two! Switch again. Now the pitcher is in deep trouble, although the batter is not feeling any too good about the situation. But the odds have passed to the batter because the pitcher must commit himself first. Once that ball leaves his fingers it is irrevocable. There is no calling it back or changing his mind. True, the hitter has only that tenth of a second in which to make his decision as to what he will do with the next pitch, but in a game of such delicate fractions of time it is a decided advantage. He knows that the pitcher cannot afford to walk him, especially if there is only one out, or none, or another man on base already. And if the bases are full the corresponding pressure upon the pitcher is all the greater. No, he must throw the ball down that nice, one-foot groove in which the bat may work to deadliest advantage. His only chance is to put so much spin, or "stuff," on the ball that when it meets the bat instead of rifling off into the outfield for a clean hit, it will deflect to the ground and give the fielders a chance to scoop it up, or glance off high into the air to be caught on the fly. But he might decide to risk it and make the eager hitter bite at one and strike out.

This goes on every minute of the game, and never seems to be twice the same, as the individual duels go on, inning after inning, changing in their nature and intensity according to the situation of the game. Pitching to batters with runners on base increases the pitcher's worries and problems a hundred-fold. Batting in pinches piles pressure upon the batsmen. The situation is always different, and they drive on relentlessly, piling up and piling up to a certain climax as the final innings of the game are reached, increasing in intensity as the pitcher begins to tire and it is a question how long he can respond with accuracy and control to the dictates of the brain behind the bat.

The game is as full of surprises as a mystery play. The plot and its ending may be perfectly apparent up to the ninth inning and the last man at bat, and then with stunning suddenness change entirely and go on to a new ending. A pitcher will often be the hero of a closely fought battle in which his side leads 1–0 for eight innings and the rival batsmen have been looking sillier and sillier as they fanned the air, clawing at curves and drops, or standing with their bats on their shoulders while the ball broke across the plate for perfect called strikes. A batter in the hands of a masterful pitcher is a pitiful sight, anyway. He releases enough energy with each swing to cave in the side of a building and it does nothing but create a mild breeze as bat fails to meet ball. He swings himself clear off his feet and sits awkwardly in the dust from the force of his useless blow. Or he stands looking like a big zany, with his ears turning a beautiful shade of cerise, while a perfect third strike burns past his bosom and the umpire calls him out and the catcher laughs sardonically and makes unpleasant remarks out of the side of his mouth.

These are moments of pure glory and unadulterated satisfaction for the pitcher and his battery mate and their adherents in the grandstands. Or the batter actually connects with the ball with a mighty swipe destined to rip the hide from it, but all that happens is that the ball takes one hop into the hands of the second baseman, who, to show his contempt for the puny effort, tosses the ball underhand to the first baseman.

Even in the ninth inning when an obviously astigmatic umpire, with two out and none on base, calls what was obviously a third strike a fourth ball, and a man reaches first base, there is no cause for alarm. The batters that day are lugging useless timber to the plate and have had no more than three safe hits the entire game. They might just as well have match-sticks in their fingers. And the next man up, the final hitter, is a weak sister, relegated to the lower half of the batting order because he has no reputation or record as a dangerous slugger. The crowd is already beginning to head for the exits, chuckling to themselves at the helplessness of the batters, admiring the skill and control of the pitcher. The catcher calls for a sizzler over the plate, loaded with spin. The weak hitter will ground it to a fielder and the game will be over. In anticipation the pitcher is already standing beneath a cooling shower, listening to the laudatory words of his comrades, and reading the "SHUT-OUT" headlines in the morning papers. Next year he must ask for a raise. He winds up—let the man on base go down to second if he wants to. Now he is in a knot. Now he unwinds. Now he pitches. And now, too, it happens. For, working silently and without warning, the poisons of fatigue in that arm that seemed to be made of steel and whipcord have worked their changes. The pitcher has given the same twist, the same flip of his wrist, the same leverage and follow-through with his body, only instead of slanting towards the batter with blinding speed, the ball comes floating down the groove, all stitches showing, and looking just a shade smaller than a full moon. The batter doesn't have to be a Babe Ruth to nudge that one. He says: "Oh, baby, come to Papa!" laces it into the grandstand for a home run, and that is that.

The game is over. The pitcher has lost 2–1. All he could do was stand there with his hands on his hips, feeling his ears growing long and furry, watching the ball sail over the whisky advertisement affixed to the top balcony. The fielders cannot even make a play for it. The right fielder dutifully has his rump pressed up against the right-field wall, but he would have to be a hundred feet tall to get his hands on that ball and he can do little more than wave it a regretful farewell as it disappears into the crowd.

There you have it. One tiny, uncontrollable slip and the hero has become the dunce, the goat, and the villain. All the failures of the batters that day are forgotten and forgiven, wiped out by that one blow. The sports-writers, some of them, angrily tear sheets of paper from their typewriters, on which they have already begun to write: "In one of the most masterful exhibitions of plain and fancy hurling ever seen at the Polo Grounds, Joie Dokes, diminutive southpaw of the New York Giants, shut out the St. Louis Cardinals 1–0 here yesterday afternoon, letting them down with three hits," etc., etc., insert a fresh piece of paper, and start all over again: "Elmer Crabtree, veteran shortstop of the Cards, hasn't been hitting the length of his cap all year, but yesterday afternoon in the ninth inning of a brilliant pitchers' duel, he stepped to the plate with two out, the score 1–0 against him, and a comrade on base due to walk, and with the count two and two on him," etc., etc., etc.

There are hundreds of these situations brought on during the course of the game, and one could write endlessly of them. I don't mean to do so. But that is why I have liked baseball and always will. It is endlessly intriguing, and when the human element is added to the weird mechanics of the sport, the wise, foxy veterans, the brash, cocky young kids, the eccentric and screwy characters who play the game, it becomes truly a part of the national scene.

But I like, too, the freedom of baseball and the physical and emotional simplicity of the relationship between player and spectator. It is the only game in the world where the onlooker is permitted to heckle, hoot, cheer, and advise the player to his heart's content. I am not particularly concerned whether it is sportsmanlike for an individual concealed beyond hope of detection in some section of the crowd, to howl, purple-faced, as a batter retires from the plate with his tail between his legs after having fanned in a clutch: "Oh, you bum! Go lay down, you bum, yah yeller. Oh, you bum!" but I know that it makes the abusive individual feel wonderful, because I have sat next to him and watched him wipe the sweat off his brow with a damp handkerchief after his tirade, tilt a bottle of pop to his lips, and then look around him to take in the admiring glances of some of the less daring and articulate fans. He has established himself as an expert and a critic. He has hoisted something off his chest. I know him, the poor little man; not man, but mouse. In the office he sits under the thumb of his niggling superior and at home under both thumbs of his wife. Taxidrivers curse him as he scuttles out from beneath their wheels, waiters ignore him, policemen bawl him out, nobody loves him, nobody pays any attention to him. But in the ball park he can rise up on his hind legs and abuse a player. It's good for him, and it doesn't hurt the player any.

So, too, the crowd as a whole plays the role of Greek chorus to the actors on the field below. It reflects every action, every movement, every changing phase of the game. It keens. It rejoices. It moans. It jeers. It applauds and gives great swelling murmurs of surprise and appreciation, or finds relief in huge, Gargantuan laughs. I can stand outside of a ball park and listen to the crowd and come close to telling exactly what is happening on the diamond inside. That quick, sharp explosive roar that rises in crescendo and is suddenly shut off sharply as though someone had laid a collective thumb on the windpipe of the crowd, followed by a gentle pattering of applause, tells its own story, of a briskly hit ball, a fielder racing for it, a runner dashing for the base. The throw nips the runner and the noise too. That steady "Clap-clap-clap-clap-clap. . . ." Tight spot. Men on base, crowd trying to rattle the pitcher. A great roar turning into a groan that dies away to nothing—a potential home run, with too much slice on it, that just went foul. The crowd lives the actions of the players more than in any other game. It is a release and something of a purge. It is the next best thing to participation.

XI

FUNNY

GAME

I HAVE always been conscious of an acute irritation with tennis-players, male and female, and everything connected with the sport. There is something wrong with that game. I wish I knew what it was. A lot of the guys who play it are all right, and so are some of the girls. Could it be that no matter how hard it is played, how many pounds are shed in a match, how brutally the ball is stroked or killed, in what state of collapse the players are carted from the courts after a hard five-set match on a hot August afternoon, it is still sissy? I have never quite dared write this before, though I have long felt it and written around it.

Funny, I used to like to go to Forest Hills and cover the National Championships for men and women, or the Wightman Cup matches, or see the Davis Cup play at Philadelphia. But my back was always up. I never felt comfortable. The atmosphere around tennis matches was always too nicy-nice. Maybe I should have stayed in the fight camps and the ball yards.

And why, for instance, when I play tennis—and I like to play, and play a lot, because it is strenuous exercise and strategically a fascinating game—do I find myself dropping into the same silly gestures, little shrieks of annoyance, flutterings, and remorseful, petulant cries over a missed shot, such as "Oh, no

. . . no," or congratulatory ones such as "Yes . . . yes, beautiful, beautiful. Oh, lovely shot!"? Those are the very things that when I used to sit in the press marquee at Forest Hills or elsewhere to watch the topnotchers, and they did them, used to make me squirm and fidget and yearn to bring the world to a sudden end by getting up and bawling: "Aw, hell, deary! Never mind the sweet nothings. Quit posing and get in there and belt that ball."

My reactions in other sports and at other times are essentially masculine. When I dub the third successive golf shot, I know what to say as I wrap the club around a tree, thanks to a hitch in the Navy and a fine vocabulary picked up at the expense of the Government. I could curse fluently for three miles out of a four-mile crew race at Poughkeepsie when I was a kid, and often found it a relief. But tennis finds me greeting a foozled shot or a bit of bad judgment like a ham actor in a play who has just heard that his house has burned down, his daughter been seduced by the hired man, and his wife eloped with a traveling salesman. All the boys do it.

Nor is this meant to be a reflection upon the men who play the game, because, with isolated exceptions, they are stout, masculine fellows, able wenchers, and good two-fisted drinkers —too good, often. They live normal lives, talk in approved chest tones, keep their hands off their hips, get married, raise families; and several of them could probably beat the hell out of me in a rough and tumble fight; but, with hardly any exceptions, when they go out on the tennis courts and get a racket in their hands, they seem to me to begin to swish a little.

It was probably unfair, in a measure, to the male tennis-players to come to their performances, as I frequently did, fresh from a couple of days at the ball park. Because at its highest development tennis will never be the delicate, hair-trigger game that baseball is, with its splitting of time and movement into the hundredth part of a second. The problems of pitcher, batsmen, and fielders are all drawn to a fine point of nerve and muscular control where the slightest slip is sufficient to ruin the day.

And yet all of a baseball-player's maneuvers, requiring speed, judgment, and sound nerves, are carried out most of the time against a background of noise that is frequently little short of pandemonium. Individual groups in the grandstands and bleachers may try to harass and rattle a pitcher by handclappings or stamping in tempo, and batsmen in a crisis, or standing at the plate in a pinch, may find a steady, unremitting roar of excitement beating at their ears. Added to this are the individual cries from members of the crowd, cries of advice, warning, abuse. And if it is a tight game between leading teams there will be too, very likely, a running fire of heckling and personal and slanderous comment from the opposing players lined up on the dugout steps.

Now, to come directly from having covered baseball to a tennis tournament and find the tennis-player nursed and coddled while he plays a game that, fast as it is, calling for a quick eye, a trained body, and keen judgment, is yet miles behind baseball, might be inclined to make one a little contemptuous not only of the game but of the players as well. When the umpire, enthroned on his outsize high chair, in itself a ridiculous affair, turns his Sunday glare at some over-enthusiastic spectator in the grandstand and makes a few severe and prissy remarks about kindly refraining from applause or comment until the rally is over, there is an overpowering desire to yell: "Oh, nuts!" or whatever the current phrase is at the time. And when a tennis-player falls down after trying for a hard shot and remains on the lawn, panting, until he has made quite sure that everyone in the gallery has seen how hard he has tried and that he would have made it if he hadn't slipped, there is also an almost irresistible temptation to holler through cupped hands: "Get up, you bum, and play tennis."

I find it hard to believe that any tennis-player is such a delicate creature and the demands upon his nerves so great that

he can be thrown out of gear or adjustment by the clacking of
a couple of portable typewriters ten or fifteen yards or more
away in the press stand where a reporter is batting out a running story for the late afternoon editions, or the clicking of a
telegraph key as his operator ticks it off into the office. And
yet, countless times, I have seen many of the boys throw a
pout over towards the press marquee or make an annoyed little
moue in that direction after missing a shot, and the audience
murmurs in sympathy with him and glares, and goes "tsk-tsk-
tsk," that such things should be.

Photographers are all but banished from the tournaments,
or thrust all in one crowd into some far corner lest the sudden
click of their lens shutters should bring on a nervous breakdown
or a sudden attack of hysterics to any of the contestants. They
are suffered to make a few sideline pictures during the preliminary warming up, and some posed shots of handshakings
at the net before the start of a match, but it is made plain that
this is all a great trial to the tennis-players and hardly to be
borne. All the officials and club members give the photographers a good glaring at while it is going on.

And once the heroes and heroines begin to pat the ball back
and forth across the net, a cathedral hush is supposed to mantle
the gathering in the stands as though something sacred were
going on instead of a game that is not particularly punishing or
dangerous.

Tennis can be a fascinating game, both to play and to watch
played by men and women of championship caliber. Once performers have achieved the technical perfection of Donald
Budge, Bunny Austin, or Baron Gottfried von Cramm, and of
course that of the great players of the golden years as well,
Tilden, Johnston, Lacoste, Borotra, Vinnie Richards, and
others, the court strategy becomes at once apparent to the spectator. The game resolves itself into a fine duel of angles,
changes of pace and speed, and the struggle of a player placed
on the defensive, to extricate himself and turn attacker and
force the play. It is artistically as well as emotionally satisfying

to see a good player increase the length of his drives, shot after shot, the way an artillerist lays a creeping barrage, forcing his opponent deeper and deeper beyond his own baseline, and then suddenly finish with a drop shot that falls just over the net, or, reversing the procedure, tease his man in towards center court and then angle him. And, by the way, when you buy your tickets for a tennis match, don't let yourself be lured into the common error of demanding seats on the side and in the center. The place from which to watch a tennis match and see what is going on is *behind* the players and about half-way up.

William Tatem Tilden, Jr., was probably the greatest tennis champion of all time. And Tilden perhaps was also the greatest offender in the matter of the effeminacies of the courts, little gestures of pique or annoyance, dramatic appeals to the high heavens, ringing cries of "Oh, sugar!" sulks and pets and glares at the gallery, but, strangely enough, I seem to have minded them in Tilden least of all. Probably it was because I always regarded Tilden as more of an artist than a tennis-player. If ever a man played a game with positive genius and all the temperamental earmarks of true genius, it was Tilden.

It may seem like a contradiction to write on the one hand of tennis as a not particularly great or taxing sport and on the other of the game giving rise to a genius. But to Tilden a tennis racket was more than merely a wooden frame strung taut with cross-hatched sheep's-gut. It was definitely an instrument of self-expression. Tilden's tennis was sometimes moody, sometimes gay and light, or swashbuckling and phonily dramatic, or stormy, with a hint of lightnings and thunder in it, or at times completely depressed, dull, and lifeless.

He was always more than just an athlete competing in national championships or Davis Cup matches. He was a unique and distinct personality, on the courts with his long, Ichabod Crane body, narrow shoulders, long, prominent jaw, small mouth, and mincing walk. He played not only tennis, but most of the time a part as well. Tilden was a ham at heart. Indeed, he was on the professional stage for a while, and once played the leading role in *Clarence*. On the courts he dramatized himself and he also dramatized his opponent if his opponent would let him. When he would turn, after missing a shot, and make his curious gesture towards the skies with racket and clenched fist, he was genuinely anguished, disturbed, tragic. He didn't give a rap about losing the point. But the great figure of Tilden the Magnificent that he had been playing right up to the hilt had let him down.

You could hardly call his poses posturings, because they were genuine. He was illuminated by his own imagination. I have seen him throw a whole set away because he didn't like it and felt that he had botched a job, like a painter destroying an irritating half-finished canvas. He was frequently guilty of what might have been inexcusable rudeness to officials as well as opponents by throwing points when he disagreed with a decision. It was rude, but it was excusable because Tilden was merely editing the game, the story he was weaving about himself as the central and important figure. He didn't like loose ends or false phrases. The hero was always Tilden, and Tilden was no hero when he batted a ball a foot out past base- or sideline and a slow-witted, astigmatic linesman called it good and gave him an undeserved point. Tilden felt the immediate switch of sympathy to the other man, and this he would never permit because it was a dramatic axiom that sympathy should *never* be permitted to leave the hero. Ergo, he gave the next point away. To him it was the sweet and gallant gesture of the duelist who refuses to take advantage of an opponent temporarily disarmed and with cool disdain steps back and waits for the man to retrieve his weapon.

But what is permitted in an artist, an individual, and a champion of champions does not go so well with the lesser fry. To digress for a moment, the only other game I ever saw that seemed to call forth the same posturings, extravagant gestures, and distinct feminisms that tennis does, is jai alai, or pelota, as played by the Spanish and Basque professionals in Spain and Cuba. This is the handball game played on a three-wall court

with the long, boomerang-shaped basket attachment fastened
to one arm. I used to hang around the jai alai frontons in
Havana just to see the boys put on their acts. Tall, lean, lanky,
black-haired Spaniards, they would, upon blowing an easy kill
shot, lean against the wall and sob, or fall flat on their faces and
lie there until comforted by a team mate and coaxed to get up,
or tear their hair, or open their arms with a wide, despairing
gesture, half to the audience, half to Heaven to witness that
this terrible thing that had happened to them was nothing but
a judgment of an angry God. But these men were Latins and
as temperamental and sensitive as women. I never understood
why Americans should go in for the same sort of thing. It must
be something about the game itself, because nearly all the players seem to do it in one way or another.

Another curious thing about tennis has been its strange development, for no particularly good reason, into a quasi-social
racket. Now, actually, the only sport that is really Social Register, at least in the East, is polo, because championship polo,
or any kind of polo, for that matter, calls for money, large
estates, and leisure time. But the polo crowd, the real blue-
bloods of sport, are a grand, rough, tough, hard-riding, hard-
drinking, hard-talking, completely masculine outfit, friendly,
easy to approach, courteous and well mannered. Whereas the
tennis crowd, in an effort to be considered social, is snobbish
to the point of appearing ridiculous, bad-tempered, bad-mannered, and frequently boorish in its behavior towards public
and press. Years ago tennis actually was what we like to call
Society. Only the wealthy could afford to own tennis courts.
The game was played mainly in and around the social centers
of Boston, Newport, and Philadelphia. The tennis clubs that
existed then were expensive and exclusive. The tournament
players were nearly all people of wealth and position, and so was
the bulk of the small audiences that used to attend the championships. There were no big gates and crowds of thirteen and
fourteen thousand.

But along with every other sport that became drenched in

the golden rain that fell in the decade 1919–29, it suddenly became nigger-rich and popular. A new crowd came in. The outfit always impressed me as being in organization, actions, and general behavior distinctly parvenu.

Twenty-five years ago tennis was not a popular sport. There was a curse on it.

The unfortunate nomenclature of the game had, I suspect, a lot to do with this. Until the advent of Maurice (Red) McLoughlin from California (1912–13) it was impossible to convince anyone that a game in which you called out to your opponent: "Forty—love!" was anything but a pastime for dudes and sissies. Then there is "deuce," and to "lob" and to "rally," a "let" ball, and a "fault"—all words that somehow do not seem to have the connotations of a manly sport. If you were caught playing the game at one of the few public courts somebody was sure to call out: "Forty—love, dear. . . . Don't get your pretty white pants dirty. . . ." Oh yes, I forgot. Tennis was played in white pants, for many years an object of ridicule and abhorrence to the more elemental citizens.

McLoughlin, the red-headed Californian, broke the ice in 1912. He came from the Pacific Coast, was just plain folks, had an ugly mug and a lot of freckles, was thoroughly masculine, and, compared to the style of tennis then in vogue, played like a whirlwind. He hit a tennis ball like a heavyweight prizefighter trying to land a knockout blow. Some of the old guard thought that it was unfair and unmannerly to hit the ball so hard and out of reach, but a lot more people thought it was swell. And he introduced the cannon-ball service. Ah, "cannon-ball"—that was more like it. A man or a boy could talk about his cannon-ball service, whether he had one or not, without being ragged. There was nothing sissy about that, and there was nothing sissy about the way, hot off McLoughlin's racket, it zipped past opponents who could do little more than stand flatfooted and wave at it as it went by. The game began to speed up. In a little over two years McLoughlin had managed to take a good deal of the curse off the sport. After him followed R. Norris Williams, another wholly masculine personality, with his trim, wiry frame, short-cropped black hair, keen, thoroughbred face, and fast, aggressive style of play. Dick Williams was one of the few male tennis-players I have ever watched who managed to be completely graceful without being effeminate.

At the same time women's tennis, which up to then had been little more than pat ball, took a sudden turn for the better with the appearance of a Norwegian girl by the name of Molla Bjursted, later Mrs. Molla Mallory. Mary K. Browne had been playing some fairly fast tennis over the years 1912, 1913, 1914, when she was national champion, but Molla, when she came to this country from Norway in 1915, had the same kind of color that McLoughlin had had. She was a brown, hard, tigerish woman, and she slugged the ball like a man. She served hard and hit fast, low, stinging drives. And shortly before the start of the second decade of the twentieth century came the whole pack and parcel of great and colorful tennis-players, Little Bill Johnston, Big Bill Tilden, Helen Wills, Suzanne Lenglen, Manuel Alonso, Vinnie Richards, Lacoste, Cochet, Borotra— names that suddenly acquired tremendous box-office value. The West Side Tennis Club at Forest Hills, Long Island, a fairly well-to-do but not particularly blueblooded organization composed half of New Yorkers, half of suburbanites, erected the first real tennis stadium the country had ever known, a steel and concrete horseshoe that seated fourteen thousand people (most uncomfortably on stone seats) around three grass courts, and simultaneously began to give itself airs.

The public, suddenly aware that there was a good show going on, clamored to see the famous tennis-players wherever they appeared. It would pay any price for admission. A tennis club had merely to announce a tournament and throngs flocked to the gates with money in their fingers. The money was welcome, but the throngs—never; and the press, which by publicizing the stars and the matches was making the gates possible, least of all. With no exceptions the tennis clubs in the East ran their public tournaments at which admission was charged, maintaining the attitude that public and press were unwarranted intruders trespassing on private property. The gate was wonderful, the publicity was wonderful, including the pictures in the papers which showed the grounds, the clubhouse, and the officials; and the show was a cinch because they got the talent and the stars practically for nothing. But the press was requested to use the tradesman's entrance and keep out of sight, the photographers were treated as though they had communicable diseases, and the paying public was dumped into unshaded, unsheltered stands in the broiling heat, heckled and bullied and bawled at by officious officials, and kept waiting from twenty minutes to an hour, frequently, beyond the advertised starting times of matches, owing to mismanagement or the temperament and caprices of the stars, and kept waiting, further, without explanation or apology.

If the tennis crowd had been real people they would have known how to handle the sudden burst of publicity and prosperity. But to a great extent the crew upon whom the handling of the suddenly spotlighted tournaments devolved were strictly nouveau-riche small-timers with a little money and the notion that the way to make people think they were aristocratic and superior was to be rude to them. They knew nothing about presenting a show from the promotion point of view and either knew nothing or cared less about the obligations they took upon themselves when they began to sell tickets, and the courtesies and comforts due someone who had paid from two to five dollars' admission to see an advertised performance.

The U. S. Lawn Tennis Association suddenly found itself catapulted into a position of some prominence and power, as having absolute authority over the money-drawing tennis stars, male and female. The players were lionized and became a social asset to the members of the Tennis Association. The stars needed the tennis association with its quasi-social connections, because the new crop of tennis-players were strictly commoners, and tournament tennis was a distinct step up the social ladder (witness Helen Wills), and certainly in the boom days the key that unlocked the doors to an easy living at no expense to them among the people that looked like the upper crust but weren't. But how were the kids who played the game to tell the difference? The tennis associations worked the stars for all they were worth, the stars worked the associations for all *they* could get; it was all one happy, snooty family who made up their own rules, apparently, and lived by them, barely tolerating the vulgar herd as long as it had money to contribute at the gate.

Money was needed more and more as the tennis stars suddenly discovered that there was a racket going on and that if the scales were unbalanced as to sharing the profits, it was against them. The tennis clubs, in addition to publicity and prestige, were hauling in gate receipts. The players' expenses began to pick up, and it became increasingly expensive to entertain them. But even with the most they could make, chisel, or hornswoggle out of amateur tennis, the players never even approached any kind of percentage of the take for which their drawing power was responsible.

The Lawn Tennis Association held a power over them that was practically absolute in spite of the fact that these men and women were amateurs and the association was both ostensibly and actually guarding their amateurism jealously. For it was obvious that if a player proved recalcitrant and suggested that he did not care to journey all the way to Maquepoisette to compete in the annual Maquepoisette invitation tournament (and besides, their liquor was lousy), he might find that when the really important (socially) invitation tournaments came along, tournaments that meant a week of high living in the utmost luxury in exclusive country-club surroundings with free meals, free drinks, free laundry (those white pants), free everything, his name might be missing from the list. Or, worse still, he might be ignored when it came time to select the squad for the Davis Cup trials.

The Tennis Association's solicitude for the amateurism of

its players was in part an honest desire to keep the sport reasonably clean and amateur, but in equal part a cool, out-and-out business proposition. Tennis more than any other sport at the time was threatened by professionalism, and the threat hit right to the wallet.

There had been a few tennis professionals, teachers of the game attached to the clubs, but they rarely appeared in public. The Tennis Association had the game and the racket completely to itself on a wonderful basis. It, or rather the member clubs, took all the swag. The players who drew the money got nothing, or at least as little as it was possible to give them. But along came, first, C. C. Pyle, a high-pressure promoter, and cleaned up on the professional tennis tour of Suzanne Lenglen with Mary K. Browne as a foil, and later a former gymnasium attendant and rubber by the name of Bill O'Brien went into partnership with Bill Tilden, organized the first professional tennis in America, and became its first real promoter. He was able to offer, not the unknown racket-stringers and instructors of the former professional tennis world, but the very stars who had once drawn the crowds as amateurs: Tilden, Richards, Hunter, Kinsey, Snodgrass, Kozeluh, Nusslein, Vines, Stoefen, Bell, Barnes, George Lott, and one or two of the Frenchmen. The professional tennis tours simply coined money. The stars were handsomely paid, the promoter made a nice profit. The matches were brilliantly staged, punctual, colorful, completely honest, and played under conditions which gave the paying public the best of it. The professionals had cut in on the sweet and easy and lucrative racket of the amateur outfit.

The U. S. Lawn Tennis Association, composed for the most part of a few near-sighted antiques in Hoover collars, wasn't smart enough to open the doors as the Golf Association had done and stage an Open Championship in which the best professionals and the best amateurs meet in a common tournament, the pro taking his winnings in cash, the amateur his in plate. Because it meant sharing the swag they fled panic-stricken or turned and fought the professionals. How panic-stricken and absurd they were is indicated by an incident that occurred a summer or so ago after Ellsworth Vines had turned professional, when officials ordered him tossed out of the marquee at Forest Hills during a national championship. As an amateur, Vines had drawn thousands of dollars through the turnstiles at Forest Hills and had further sacrificed many years to the thankless job of Davis Cup play. But when he became a professional, or, as we used to put it, "turned square," and began to reap some of the financial benefits of his work and skill, he became a pariah, not fit to be in the same inclosure with amateurs. Wow! It was ridiculously easy to read their scared tuppenny minds—if all of the stars turned professional, no more big gates, no more importance, no more social prestige, no more pictures in the paper. And in the meantime they had their clubs and, above all, that big stadium on their hands.

The tennis-players themselves, with a few exceptions, very quickly took their cues from the people who were patronizing and promoting them and learned how to be snobs, bores, boors, and general pains in the neck. Most of them were of the new generation, with no idea how to evaluate and accept the publicity and adulation that were showered upon them. Many of them felt that when they were accepted into the circle of the tennis crowd they had come up in the world, and so they modeled their attitudes and manners upon those of their hosts, which for the most part were bad. They came to look upon themselves as rather exceptional creatures, which none of them were; outside of being able to play tennis, they were for the most part a set of pretty dull young men and women.

Tournament tennis is exacting. To remain in the select circle you had to be a winner. To be a winner you had to play all the time, winter and summer, at home and abroad. It left very little time for intellectual development. The phrase "tennis bum" was coined by George Lott, an amateur star who later became a professional. It described trenchantly and graphically the young men caught in the toils of the tennis-social racket, wasting some of the best years of their lives for the benefit of what, examined over the record of the past ten or twelve years, seems to have been a worthless and useless crew. I feel somehow that I am going to be able to bear up rather well, away from tennis-players, clubs, and officials.

XII

PUNCH

WITH

HIM

FIGHTERS HAVE always fascinated me. Prizefighting is a swinish business, but the men who engage in it as a profession are, in many respects, human beings. They eat, sleep, walk, talk, drink, live, and love, but withal are a strange people and to me always a race apart. Probably it is because I am myself not a combative type that I have never quite been able to understand what makes a prizefighter tick and have therefore looked upon these relatively simple creatures with awe and some bewilderment.

I cannot, for instance, understand how it is possible to step up to a beaten, semi-conscious man whose hands are down at his sides, whose legs are wobbling, eyes glassy, head relaxed and rolling drunkenly on his neck, and slug that defenseless man on his chin as hard as it is possible to hit him. I have, in my lifetime, hated intensely, and wished to see a man destroyed. But once he was helpless and wounded, there was nothing left but pity; no hatred, no driving forces left. Perhaps it is because the prizefighter conducts his labors utterly without any emotions whatsoever, certainly without hatred for his opponent, that he is able to operate in such a wholly cold-blooded and efficient manner.

As a matter of record, the only really emotional prizefighter I ever knew was Jack Sharkey, and he was therefore a bad one. He was a brilliant boxer, a good, punishing hitter, and something of a master technician, a thorough workman with every known type of punch or attack, but his emotions nearly always managed to get into the way of his work. He was always bursting into tears or having hysterics, or waving his arms about, exposing his chin, or threatening to jump out of the ring—obviously a handicap. Sharkey was one of the few fighters on the big time that I have ever known who had to cook up a mad-on at an opponent, or dramatize himself before he could do justice to his task. And then his emotions, hatred, rage, jealousy, pride, or whatever they were, would get him into trouble.

Another puzzle that I have never satisfactorily solved is how men can be friends and sometimes close companions, as many fighters are, having been buddies in their amateur days, or stablemates—fighting for the same manager—at one time or another, and then step into the ring with one another and fight, slug, cut, and bruise and practice upon one another every cruelty and foul trick that is in a fighter's repertoire.

I suspect that I have always been much too romantic, sentimental, and imaginative to appreciate the true hardness and grimness of what is known as the Sweet Science; perhaps I have always approached the ring from the fiction-writer's angle. But I seem to see myself standing in a prize-ring, bare to the waist, gloved, waiting for the bell, and looking over across at the other man, a friend, and hearing myself say, a trifle maudlinly but in the best dramatic tradition: "You are my friend. I have known you, broken bread with you, shared a little of both joy and sorrow with you. I cannot lift my hand to hurt you."

If there are any friendships among fighters, they manage to cease inside the ropes. Men whale away at one another with complete and unmerciful ferocity while the fight lasts, afterwards grin at one another through blood and sweat, shake hands, and that is that. I have asked many fighters how they felt about this, how they could bring themselves to cripple a friend and knock him out if they managed to get him going. None of them were ever able to give me an intelligent answer, or any kind of an answer beyond: "Oh, I dunno. It's different when you're in the ring. We got no hard feelings afterwards." Well, I suppose the manufacturer or the merchant cuts his pal's throat just as cold-bloodedly with a "Sorry—business, you know."

There are two kinds of prizefighters, apparently: rough and dirty, and gentlemanly and dirty. My favorites have always been numbered among the former. I have as little patience with the attempts to whitewash the ring as I have with the phony dodges used to scent horseracing or college football. A fight is a fight and there is rarely ever anything pretty about it. The ring is a dirty game and it smells bad. But it is exciting, colorful, Rabelaisian, earthy. It attracts the rabble and the unwashed. It stinks of bodies and liniment and leather and blood and it appeals to the so-called lowest instincts of humankind. But they are still humankind's instincts, and therefore important. I resent attempts to prettify something that isn't pretty, however, and I never had much use for the dandified fighter with his hair parted in the middle and slicked back, with his dancing-master form and his penchant for smiling and shaking hands, especially immediately after he has fouled an opponent by sticking his thumb in his eye.

Not that I am particularly outraged by fouling or thumbing, or share the indignation of the crowd, quick to rise to a wholly spurious and phony anger if one of the boys lets one go that isn't exactly on the belt line. It is phony because it is shared usually only by one half the crowd, the half that has bet on or favors the man who has been nudged below the equator. True, there are rules for boxing just as there are for every other sport, but I have always felt that in a way they were false and insincere rules. When two men are loosed in a ring it is still fundamentally a fight. The gloves they are wearing are chiefly a concession to the wowser element, and the rules about hitting low, backhanding, gouging, biting, and hitting on the back of the neck, purely formal. Gloves are really more of a protection to the hands of the hitter than to the face of his opponent. A glancing blow of knuckles encased in leather can and does cut as cleanly as a surgeon's knife. And the first thing an experienced fighter does in his corner or in the dressing-room, in whichever the mittens have been laced on, is to break them—that is, work the padding away from the knuckles.

What remains of our sense of decency has, in public competition, outlawed gouging and biting, kicking in the groin, and applying the boot to a fallen opponent—though those things are done all the time to the delight of the audience in modern catch-as-catch-can wrestling exhibitions and frauds—but, fundamentally, when the gong is struck, two men are unleashed against one another for purposes of destruction. Our present state of civilization and temper is such that it demands that the manner of this destruction shall be hampered by tying up the hands of the combatants in little leather bags instead of furnishing them with knives or axes. And yet these are only temporary hindrances and may be changed as we continue to change. Indeed, in recent years the New York State Athletic Commission has rearranged the most precious and catholic rule of the prize-ring and fair play so as to read that a fighter who has been felled by a blow struck below the belt and who has failed to arise before the count of ten has been completed shall be ruled to have been legitimately knocked out. Thus, rules change and vary, but the basic idea remains the same. Two men are to try to do one another as much injury and damage as they possibly can within an allotted space of time, and when the time is up, the least damaged man, if he has also dealt out the greater part of the punishment, is adjudged the winner, and everyone goes home dissatisfied and there are endless arguments. There is only one satisfactory ending to a prizefight: that when one of the fighters is unconscious on the deck, unable to rise, and is counted out, or is in such a helpless state that the referee intervenes mercifully and rules that a technical knockout has been scored.

As I look back over more than a decade of fighters I knew and saw in action, the perfect fighter, to me, next to Dempsey, in type the pure, unspoiled standard-bearer of the prize-ring, was a middleweight from Nebraska by the name of Ace Hudkins. He wasn't the best fighter in the world; indeed, he was never a world's champion; but he was tough, hard, mean, cantankerous, combative, foul, nasty, courageous, acrimonious, and filled at all times with bitter and flaming lust for battle.

If there was a kindly trait in Hudkins, I never knew it. He was as bad outside the ring as he was in. Too, he was completely careless of his own person in a fight. He never bothered to box, or jab, or duck, or go through the orthodox picture-book maneuvers. When the signal was given, he did an about-face in his corner, came forth, and immediately began to batter and claw at his opponent as though he wanted to kill him. He very probably did.

He weighed usually around a hundred and fifty pounds and had sort of pinkish, tousled hair, a long, stubborn jaw that always showed a four-day stubble of beard—it was useful to rub against an opponent's skin in the clinches, to make it raw and sore—and a pair of the most baleful and vindictive blue eyes ever placed in a human head. His lips were thin and his teeth always bared in a snarl. He was utterly vicious, truculent, and brutal. He would heel, rip, thumb, and butt with his head. He was meant to be strictly a rough-and-tumble bar-room fighter. He was a bad, bad boy in the ring, and outside it, too, where his fondness for packing a cannon got him into several entanglements with the law. Had he lived some eighty years earlier in Nebraska, he would have become a killer pure and simple, another Billy the Kid perhaps, and would have died with his boots on, his skin full of lead. He was so tough and brutal in the ring that the late Commissioner Muldoon, who in the later years of his life developed an astonishing set of inhibitions, barred him from New York rings simply because he was everything and all that a prizefighter should be.

I remember the first time that Hudkins came east to fight. He was then no more than a lightweight with a fair Western reputation. We had a little East Side ghetto fighter by the name of Ruby Goldstein in New York City, one of those fast, smart little Jewish boys with a straight left followed by an even straighter right that could knock your brains out. Ruby's ego had been nicely inflated by a series of set-up fights in which he slaughtered an astounding list of pugilistic sacrifices. He thought that he was unbeatable and that he could stiffen anyone he could hit. He was pretty good, too. It was thought that he was ready to step out a little, so this unknown from the West by the name of Ace Hudkins was brought on, and they fought one night back in 1926 at the Coney Island Stadium with the rumble, roar, and crash of the roller coasters and the ceaseless din of the Surf Avenue barkers in their ears.

It was a pleasantly entertaining little match for three rounds between a mauler and a deft boxer. And then in the fourth Ruby let the right go straight down the groove, and down went Hudkins, just like the rest of them—stiffened. He never moved for four seconds. Goldstein turned his back and walked casually over to a neutral corner, mentally dusting off his hands. The night's work was done. It was not quite done, however, for at five Hudkins stirred, at six he rolled over. At eight he was on his hands and knees and at nine he was on his feet, his teeth bared, and his ominous blue eyes and curled lips giving his face a look of depraved and primitive savagery. His breath was whistling through his teeth, his knees were trembling a little, but he was swaying back and forth just like a cobra preparing to strike, and his hands were up and cocked. That was what little Ruby saw when he turned around to watch the referee complete the formality of counting his opponent out. Thirty seconds later Goldstein was draped over the second rope strand like a wet dishcloth hung on a rack to dry. He no longer heard the roller coasters or the carousel music or the sharp snapping of the cheap rifles in the shooting galleries. He woke up some time later in his dressing-room and never could fight a lick thereafter.

There was no mercy in Hudkins, no latent love for man, and no one ever, that I remember, took the trouble to send out press-agent stories that he was kind to his mother. I never saw him wear a bathrobe into the ring, but merely a short jersey with a stand-up collar. His nose was flat and his ears were thick. He liked to maul, to hold with one hand and strike and claw with the free one, or rest his stubble chin on the shoulder of an opponent and with both hands rip out his belly. He laughed when he was stung, a nasty, sneering laugh, and he was stung often because he couldn't box very well and never cared to try. All he wanted to do was fight, fight, fight. Never mind the pitty-pat, you-jab-me-and-I'll-jab-you stuff, the shaking-hands, the stepping back and giving an opponent a chance to recover his balance after a slip, the apologizing for fouls, intentional or otherwise. Civilization and the niceties had just skipped him. Well and good. This is what a fighter should be like to deserve the name. The important thing in his business and his life was to win, not how he won. Let the apologists sing: "It isn't how you win or lose, but how you play the game . . ." or however the doggerel goes. Ace knew better. And so does any fighter bent on conquest.

There was another fighter who was a particular pet of mine—curious how one adopts these brutes—a black-haired, shuffling, heavy-browed German-American by the name of Paul Berlenbach, an ex-wrestler, ex-amateur boxer who became the light-heavyweight champion of the world. His nicknames were "Punch 'em Paul," "Paralyzing Paul," and "The Astoria Assassin." Berlenbach was a simple boy from the Yorkville section of New York, untutored, unlettered, slow-witted, slow-moving, and wholly lacking in animation or imagination. I have come into his dressing-room many times before important fights and found him stretched out on the rubbing-table fast asleep. They would let him sleep until it was time to lace on the leather and go into the ring.

But he had a magic, this boy. It was a numbing, paralyzing body punch that caused his opponents suddenly to crumple up as though they had been struck by a .44 slug. It was a slow punch, too. None of your quicker-than-the-eye Joe Louis drives that are so swift that they blur on the camera plates. Sometimes Paul seemed merely to be dropping his right hand to the side of an opponent, in the manner in which one places a friendly hand on someone's shoulder. Sometimes he would hit his opponent on the chin, but more often he just hit him in the side and caved in his ribs. Often it would happen in a clinch and you wouldn't see the blow at all. His opponent would suddenly wilt, go limp, collapse to the floor, and stay there.

Berlenbach had very little to offer in the way of defense, a matter which later proved to be his destruction, because he came up against hitters who measured him before he could get close and punched him silly. His only method of fighting was to shuffle in, pawing with his left glove like an awkward bear, and then sweep his right hand to the body. He had a funny little jiggy step he would do to wind himself up to start an attack, and he did it every time he was disturbed or pushed or knocked off balance—one-two-three, hoppity-skip, and then would come the relentless shuffle forward again, head sunk low between his shoulders, black eyes squinting out of a dead-white face screwed up in complete concentration on his work, his left foot leading him on, his right foot dragging after.

I suppose that he was fascinating for the same reason that Dempsey was fascinating, the same reason that the Negro Joe Louis is coining a fortune in spite of his defeat by Schmeling, because he had the power to destroy, to blast men like the ancient gods. It is a power given to very few fighters. They score their knockouts here and there, but not to many is given the aura of approaching and inevitable doom that Berlenbach carried with him.

With his black hair standing up stiff and straight, pompadour style, somber eyes, black tights, pale skin, and sloping shoulders, he needed nothing but the black mask over his face to make him look like a medieval executioner. His victims were more than half hypnotized by the time the bell rang and they had to get up to face him. Joe Louis had the same effect on many of his early opponents. It is a powerful factor in the lethal quality of a punch if the recipient-to-be thereof is half scared to death before he gets it. Even if it isn't quite as hard as necessary to lull him to sleep, the first hard poke he gets he is liable to say to himself auto-suggestively: "Oh, oh! That's it. Here I go."

But Paul was vulnerable. He was too slow and methodical in his attack to have it constitute a defense. Dempsey never had to bother to defend himself during his heyday because he kept the other fellow so busy trying to survive. But every time Berlenbach fought, it was like a division going over the top and walking into machine-gun fire. Those that survived the head-on deadly blast and reached the machine-gun nest blew it up and bayoneted the crew. But the price was always high. Very often Berlenbach waded through sheer hell on wheels to reach his man, taking a brutal pounding about the head until he could herd him into a corner, pin him there, and work his magic on him. Once he had him there, one or two applications usually sufficed. But Paul walked through one barrage too many. The first really sharp and deadly hitter he met in his sensational rise, a French-Canadian by the name of Ovila Chapdelaine who fought under the name of Jack Delaney, knocked him out. Or, rather, he stopped him. Nobody ever really knocked Berlenbach cold. But he had a curious and, for a fighter, a fatal weakness. Punches around the temple and high on the head made him dizzy and caused him to reel helplessly around the ring like a Saturday-night drunk. The technical knockout didn't stop him, however, because he had an antidote for his weakness —his total lack of imagination. His capacity for thinking was, I suspect, limited, and his capacity for memory practically nil.

Long after his career was over and he had been stopped and knocked loose from his senses many times, floored, and saved by a humane referee, I met him over in Astoria one day, and he mumbled that he was training for a come-back; he had had his hands fixed. "That's all that was the matter with me," he said; "my hands. . . . Nobody ever hurt me or knocked me down, isn't that so? I'm gonna make a come-back. . . ." They are always making come-backs, these derelicts of the ring. And he was talking to a man who had seen every one of his fights and suffered through more knockdowns than he could count. But before he retired, he did go on to win the world's championship at his weight, 175 pounds, and made himself a comfortable annuity and quit the ring, a thoroughly unhappy young man with sufficient income to live on the rest of his life, and nothing, nothing whatsoever, to do to occupy his time.

The man who knocked him out the first time, Jack Delaney, was another of the great romantic ring characters of that era, a light heavyweight too, and likewise eventually champion of the world. He won it from Berlenbach in the third of four fights that they had.

He was one of the handsomest men that ever stepped into a prize-ring, tall, slim, lyrically graceful, with curly dark hair and flashing teeth and eyes. He was a brilliant boxer with a picture style, a long left arm extended and used like a rapier, and his right hand, the killer, cocked at his chest ready to burn through an opening. He moved, or rather he glided, like a ghost. One was never conscious that his feet were moving, and he carried himself like a king, head held high, with a proud and regal bearing. He was supposed to have Indian blood in his veins and he would truly stalk his prey like a redskin, waiting patiently for the opening, fiddling and fencing and scoring with his left, but watching with his sharp, black eyes for that momentary slip or lapse into carelessness. When it came, his right would flash and generally it was all over. He was one of the few fighters who was a one-punch knocker-out. He was also one of the few fighters who knocked a man out twice on the same night. He was matched once with a very good Negro fighter by the name of Tiger Flowers—Deacon Flowers they called him, because he was a dignitary of a small Southern church and he always read the Bible in his dressing-room before going into the ring—well, anyway, it made a good story, whether he did or not. Delaney floored Flowers with that whistling right hand after a round had passed, and Flowers was counted out. But there was a dispute over the manner of the count, Flowers's manager claiming that the Negro was up off the floor before ten. The fans took sides and it looked as though there might be a riot. An unprecedented thing, Flowers asked for another chance, and, still more unprecedented, Delaney gave it to him. It staved off what might have been a nasty brawl around the ringside. They boxed nicely for another round and then in the fourth Delaney let that old persuader go again. This time Flowers didn't get up at all. When he came to, he went around to Delaney's dressing-room and shook hands and said: "Ah wants to thank you, Mr. Delaney, and tell you that Ah is convinced."

Delaney was throughout a romantic character. He had been bought by his manager, Peter (the Fox) Reilly, for nine hundred dollars when it looked as though he was through because of bad hands. Reilly ran him into a half-million-dollar property. He was married to a pale, pretty wife whom he seemed to adore. He was ostensibly a child of nature who loved to fish and hunt in the wilds, and when his training and his fights were over he would retire to a woodland lodge he owned in New Hampshire on Lake Winnepesaukee and commune with nature.

Sports-writers who visited him there were impressed with his simplicity. He seemed such a plain, happy woodsman at heart, with his love for nature, and his keen eyes that made him a fine shot, and an accurate hand at throwing a knife, Indian style. It was early to bed and early to rise. Never was there a drop of liquor to be had or seen at his camp, and the gentlemen of the press who were used to strong stimulants pocketed their various types of thirst during their sojourns there out of respect for the wishes of this simple soul, and drank milk, or fruit juices, or water, as he did.

There was only one serious trouble with Delaney, and that

eventually speeded up the finish of his career in the ring. He drank. He went off on protracted sprees that lasted for days. Actually, one of the greatest managerial and press-agenting jobs for preventive publicity in the history of boxing was turned in by Pete Reilly; not until long after he was through with the ring did anyone ever find out that each and every one of the disasters and catastrophes that eventually met Delaney in the ring and cost him a chance at the heavyweight championship was caused, directly or indirectly, by his having been on a bender. So well did Reilly build up his character of nature's child that no one ever dreamed the real reason why no liquor was in evidence at Delaney's camps.

In 1927 Delaney was matched with Jim Maloney, a second-rate heavyweight from Boston. Had Delaney knocked Maloney out, as he was capable of doing, he would have been rewarded with a chance at Gene Tunney and the heavyweight championship, plus a three- or four-hundred-thousand-dollar purse. Maloney won the decision in ten rounds. Delaney never let his right go. Years after the fight Pete Reilly told me what had happened. Delaney had escaped from his training camp while preparing himself for this match and had gone on a three-day toot. During the course of it he took a punch at the head of a Pullman porter on the New York, New Haven and Hartford. The porter ducked and Delaney mashed his right hand into the steel side of the car. Not even Reilly knew that. The wise, gray-haired little manager found it out under most unpleasant circumstances. When during the course of the fight with Maloney it was obvious that Delaney was losing and wasn't shooting that right at his big, lumbering target, Reilly commanded, implored, cajoled, pleaded with him to throw it and knock Maloney out. It was while sitting on his stool between rounds that Delaney for the first time revealed to Reilly that he couldn't use it. It was useless. "I felt," said Mr. Reilly, "like hitting him over the head with the bottle."

The last time I ever saw Delaney fight, he was apparently drunk in the ring. Gone were his fine slimness and keenness and regal bearing. His face was bloated and puffy, and he was so tight that when the bell rang for the opening round he didn't hear it, but stood stupidly staring in his corner while his opponent, Jack Sharkey, ran over towards him and then stopped in mid-ring, dazed by Delaney's amazing attitude, wondering whether *he* had heard aright.

That was one of our more charming evenings in the New York prize-ring, anyway. Rickard and Tunney were in Miami preparing to sign Tom Heeney for a championship match with Tunney for the world's heavyweight title. Delaney and Sharkey were matched, and Buckley, Sharkey's manager, wired Rickard frantically not to sign Heeney until after his man had fought Delaney. Everybody was around saying that the outcome had been arranged. And Delaney was drunk. And after the fight Sharkey was accused of having been hopped up with drugs to enable him to vanquish a man who wasn't going to win anyway. It wound up in a blaze of glory and laughter, with Delaney being counted out while crawling around on his hands and knees like a man looking under a bureau for a collar-button, munching stupidly on his red rubber mouthpiece half protruding from his face, while Sharkey slithered along the ropes weeping like a fifth-rate ham actor. It was a dilly. When Rickard had the news of it in Miami, he laughed too, and immediately signed Heeney. That dear prize-ring. Maybe I am going to miss it after all.

XIII

PIGS

AT THE

TROUGH

THE NEXT time you are in or about Rome, take a day off and drive up to the famous walled city of Tarquinia. There is a museum there, for Tarquinia is built upon or close to the site of the stronghold of the ancient Etruscans, a race of high civilization, older than the Romans by a thousand years, perhaps, and you can get the curator or watchman to take you on a little trip, a mile or so out of the city, to visit the painted tombs of Etruria.

He will fetch an acetylene lantern and an enormous iron key-ring on which are large and medieval-appearing keys, and climb into your car with you. They have built stone kiosks, looking like our subway entrances, over the opened tombs, barred and locked them. The curator selects a key from his bunch, the lock grinds and complains as he opens it. He lights his lamp and leads you down a flight of slanting, slippery steps. At first in the semi-darkness of the tiny chamber you see nothing. But then, as your eyes grow accustomed to the light and he plays his flickering yellow beam on the walls, you find yourself looking at wall paintings, frescoes of a vanished race and civilization, as fresh in color and life, almost, as the day they were painted, more than two thousand years ago. And there, on one of the walls of a tomb belonging to a deceased man who was apparently in life a devotee and patron of sports, is a painting which is in itself almost the whole history of the ancient and dishonorable game of boxing.

It depicts two boxers squared off to one another, almost in the modern orthodox position, left hand and left foot extended, right hand cocked at the chin, arm bent at the elbow. One of the boys in the painting has his hands set in the usual manner that you will see today in photographs of a couple of fighters posing without boxing gloves on; that is, with the fingers held together, or curled into a fist. But the other has the thumb of his left hand nicely extended away from the side of the hand, cocked and ready to poke it into his opponent's eye. The artist who carried out his commission in that house of the dead had a sense of humor. He couldn't resist the temptation to immortalize what even then must have been one of the oldest tricks in the ring, the left lead to the eyeball. You say: "Excuse me," if you are caught out at it, and extend your hands in a quick, gallant, frank gesture of apology. Then, while your opponent is blinking through the tears and trying to get his sight back, you hit him quickly and violently on the chin in what is nothing more than a humane gesture to put him out of his misery. It's still done.

And, incidentally, the boxers of Etruria antedate the brutal cestus of the Greek and Roman arenas. It was our Mr. Tunney, a heavyweight champion with quasi-cultural leanings, who used to like to advise after-dinner gatherings that boxing in the olden days began with the use of the cestus, that contraption of leather, studded with iron, bound around the fists and wrists. But Mr. Tunney was falling into a common error. It didn't. The Etruscans wrapped their knuckles and reinforced their wrists with soft bandages, because they, too, had made the discovery voiced not long ago by Monsieur Leon See, the French boxing manager, that the hand was never by nature intended to be a striking weapon, and that it was always getting out of kilter when used for that purpose. The pug of today, before he draws on his six-ounce fighting gloves, wraps his hands and wrists with the same kind of bandages and uses the same manner of bandaging that you may still make out on the long-vanished battlers of Tarquinia. The modern sometimes has a slight improvement which he adds if he thinks he can get away with it to aid him in his work—namely, a length or two of bicycle or hard adhesive tape over the knuckles, which does away with some of the anatomical faults in the structure of the hand and makes it more effective as a bludgeon. He thinks it is a new idea. It isn't. The Romans thought of it a few centuries before.

It must be fairly obvious that the first play-fighting or boxing in its rudimentary stage was done with the bare hands. The earliest known hand-bandages are those depicted on the Etruscan tombs and were used, as I have indicated before, not to spare or protect the party of the second part so much as to conserve the hands of the other party. It was the Roman who found the soft bandage too tame. One might almost measure the degeneracy and decline of Roman civilization by the increasing refinement of their boxing weapon.

The soft bandage protected the hands all right, but it also in a way spared the features on which it landed and got to be a bore. Good stiff leather wrappings, it was found, safeguarded the hands even more, but also made nice clean gashes in faces and bodies. There was blood, but not enough. The leather was then reinforced and studded with knobs and strips of iron that were capable of smashing in the side of a man's head—and did. This brought the spectacle of the boxing match neatly up to the Roman standard of entertainment. The penalty for being a bad or a careless prizefighter was to be a dead one.

Boxing is in many ways an exciting, interesting, and healthy sport. It calls for courage, speed, stamina, a good eye, and something of a brain. It is also a silly game, this gratuitous exchange of punches on the nose and in the stomach, but a great many people seem to enjoy playing it and watching it played.

There has never been anything essentially wrong with the pastime. The trouble has always been with the people who take part in it, promote it, foster it, and make a living out of it. As a sport it is innocent enough, but as a business or profession it calls for certain swinish and brutish attributes in the participants if it is to be conducted successfully. It therefore should surprise no one when the pigs gather at the trough. In recent years boxing has been a source of untold wealth, unheard-of fortunes. All the more legitimate reason, then, for the swine to grunt and snort and snuffle and jostle. The greed for gold would quite naturally remove whatever vestige of decency there might be in human relationship to and attitude towards the sport. Boxing, we all agree, is nice exercise, but prizefighting smells to heaven and always has.

The hierarchy of modern prizefighting begins at the bottom with the backbone of the kingdom—the common pugilist. The next rank higher is the prizefight manager who operates and exploits him and the gangster back of the manager. Thereafter come the fight promoter and, at the top, the cheap politician. In the heyday of the American prize-ring during the golden era, the public used to dump two or three million dollars into the trough at one time, every so often, and how the boys would go for it!

The eventual fate of the modern prizefighter is not far removed from that of his ancient brother. With but few exceptions he ends his days broke and broken. His brain or his eyesight is invariably damaged and his money dissipated. He trades his body for temporary luxury. He is but rarely able to enjoy his earnings, if he has managed to salvage any, in health and comfort, when his day is done. And the average active life of a public brawler is between seven and eight years.

The layman is often surprised that a fighter can age and go to pieces in what seems to be comparatively few fights. It is quite true that he takes his most severe beatings in combat with the six-ounce gloves, and that very often he is badly injured around the head when he is on the verge of being knocked out and can no longer roll with a punch or defend himself and is struck about the skull with the full force of an opponent's punch. But what even the boxing fan forgets is that the fighter receives a steady, daily battering about the head and body in his training periods in spite of the fact that twelve- and fourteen-ounce "pillows" and head-guards are used. A heavyweight champion will sometimes train for two months before an important fight, and the older he gets, the longer he must train to get and keep in condition. Most fighters, even when there are no matches scheduled immediately, make it a practice to go into the gymnasium two or three times a week and box. Eventually the system can no longer absorb and throw off the effects of this steady punishment. Minute injuries to the brain become exaggerated. The optic nerve is damaged by the steady pounding upon the frontal bone and the bony ridges over the eyes. The speech centers are disturbed from injury to both the larynx and the brain, and eventually lesions and blood clots formed by constant concussion and shock affect the locomotor areas of the brain, and the fighter acquires the halting, half-limping walk so elegantly described by one of the terms of endearment invented for prizefighters—stumble-bum.

The changes worked in fine-looking, clear-eyed youngsters who adopt the ring as a profession are sometimes shocking to observe. You see them at the start fresh and unmarked and you live through their gradual disintegration. The knotted ears and the smashed noses are the least of their injuries. Their lips begin to thicken and their eyes seem to sink deeper and deeper into the cavernous ridges above them, ridges that are thickened and scarred from battle. Many of them acquire little nervous tics. Their voices change to husky, half-intelligible whispers. Some of them go blind—Dempsey today lives in mortal terror of blindness. Their walk is affected. And, worst of all, sometimes they cannot remember, or they say queer things. The industry laughs and says: "Don't pay any attention to him. He's punchy!"

In exchange for this, under the present system, the fighter is technically entitled to make away with the lion's, or rather, to continue the simile, the hog's portion of the swag. Out of his share of the gate, which legally, in a championship fight, consists of 37½ per cent for the champion and 12½ per cent for the challenger, he is entitled to retain for himself 66 2/3 of the money. The other third he hands over to his manager in return for the services rendered him by that individual. And in New York it is illegal for a boxer not to have a manager, no matter how clever he is or capable of looking after his own business. The state says that he must have one in order to be able to receive a license to box. The state in this instance consists of the politicians who head the hierarchy, three in number, commissioners, with their minor satellites, appointed under the Walker Boxing Law. It is exceptional actually for the fighter to get one third of the money that is coming to him.

The two-thirds, one-third division of the purse between fighter and manager is determined by rule and law, but there is nothing to prevent a private agreement between fighter and manager whereby their earnings are split fifty-fifty, and upon more than one occasion a fighter has had to content himself with twenty-five per cent of the booty, the other seventy-five per cent being whacked up amongst a board of managers, camp followers, chiselers, and racketeers. "Pieces" of fighters are sold like shares in a company, on spec, or in times of trouble when debts pile up. Max Baer once achieved something notable when he sold more than one hundred per cent of himself to various parties in return for ready cash. He excused himself on the grounds that he thought he owned a thousand per cent of himself.

But there is also the little matter of expenses, whereby the careful manager is able to reduce the size of the portion which he must hand over to his bum, as he is frequently apt to call him. Often he is moved to increase the size of these expenses more out of compassion than self-interest, because, his bum being a person of low origin and simple tastes more often than not, would obviously be at a loss to know how to spend the money or what to do with it if he had it, so why give him any? Some of the expense accounts rendered Carnera during the period of his systematic fleecing ought to be salvaged and placed in the Smithsonian Institution.

There is practically no limit on what may be charged to a fighter as expenses by his manager, including bribe money to newspapermen (which in these days is rarely if ever paid or accepted any more, but the fighter is not supposed to know the difference and usually doesn't). A sports columnist or boxing-writer will prepare a legitimate and sincere analysis or appreciation of a fighter and his qualities and ability for the pure story and reader interest that it might have. There is nothing to prevent the manager from taking this piece to his bum the next day and saying: "See what Joe Doakes wrote about you today, kid? Cost me a grand, but it's worth it, ain't it? See, he says here you're a killer when aroused." The fighter's vanity is tickled. He is pleased and the manager pockets the thousand, kicking himself for not having said fifteen hundred. He might just as well have. Or the manager can come to his big dope and say: "It's okay, kid, I got you a match in Chicago. We'll draw plenty of sugar with it. But I had to 'see' some of the boys before they'd let me in. You know how the Big Fellow is. But we got protection. Only cost me five grand out of our end." Maybe he had to pay it, and then again maybe he didn't. The fighter never has any way of checking or finding out. Such transactions are never made a matter of record.

There are training-camp expenses to be charged, expenses for travel, long-distance telephone calls, entertainment which can and does often run into thousands of dollars, kickbacks to matchmakers whether they occur or not (the kickback is a fee that the matchmaker as a part of his private graft requires of the fighter's manager in return for putting him on the card). The fighter rarely asks to see the manager's books. If he were to do so he would find either that the manager hadn't kept any books or that if he had, the fighter couldn't make head or tail of them. The take from such items as those mentioned is especially rich in the instance of a foreign fighter coming to these shores and not speaking the language. If he has been brought over by a foreign manager, that individual soon discovers that it is impossible to operate here successfully without cutting in an American manager. And if the pug is any good, as was the case with Schmeling, the foreign manager is very quickly eased out and the locals get everything. In the case of some American fighters the good work is further simplified by the fact that they are unable to read or write. The manager is well aware that if it were not for his own brilliant brain and untiring labors, the bum would be working on a truck or living on relief, and if he isn't over-scrupulous in his finances with his clown, he is only giving himself his due. After all, all the big dope has to do is get in there and get hit on the chin.

There are occasionally fighters who are able to combine intelligence with the other prime characteristics required of a successful pugilist: to wit, cruelty, ferocity, lack of imagination, and no ethics, morals, or scruples. Sport does not enter into the business at any time whatsoever. The student brawler learns from the very first that the important thing is to win, never mind how. He is never taught that he has any obligation to the public that pays to see what it hopes will be an evening of stimulating entertainment. If a boy can win by hanging on and doing as little fighting as possible, then that is the way to do it, as long as it goes into the record books as a victory. The public has a mercifully short memory and, unless reminded by watchful sports-writers, the next time he is presented, remembers only that he was the winner—not how he won. If a fighter can manage to get away with a dirty trick such as thumbing, gouging, heeling, butting, ripping, or hitting low, he feels that it is all right to do so if it will help him to win.

As a matter of strict truth, the fighter really could not get on without his manager to handle his business, his matchmaking, and his conniving for him. Successes in the ring are rarely if ever accomplished on merit. They are all schemed, chiseled, and bargained for. The cross, the double-cross, and the triple-cross play an important part in the rise of any champion. It is by no means sufficient for a fighter merely to have big muscles, speed, courage, and a devastating knockout punch. If he hasn't a capably crooked little manager to maneuver him into the spot where he can use that muscle to best advantage, he will never get past a six-round bout at his local club or the American Legion smoker. Championship matches and fights leading to them are made in the manner of big business deals. They are never signed and sealed until each side is convinced that it has every bit the best of it, with the judges and referee sewed up as well. The manager does all this. The fighter is merely the instrument.

I have never been able to feel particularly outraged at the machinations of prizefight managers, though their callousness and brutality towards their charges is something else again. For the most part they play in their own leagues and confine their petty larceny and swindles to one another. And if occasionally the public is caught in the middle and is bilked by a prearranged match, it is generally the fault of that public. There are usually from two to a dozen boxing-writers either hinting or making the plain statement that there is something curious in the wind with reference to a scheduled match and that inasmuch as all parties concerned in it are thieves and second-story men and have never fought an honest match it would come as a complete surprise if they were to begin at that point. They will indicate that they must consider the entire menage engaged in putting it over is slipping badly if it turns out to be honest. And that is usually the signal for the customers to storm the gates. If there is a phony coming off, they want to be there to see it.

The only pity is that the fight manager on the whole cannot be more decent and honest with his bum and content himself with cheating his rivals in business. A few of the men who own and operate stables of fighters are decent and reputable, but the majority are not. Some of the sheer cold-blooded heartlessness shown by so-called human beings who have the health, sanity, and lives of other human beings in their charge is sickening. A manager will coddle and protect a champion or money-making fighter because he is his meal ticket and a valuable piece of property which he doesn't want to see damaged because he will be out of pocket. But he will send a run-of-the-mine bruiser of the type generally known as a "club fighter" or crowd-pleaser out, round after round, cut, dazed, semi-conscious, bleeding badly from wounds that he is either too stupid or careless to attend to, to take a further beating or get knocked out. If there is any feeling of humanity or mercy in their dark souls they keep it for themselves. The only man I ever knew who I ever thought had any feeling for his fighter was a chap from the Middle West by the name of Jack Hurley, who managed a tough, hard-hooking little welterweight, Billy Petrolle, who also went under the exciting nickname of "The Fargo Express." As long as "the old man," as Hurley called his fighter, was in there popping the other fellow—and how he could pop them!—and not catching too many, Hurley let him go. When they began to pop Petrolle, Hurley retired him and refused to let him fight again. But for every Hurley in the game there are a hundred swine who rub a filthy towel over the pulped faces of their fighters, give them a swig out of the bottle, and heave them up out of their stools with "Go on out there and fight, you tramp. You're layin' down on me," and a few minutes later haul them back to their corners, douse them with water to bring them to, and boot them back to their dressing-rooms. I remember particularly one kindly old gentleman, a veteran fight manager by the name of Charley Harvey. He was a mild, sweet-looking old soul with innocent blue eyes and a walrus mustache. And I watched this man one night pick his beaten half-conscious fighter up and shove him out to destruction. The fighter was Tom Heeney and his destroyer was Gene Tunney, then heavyweight champion of the world. Harvey had neither the courage nor the decency to stop that fight at the end of the thirteenth round. Years later he let another of his boys, Steve Hamas, take such a brutal beating at the hands of Max Schmeling that

Hamas went to the hospital when it was over and never has been the same since.

There are a great many reasons for fixing fights, and they are all good ones. A writing-paper manufacturer who did not see that his product was given every advantage over other similar products and who failed to take advantage of rival business concerns would be considered a poor business man indeed and wouldn't last very long. The hue and cry that is raised at the idea of a fixed fight is pretty nearly as phony as the fight itself. People who attend prizefights are old enough to know that it is not a sport but an industry, and that if they are permitted to witness a contest that is fought strictly on its merits they are just lucky. It is paradoxical, however, that most of the big heavyweight championship contests are honest, especially when fought by two reasonably young men of equal fame and ability. This is because there is so much money involved that neither one nor the other of the parties concerned is able to muster sufficient cash or even promises to make it worth while for either champion or challenger to do anything but his best.

The most common form of business arrangement where championships are involved and there is no out-and-out arrangement for the champion to lose or the challenger to take a dive is the continuing contract whereby the challenger, if he wins, guarantees to pay the defeated title-holder a percentage of his earnings as champion on his next two or three fights. Thus, if the incumbent champion is able to stand off the challenger in the fight, he still has his title and his earning capacity. And if he loses, he continues to share in the profits of the championship for a time. On the face of it a fight under this arrangement is perfectly honest. Both parties are trying—well, maybe. But there is always the chance that if the champion gets a clip on the chin and finds himself on the floor he may decide to stay there. After all, it will be easier to let the other fellow do his fighting for him for a year or so.

Sometimes, however, when it is evident that the challenger is more colorful and will have unquestionably greater earning capacity as a champion than the incumbent, the managers of both champion and challenger get together and form a species of syndicate or pool. A championship match is arranged. The champion with suitable pantomime succumbs in great agony to a violent slap on the scapula, and all the members of the pool then share in the subsequent prosperity of the new champion. This is definitely the system employed throughout professional wrestling.

But most of the deals and dickers occur, on the whole, before the championship match is reached. Let us say that a new heavyweight appears, a colorful chap with a knockout punch. It is necessary to provide him with a record for advertising and publicity purposes since the first question asked by the patron of boxing shows when a new phenom is introduced is: "Who did he ever lick?"

A tour through the country is then arranged in which the rising candidate meets and by agreement, wherever necessary, knocks over a series of trial horses who for a consideration agree to collapse in whatever round is deemed advisable. This matter of the round is frequently of great importance. If the reigning champion, in his day has knocked out Joe Punk in five rounds, that is considered par for the course and it is held good business for the new candidate to accomplish the same feat in two or three rounds, or two under par. Occasionally a trial horse is discovered with scruples or ambitions, or a girl friend, who will not listen to reason in the little matter of offering himself as a victim. In such cases, if the aspiring candidate has the right kind of connections, it has been customary to threaten the trial horse with sudden death by firearms. Moral scruples are then likely to strike the trial horse as hardly worth while.

The late W. L. (Young) Stribling, a famous and curious heavyweight prizefighter who was killed in a motorcycle crash (he was afraid of nothing that rolled on wheels or flew on wings, but was a coward in the ring), had an even more foolproof system for compiling an impressive knockout record and incidentally picking up a little spare change. He traveled with a motor caravan through the South and the Southwest fighting his chauffeur. This chauffeur would move on ahead to a sizable town that harbored prizefighting and establish residence and training quarters under the name of Smith or Doakes with an appropriate prefix such as "Butch," or "Red," or "Spike," or "Kayo." Stribling would come along, a match would be arranged, and Strib would knock him out in a thrilling fight. It should have been thrilling. It was rehearsed often enough. Then the caravan would move gayly on to the next stop, a good two or three hundred miles away, so that there would be little or no danger of repeaters among the audiences.

The layman is often puzzled as to why, if the candidate to be built up is any good at all, it is necessary to prearrange fights with a collection of stumble-bums, tramps, and has-beens. The truth is that it is not easy to knock a man out, no matter how bad a fighter he may be. And the trial horse, if nothing else, has garnered experience during his years in the ring, and an experienced fighter if he wants to dog it can usually avoid being knocked out. To have such a clown recorded as having lasted ten rounds with the candidate is considered very damaging to his career and clear evidence of poor management. One reason why the sports-writers helped to create such a furore over Joe Louis was that his early amazing knockout record was honestly come by and the writers knew it. It is almost impossible for a Negro to get a white fighter to take a dive for him, whereas the Negro is, under certain conditions, *ipso facto* supposed to obey orders whenever requested. Louis had to carve out his record with his fists, and did.

There are other legitimate reasons, however, for rehearsing the outcome of a scheduled fight. The ramifications of the business of professional boxing are so tortuous that they might well take a whole book to describe. But one example may serve the cause of enlightenment.

Smith and Jones are two old-line fight managers with large families to support and expensive tastes in silk shirts and shiny cars. Smith is sole proprietor of the middleweight champion

of the world, a nice piece of property, and also numbers among
the collection of big and little bums in his stable an up-and-
coming young lightweight. Jones, on the other hand, is the
owner of a rather ordinary but capable and crowd-pleasing middleweight, and also listed among his possessions of run-of-the-
mine clucks is a lightweight who was once the champion of the
world but has fallen upon evil days and is now close to being
washed up and ready to be discarded.

Smith and Jones meet on the road, on a train, or in a hotel
(usually the bathroom of a suite, where, for some strange reason, a great deal of prizefighting business is transacted), and
they promptly put their heads together for mutual advancement and benefit. Smith says: "Looka! Your lightweight, the
ex-champ, isn't going any place. He's ready for the cleaner's.
This lightweight kid I've got is pretty good, but needs building
up. I got a good chance to steer him into a match with the
champ. How about your bum lays down to him maybe in
Cleveland or Pittsburgh, and next year, if he's still up there and
drawing good, I give your middleweight a shot at my title?"

Here is a sound business deal and one that bespeaks excellent good sense. Goodwill is as vital a commodity in the prizefight business as it is in another; indeed, more so. When
prizefight managers fall out they don't seek revenge or satisfaction by trying to get their fighters to knock the other fellow's
fighters out of the ring. They have a much more cruel weapon.
They won't let their fighters meet, because by fighting they
would give the other fellow a chance to make money. The
man with the champion holds the monopoly. It is necessary
to deal softly and kindly with him, if he is to consent to risk
such a valuable property in competition. Jones's lightweight is
indeed going nowhere but to the graveyard of fighters and his
usefulness is practically over. Jones therefore sacrifices a pawn
with pleasure and avidity to jeopardize the position of the
king. It is well worth it to get the chance at the middleweight title and the cut of the big purse that goes with it,
not to mention the chance at the championship itself. And,

strangely, when that middleweight championship match is eventually made, it is quite likely to be contested strictly on its merits. Fight managers are queer creatures, with their own codes of ethics and morals. Frequently one manager will let one of his boys take the plunge for another manager with no immediate reward in sight, merely to do him a favor, or to return a favor and establish and keep goodwill.

There is still another angle to the fixed fight which has as its basis a sound consideration of dollars and cents, and that is the occasional custom of road-showing a fight. It must be remembered that a good fight is a highly perishable commodity. It isn't like a play or a picture. It happens just once and then is a thing of ring history. The films have a record of it, it is true, but that isn't the same. And it is highly painful to a manager or managers of prizefighters who succeed in producing a fight that pleases and entertains a great number of people to see the thing ended there with no further collections possible.

And so, in a small way, if Joe Doakes and John Smith stage a great fight in New York, one about which the experts and critics have written lyrically, the obvious next step is a return match in Chicago, Philadelphia, Los Angeles, or San Francisco, and from there just another slight jump in the direction of a permanent road show that is given wherever and whenever the traffic will bear it. There are all kinds of variations of this idea, from the definitely prearranged affair where the managers get together and one of them says: "We will go a good fast dror in Detroit, and then come back again in Scranton," or "Your bum, he win in Boston, but my bum win back in New York on account he's got a good following there," to little private schemes cooked up solely between the manager and his own fighter, some time during the progress of the match itself, in which, once it is apparent that they have the upper hand, they decide not to win too decisively in order to be able to get the bum back again for another purse, either in the same town or in a neighboring one. It is all, as I have suggested, sound business and showmanship. But the thing that makes it swinish and quite bestial is that the commodity trafficked in is human flesh, housing, even at its worst, a human soul.

The promoter rarely if ever bothers with fixing a fight. He is dealing directly with the public and must sell them tickets and get their money from them, and it is more to his interest to serve up an honest contest if he can. And besides, he doesn't have to. The managers take that matter right out of his hands. It was said that Rickard would not tolerate a crooked fight, and yet plenty of bad ones took place under his promotion. There is simply no way that a promoter can control the integrity of any of his fights except to blacklist those managers and fighters who have a reputation for being shady or who have ever been mixed up in a crooked ring deal. That would leave about half a dozen with whom to carry on business, which isn't enough.

The man at the head of the whole business, the politician, takes his pickings in patronage and favors, which are his form of currency. The cheap, semi-racketeering type will steal petty cash if there is any they can get their fingers on, but the big ones like the members of the New York State Athletic Commission keep their hands clean, although it is possible to read politics of some sort in three quarters of the things they do and the ukases they issue. Not even the most ardent believer in the purity of a political boxing administration could quite stomach the innocence of the order that once went out from the commission offices that all fighters must wear trunks of a certain color, the make of one certain manufacturer; such a roar went up that the commission had to amend it hastily to mean any manufacturer. And it was as chairman of this commission that Jim Farley acquired the popularity and the prestige that eventually rode him into the national picture as Democratic Chairman and finally Postmaster General of the United States and dispenser of patronage under the Roosevelt presidency.

In local politics the boxing patronage is highly important. More good can be done for the party with a free fight ticket than with a five-hundred-dollar bill. And a promoter can be bled for plenty of complimentaries and passes because he is rarely anxious to buck the governing politicians, with their absolute autocracy over the sport and complete licensing powers. And besides, they always have the trump card. They can always call up their old pal the fire commissioner and have any club shut down as a fire hazard. It has been done. A fighter with the wrong political affiliations might even find it difficult to secure official sanction as a challenger for a title. A hostile commission can very easily hornswoggle a fighter out of a favorable match simply by refusing to license or sanction it. It was purely politics that drove the first Dempsey-Tunney fight to Philadelphia.

The politicians manage to get a finger in the pie in the awarding of stadium-construction contracts, the ushering jobs, the program and soft-drink selling concessions, and sometimes even the assignment of the motion-picture rights. It is not necessary to graft here, but merely to see that right-thinking parties secure the lucrative contracts and jobs, parties who have influence and who will wield that influence and show proper gratitude at the polls when the time comes. A favor to a fighter of Irish extraction is good for the Irish vote, a fish tossed to an aspiring Negro pugilist takes care of the Harlem constituency. There is really no need to crowd and jostle at the boxing trough. There is room enough for all the pigs, both great and small.

XIV

COME ON—

MY HORSE!

ALL I know about the ancient and occasionally honorable sport of horseracing is the excitement of going down to the betting pits and watching money change hands. I probably knew and wrote less about horseracing than any other game. And I suspect that this may have been the case because the ponies always seemed to me inseparable from page upon page of tiny numerals in fine print, figures that smacked unpleasantly of mathematics, a subject that has been distasteful to me ever since I found out, in early youth, that it is true that they cannot and do not lie. I suppose if I set my mind to it I could read the chart of a race and gain a fairly comprehensive idea of how the race was won and the position of the various horses throughout the trial. But the hieroglyphics of the sport have always repelled me and I could never bring myself to study a form chart of a clocker's tabulation or a solidly massed page of past performances.

Still, when I went to the races occasionally, I liked to bet and, above all, I liked to win, which I rarely did because I was always betting with scared and poor money, a trenchant racetrack phrase. But I always recall vividly the thrill of taking my day's program to an expert, possibly some veteran turf-writer, or a famous brother sports columnist whose specialty was the ponies, like Bill Corum or Damon Runyon or Joe Williams, or perhaps one of the visiting millionaires or celebrities or politicians, who must surely be in contact with good information, and asking him to mark it for me with his choices. There are a great friendliness and generosity in racing people. They will always share tips, good things, information, hunches, etc., provided you are a gentleman about it and are not inclined to hold them personally responsible if the tips do not mature. There is even an eagerness, almost, to pass these tips along as though they gained strength by having other supporters, or perhaps there is a propitiatory thought behind the kind deed. I do not recall ever having had any hesitancy or conscience about thus picking the brains of the experts—I was perfectly willing to swap hunches on the outcome of prizefights or football games —and I was always as happy as a child with my marked program, especially before the races were run. I always felt that I held a practical fortune in my fingertips. Those penciled check marks, or rings drawn around the exciting and intriguing names of horses, represented vast sums of money for which perhaps I should not have to do any work. Who could tell? A year in Europe and freedom and independence, time to travel and write a book, a new car, a paying up of all debts, the feeling of having for the first time in my life a lot of money that I could spend, if I liked, for new clothes, books, phonograph records for my collection, a lot of new dogs—perhaps a motor boat. . . .

There is no more thrilling place in the world than a racetrack unless it be the Mint, because there is so much money about. And in the Mint it lies in cold, austere, static, unapproachable piles. At the racetrack it is red-hot, alive, pulsating, and constantly changing hands. You keep seeing it. Lucky bettors come away from the paying windows with their fingers full of green- and yellow-backs which they stuff into their pockets without counting. Everyone in the long queues up to the betting grilles has money in his or her hands. The white numbers up on the great, black odds and results boards mean money.

Everyone is talking money, handling money, feeling money, making or losing money.

And the turnover is so rapid and satisfying. To anyone accustomed to earning money the hard way, through a week's work at an office or shop or factory in exchange for a predetermined amount in a pay envelope or a printed check, or three weeks' labor on a story or article and a month's delay until it is sold and turned into actual cash, the speed of the racetrack is utterly fascinating and sometimes completely demoralizing. Everything is on a cash basis. Twenty minutes sees the whole transaction finished. You buy your pari-mutuel ticket or place your bet with the bookie and stroll out onto the lawn to see the ponies run, or, rather, to watch your investment mature—or fail. The physical running of the race, once the seemingly interminable yet thrilling and nerve-tingling delays at the post are over, occupies from one to two and a half minutes. By the time you have wandered back to the betting ring, the pay-off is up on the boards, and the pay-off windows are open. The men serving them are crisp, pleasant, and friendly. It is no money out of their pockets. They slap the pile of bills and the loose breakage silver down on the counter and thrust it out at you, and there you have it. True, the action in the gambling-house is even faster, where the spinning ball, the tumbling dice or the turned-up card can make your fortune in a few seconds. But anyone can go to the racetrack and very few can patronize gambling-houses. The gambling-rooms are too tense and solemn. They have an atmosphere all their own, but to me it lacks the thrill and the real money fever of the track.

Somehow, my most vivid and pleasant memory of horseracing is not the Kentucky Derby, or the Preakness, or the big stake races at Belmont Park like the fifty-thousand-dollar Futurity, but the main street at Saratoga Springs, the little upstate New York spa just below the foothills of the Adirondack Mountains which for one month of the year—August—becomes a horse town. And just because it is a sleepy, and, except for the massive Victorian wooden hotels like the Grand Union, ordinary ugly American country town, it takes on a life, a sparkle, and a coursing excitement that is completely fascinating.

I am thinking again, as I write, of that main street with its inevitable knot of standers-around outside the Western Union office, waiting for answers to appeals for more money—fresh scratch, as they call it—the touts and the chiselers and the hangers-on lingering around in front of the hotels; but most of all I remember the shops. Here you will find transplanted a little piece of Fifth Avenue, New York, or Michigan Boulevard, Chicago. There are shops exhibiting lovely, expensive gowns, perfumes, jewelry, furs, objets d'art, and, above all, open-front stores from which the plate-glass windows have been swung outwards and in which stand, half encroaching on the broad, tree-lined sidewalks, so that as you pass on a stroll you have to walk round them, the biggest, handsomest, shiniest motor cars in the world.

There is nothing quite as alluring in a show window, unless it be beautiful furs or fur capes and wraps, as a cream-colored chrome-nickeled car with smooth, Spanish leather upholstery, black and silver dashboard dials and gadgets, wire wheels with crimson spokes, long, shapely hood that promises power and smoothness at leash, spare tires in cream-enameled, chromium-plated covers, smart trunk in the rear, and gleaming accessories. Heaven help you, how you want it! Nothing seems quite so thoroughly calculated to arouse cupidity and covetousness.

The inference, of course, is obvious. There it stands in the brilliantly lighted window, grinning at you, with the white incandescents gleaming from its lovely skin and beautiful ornaments, suggesting: "Go on, make a killing tomorrow and drive me home. One good day at the track, buddy, and I'm yours, paid for, to keep for yourself until I fall apart. You come back from the track tomorrow around six o'clock with five thousand dollars on you and you drive me right out of this store and park me in front of your hotel. I think I'd like you. You and I could be friends."

It sings its seductive song to bum and millionaire alike. It recognizes no class distinctions nor any such thing as anyone too poor to buy. The cars along Automobile Row on Broadway are distinctly snobs and avert their headlamps from the poorly dressed passer-by who presses his face hungrily against the plate glass of the show window for a moment and yearns for the beautiful luxury within. They know a prospect when they see one.

But at Saratoga everyone is a possible customer, a potential millionaire. The shiny cars talk the language. "What have you got on you, brother, a fin? That's enough. Five bucks buys me tomorrow night—if you guess right tomorrow afternoon. Or never mind the guessing. Just go on out there and be lucky. It may be your day. No work. No trouble. A ten-to-one shot in the first race gives you fifty for your five. Bet it back at eight to one and you've got four Cs. Split the four hundred in case of accident and hit a five-to-one shot in the third heat, and you've got twelve hundred. Skip the fourth race, which is too tough, but there's something pretty at five to one that ought to be even money running in the fifth. Shoot the grand. If he comes down in front, that's five grand, and I'm yours. Never mind those other races. Remember me. I'm waiting for you back here. Grab a cab and come on back to town. You've got the sugar in your kick. Hand it over, climb into my front seat and feel that cool, smooth leather. Custom-built I am. Listen to me purr. You'll have to strain your ears, I'm that silent. Okay, brother. See you tomorrow night. With the dough!"

It can be done. It has been done. That's what all those lovely, expensive things are there for, to excite cupidity and keep you from returning your money whence it came—the track. Turn your winnings into lovely merchandise, they say, that Paris evening gown, that chinchilla cape, that sapphire bracelet. By sundown you may be able to walk in and buy them. A little of the right information, a little courage, a little luck . . .

In the meantime you may pick up your sporting sheet or racing paper or a pamphlet or magazine and read about the Sport of Kings and the self-sacrificing millionaire sportsmen grouped together to further the happy philanthropic work of improving the breed of horses.

This is a long and complicated business, fascinating to some, tedious and obstetrical to me. May Day's sire was May Flower, Derby winner, and his dam, Happy Day, one of the few fillies to win the Preakness. The production of May Day took time, money, brains, and organization. There is a background of lovely, rolling stock farms, stables, private training tracks, blue grass, or deep green, picturesque Southern mansions, or stately Northern villas, wealthy sportsmen giving gratuitously of time and money in order that the horse of tomorrow may be better than the horse of today—truly a hobby of luxury, since the horse of today or tomorrow has no more practical value in a mechanized age than the sailing vessel of yesterday.

Racing associations, jockey clubs, and the like are generously endowed, beautifully horticultured laboratories and testing plants for this noble experiment, gathering-grounds where in pleasant surroundings and under proper conditions the sportsmen may bring the results of their labors and experiments and try them out. These plants have the shape and construction with which we are familiar today because the sportsmen are not particularly interested in the intelligence of the horse or in arriving at a strain that will be able to climb trees, perform lightning calculations, or draw a greater pay load, but rather, by sheer coincidence, deal only with the improvement of two signal qualities—speed and stamina.

What has this to do with you or with me as we stand by the rail, or sit in the grandstand, trembling a little, field glasses pressed to our eye-sockets so that the pressure hurts the frontal bone, watching those bobbing heads and bright-colored jocks streaming around the track? All we care about is finding our horse by color, silks, or number. Our hearts pound as the patterns change and first one nose and then another is in front. Breathless, sweating, close to fainting with excitement we are, because if that chestnut pony with the number 5 on his saddle cloth, and the monkey dressed in yellow silks dotted with red, sticks his muzzle out in front and keeps it there past the wire, we shall have six hundred dollars, whereas we only had twenty before.

What has this, then, to do with us? Everything, and yet very little. It happens to be the front for the most fascinating gambling game ever devised. And we must have a front, because we know that gambling is wicked, a great sin, and generally prohibited.

I found that this front never interested me particularly, even though it was a good one and picturesque, but it was still a front and therefore, to a certain degree, false. And it is the more false in that its main premise has never proved accurate, and its promise has never been fulfilled.

The premise was that this interesting, exciting, and lucrative hobby of breeding horses that would run faster and farther than their ancestors should be left in the hands of the aristocracy, it being considered, along with many other things, much too good for the common people and also much too dangerous for them, since the common people were frequently overcome by avarice and greed for gain, and the honesty of the laboratory tests at the racetrack must be guaranteed.

The dignified millionaire socialites and sportsmen and their famous consorts who appear so often in the Sunday rotogravure sections could never be suspected or accused of trimming, sharpshooting, cheating, or double-crossing. So long as the sport remained in the hands of these wealthy patrons, the public would be protected. The premise may be socially sound, but it doesn't work. The promise has never been kept, because racing has always been a dirty and crooked game, like any gambling device, and always will be. There is only one legitimate reason why horseracing is in the hands of the wealthy: it takes money to raise, breed, and train horses. But as a protective device it fails.

It is possible to find occasionally an honest wheel and a

square dice table in a gambling casino that is satisfied with the house percentage, but it is the exception to the rule. And even if the house is honest with the small fry, sooner or later along will come a sucker with a hundred-thousand-dollar roll just begging to be clipped. He gets clipped. Horseracing is a simple gambling game and nothing more. Occasionally it is quite honest and clean—some tracks more so than others—and run in the way that the aristocratic patrons would prefer, but more often it is not. Nor is there anything in the book that guarantees that because a man has wealth and family, he is above an occasional bit of trimming. Very few large fortunes were piled up by strict adherence to scrupulousness all the way. Be that as it may, however, the famous coterie of wealthy and socially prominent millionaires, as they were called during those bold, gay days after the war, have never been able to protect the public from the fixer, the sure-thing gambler, the horse-doper, the sponger, the ringer, the gangster, and all the rest of the unholy crew that operates for quick, illicit profits.

The patrons of the gambling device known as horseracing have tried to operate it honestly for the most part, have employed private detective agencies to protect their tracks, and have appointed trustworthy and honest stewards and officials. And yet they have not been above occasional manipulations of their own. Every horse entered in a race is theoretically supposed to be permitted to try its level best to win that race, and yet very often at the tracks you will find newspapermen and turf-writers scurrying about trying to dig up information as to whether a certain owner is trying with his horse in a particular race. Legally and ethically he is always supposed to be trying, but sometimes it is more convenient and practical to let a horse run merely for the exercise. The news gets around the clubhouse quickly enough that an owner is not backing his horse, but it doesn't get out so quickly to the run-of-the-mine spectator and bettor, with his two or five dollars clutched in a sweating fist, in the grandstand or infield.

Nor has it ever been possible to restrict the game wholly to

those fine old families who might occasionally, for the fun of
the thing, swindle one another a little, or pull off a coup, but
who would never knowingly or willingly stoop to tricking the
public. Disreputable characters are as quick to learn the art of
putting up a front as anyone—a little quicker, even, in fact—
and anyone who has no criminal record, but who has sufficient
money and the appearance of a gentleman or gentlewoman may
own, enter, and race horses.

Gangsters of New York, Chicago, Philadelphia, Pittsburgh,
and other cities manipulated and raced horses under dummy
ownership. Paddy Barrie, the English racetrack crook and
ringer of horses, raced horses in America with a pretty girl front-
ing for him. The pretty girl was his sweetheart. In this respect
the fine old families have been a hindrance rather than a help
to racing, because, as is common with fine old families, fear
of scandal that might pull the entire house of horseracing down
about their ears often prevented them from taking immediate
and drastic action where it was called for. When you are operating on the postulate that racing can exist only because it is
in the hands of impeccable people, it becomes increasingly
difficult for these people suddenly to announce that Psmith,
Bbrown, and Jjones have been discovered to be thieves, crooks,
and rascals who were fixing races and hopping up their steeds
with cocaine or Scotch whisky and have been turned out. They
do announce it because they are honest people, but it hurts
and one can understand their reluctance. After the first flush
of congratulation has died down, the public is bound to wonder
how Psmith, Bbrown, and Jjones hoodwinked the racing fathers as long as they did, and how many more of these rascals
there are still running ponies, unsuspected and undiscovered.

I have never been particularly scandalized by instances of
crooked work at the barrier simply because I look at horseracing less as a sport and more as a game of chance, and most
games of chance are crooked. If I go to a gambling casino at
Miami Beach or Saratoga or Newport to play the wheel or the
bird-cage or buck the house at blackjack, I know that I am

taking my chances on getting a square shake, and the fact that the house is owned and operated by someone called Colonel Jenks instead of plain Mr. Jenks or Butch Jenks does not increase my confidence to any extent. I hope that because I am small fry—that is to say, a little sucker with no more than fifty or a hundred dollars to lose for a night's excitement—I will be permitted to try my luck against the normal house percentage. But I realize that if I walk in as a wealthy man willing to lose fifty or sixty thousand dollars at the dice table, Colonel or no Colonel, I am more than likely to be assisted at the losing thereof. The fact that gambling is outside the law makes the problem of trimming the sucker that much simpler.

Racetrack betting is now legalized in many states, and taxes on it are an important part of the state revenue. In 1935, for instance, a total of $75,000,000 was bet through the machines. In California and Rhode Island the state collected a million dollars in taxes on wagers. But in spite of the fact that it is legal, the tracks are always keeping a wary and nervous eye cocked towards the Methodists and the Baptists and the rest of the wowser element. They like to maintain the happy fiction that it isn't really gambling at all, but merely a profound and innocent enthusiasm for the improvement of the breed of one of nature's noblest animals, practiced as a luxury and hobby by the aforementioned fine old families. To back the results of the experiments conducted by one of those over a period of years, by a modest wager, is merely to express concretely the approval of the methods of that family and loyalty to them.

The Whitneys, the Vanderbilts, the Bradleys, the McLeans, and people of that class who own stables or, banded together, operate racetracks or are members of the boards would be considerably hurt if you referred to them as large-scale gaming-house proprietors. But both they and the sport would be much better off if they would all state frankly at the beginning of each season:

"Ladies and gentlemen, our gambling pitch at Westchester

Park will be open for business on the first day of May and you may come there and bet your money on the results of the card of seven races a day. No expense has been spared to secure the best grade of horses so as to give you keen and fair competition, and, too, every effort has been made to guarantee honest gambling, as far as it is possible. We beg to remind you that no game of chance has yet been devised by man that cannot be tampered with, and racing is not only no exception to this rule but one of the weakest in structure because there are so many sources of attack. As you know, there can be dirty work with the horse, the jockey, the stable staff, the trainer, the officials, and finally the owner. Horses, jockeys, owners, and trainers will be ruled off this track at the first suspicion of malpractice. We do not do this because of our great love for the horse as a noble steed, or because of our great love for you. We do this because we wish you to keep on patronizing our track so that we may continue to collect a legitimate profit out of your entrance fees and your wagers."

It is not by any means necessary to go to the track to bet on the horses, but for me and for most people the excitement of winning or losing money is enhanced by the spectacle of the running ponies. It becomes a story, and as in the case of the Kentucky Derby when the best three-year-olds in the country race a mile and a quarter with more than a million dollars bet on the outcome, a good one. You may lose your money, but you get something for it, a thrill, color and excitement, as in playing those automatic crane boob-traps that by the insertion of a coin can be made to operate and grab for a valuable article lodged firmly in grains of candy. In ninety-nine cases out of a hundred the tongs of the crane slip off the object, but slip you as largess a few grains of sweet. It leaves you feeling not quite so bilked.

You may look at the pattern of a horserace from two points of view: that of the artist who sees color, life, and rhythm in the streaming pack and the bobbing heads, or that of the other ninety-nine per cent that sees only a financial transaction taking place before their eyes, an investment imperiled, losing ground, gaining, improving, and finally winning or hopelessly falling through.

I have managed to miss, in my years of sports-reporting, the colorful characters who infest the racetracks, the horsy men with the queer nicknames and the queer clothes and the strange habits, who follow the horses day in and day out, rich one week, living on the cuff the next, always with a fortune just round the corner. These are the professionals of the horse gambling business, every bit as distinctive and individual as the old-time professional blackjack- and faro-players, with their own language, customs, and morals. They are a part of the *mise en scène* of the racetrack, as much as the red-coated leader of the parade to the post, the jockeys in their bright parti-colored silks, standing on the scales with their saddles over one arm, the swans floating on the artificial pond in the center of the plant, and the bugle calls to saddle and mount.

But I have at times been quite close to what is horseracing because I am and have been a hungry, greedy, covetous man myself. I have mingled with the betting crowds and felt the pounding of the thousands and thousands of pulses in my own wrist and throat. Herein lies the turf, in these other eager, greedy people, all swept together by the common fever engendered by trying to obtain something for nothing.

Their eyes sparkle, their clothes are awry, they sweat, and not alone from the summer humidity; they buzz about the lawns and the paddock, nervously moistening their pencils at their lips and marking their programs, quizzing for information and more information, weighing chances, haggling with themselves, seeking advice and discarding it summarily, or weighing it against other advice already received. They examine the horses in the paddock, trying to read the riddle of success or failure in the animals as they are led about the inclosure or stand tethered beneath shading trees, and unconsciously ascribe human attributes to them, by taking into account facial expression, carriage of head, and general bearing and demeanor. A word or two with the jockey or one of the handlers will bolster their courage amazingly. They have a desperate, hungry longing to be on the inside, to learn something that will justify them in risking money gained through labor on the chance of increasing it, ten, twenty, who knows, fifty or a hundred fold.

They fight their battles between caution and boldness, prudence or rapaciousness, and you see the struggles writ plainly on their faces. Shall they put it all on the nose to win—everything or nothing—or be content with less profits and take the more certain road of the place or the show bet, which gives them two or three chances, respectively, to collect, instead of only one, but of course at shorter, less glamorous and exciting odds. They stick their noses into their dope-sheets, burrow into the opinions of the experts, and still cannot decide; still they seek some further assurance.

Nor are they particularly concerned with whether a race is honestly run so long as they are on the inside of the proper information as to which horse has been fixed to win. This is a true but curious commentary upon the great efforts made to put up a front for racing and give it the appearance of sport for sport's sake, beyond reproach. Find out which way the big money or the big influence is betting and bet with the money and the influence. The small fry around a track feels that a tip from a celebrity or a visiting politician is worth more than all the dope-sheet and experts' consensus, because he suspects that in all probability the celebrity has been made privy to some inside information that has been denied to the public, that the big shots get together and talk things over, that they know what is going to happen—which is why they are big shots, anyway.

The morals of the bettor are curious and convenient, and most bettors are not much more honest than the men who rig the races. Were one to be approached by an individual who was to say: "You don't remember me, but you once did me a great service, years back, and I feel that I can repay it now. There's going to be something doing in the third race. The boys have been able to bag this one. Silly Celia can't lose. Bet your roll on her. She'll be fifteen to one or better" would he rush off to the stewards shouting: "Stop the third race, it's been fixed"? He would not. Not one man out of a hundred would do anything but get a bet down on Silly Celia. After all, *he* didn't fix the race, and if he happened to hear about it—well and good. There must have been plenty of fixed races that took his money and about which he never heard anything.

The dirty work goes on as it always will. The ringer paints and substitutes the fast horse for the old skate he has been made up to resemble. The hop men needle their horses with a preparation of cocaine, and run them hot or run them cold according to the coup planned; the fixers buy or bulldoze the jockeys, or arrange to thrust their cruel sponges up the nostrils of thoroughbreds favored to win, or lame them, or see that they get bumped at the turns. And the public apparently is never particularly outraged at these swindles when they are exposed, nor even especially interested, beyond enjoying the reading of a good story about an exciting coup brought off under the noses of the stewards and the Pinkertons. Most of them wish that they had been in on it for a little bet.

No, the essence of racing is not to be found either in the manipulations of the inevitable crooks that fasten onto any game where there is easy money to be had, or in the pleasant fairy tale that the whole thing is a vast philanthropic scheme to improve horseflesh, the hobby and pastime of altruistic millionaires. It is to be found rather in those hot, excited, trampling, flushed crowds of two- and five-dollar betters moiling and pushing and milling about, asking their interminable hopeful questions: "What do you hear? . . . Who do you like in the fourth? . . . What is Soandso betting on? . . ." looking eternally to Lady Luck to make ten dollars grow, magically and thrillingly, where but one was before.

X V

KEEP

YOUR HEAD

DOWN

IF THE father of modern chemistry was the search in ancient laboratories for the philosophers' stone, and the discovery of the Pacific Ocean the result of a similar quest for the Fountain of Youth, then the golf industry in the United States is based on the seeking of a magic implement or means by which a semi-portly broker or merchant can stand on the first tee of his golf club on a Sunday morning, lash out a 230-yard drive straight down the middle, and follow it up with an iron shot that splits the pin all the way, and which will enable him never to take more than three putts on any green. Or perhaps Mr. Joe Cook, the comedian, has expressed even better that terrible yearning in the human soul. He has constructed a single golf hole on his estate at Lake Hopatcong, a short iron shot to a punch-bowl green. Land anywhere on the green and the ball immediately gravitates towards the hole and rolls in— hole in one. It is significant, however, that Mr. Cook has not yet invented any contraption that will enable certain incurable dubs to hit the ball from the tee so that it will land on his trick green.

The game of golf is a mystery, as much of a one as the universe and the solar system, electricity, or ionic affinities. Because he cannot solve it, the busy American golfer turns to magic, cure-all gadgets, old wives' tales, books, witch doctors and medicine men. He is forever searching for some secret that he fondly believes will be the key to the miraculous transmutation of himself from an execrable duffer and golf clown to an envied player who can tour any lay-out in *circa* eighty strokes or less. Golf makes a simple-minded, superstitious peasant out of an otherwise apparently intelligent person. Result—modern golf. It is not in the nature of any American business to withstand taking a sucker who is begging to be taken. And if it does withstand, it doesn't last very long as a successful business. Somebody else with fewer scruples and more acumen comes along, garners the boob, and banks the dough.

Hundreds of thousands of people in Bob Jones's time trailed in his wake and pursued him over hill and dale because they thought that he was a magician. He had the Touch, and they were trying to pinch it from him. They watched his hands, his feet, his hips, the angle of his head, argued and discussed which eye it was with which he looked at the ball, studied his knuckles, devoured his articles, and eventually purchased thousands of sets of implements designed by him. They would rush away from the big tournament, pile out to their golf clubs, and hurry to the first tee to try out something they thought they had gleaned from watching the Master. Thousands of people who don't play tennis, baseball, or football go to tennis, baseball, or football matches. But the golf gallery is all golfers. There were two things that contributed to the post-war golf boom that saw a game turned into another important industry: money and the leisure time that went with it, enabling people to get out and play, and the coming of the prophet Jones, to whom All Things Were Clear and Patent. The habit has persisted, and a crowd still gathers, though not quite so large when any of the minor disciples and doctors of the cult are scheduled to give a practical demonstration of miracles.

The average American business-man golfer has little time for the game and even less patience. He either does not know or will not learn that to swing a golf club in a proper arc calls for more co-ordination, timing, instruction, and practice than perhaps any other sport with the possible exception of pole-vaulting. A minute error in a golf swing is so quickly multiplied, exaggerated, and penalized that by the time the club-head reaches the ball, the swinger might just as well be wielding a broom. There is actually only one way to make a golfer, provided a man has any aptitude for games and co-ordination and isn't trying to swing past a bay window that obscures his vision of the ball at his feet. And that is by good instruction, patience, and practice.

The man setting out to learn the game can always acquire the first, because we have the best golf teachers in the world. But the other two? That is something else again. This being a mechanized era, the player expects his faults and defects to be corrected and compensated for by his tools. The golf-club designers have done this as far as they are able by giving him irons and woods so matched, weighted, and balanced that they all swing alike. The only trouble is that he swings them all badly. And they have invented and perfected an enormous heavy-headed blasting club that will explode a ball out of sand if the wielder hits within a foot of it, and explodes most of the trap out with it. This is the closest thing to a foolproof golf club yet marketed and it has made the duffer happier because he has no interest whatsoever in the delicacies and niceties of niblick play out of a bunker. All he wants to do is get out.

The designers have done what they were able to, but it hasn't been enough for the dub. Because he will not practice. He has very little time, anyway, and except when on vacation, most of his golf is confined to Saturday afternoons and Sunday mornings. And, furthermore, he is not particularly amenable to instruction—that is, not until it is too late. When he first begins to take lessons the swing feels all wrong and the grip is awkward. Well, it is. The natural tendency is to take a baseball grip on the end of the golf stick and soak the ball with the right hand. But the club is held in the fingers with the hands in a strangely unnatural position, and the impetus for the blow comes from the left hand. The beginner immediately thinks that the professional is trying to school him in a style to which he is not physically adapted. As soon as he gets out of sight of teacher he does it in his own way, the one that feels natural to him, hits an occasional good shot quite by accident, and is heard announcing in the locker-room: "Ya gotta keep away from those damn pros. They'll ruin your game."

He wants to learn it all in six lessons. He won't spend time on the practice tee because he wants to get the boys and go out and play. After all, that is why he has taken up golf. And so inside of a month he has joined the cult and is looking and hoping pathetically for the magic. The word is passed around from mouth to mouth faster than a new remedy for a cold: "There's a fellow has a new book out on golf. They say it'll take ten strokes off your game. It's marvelous." The only way to take strokes off your game with a book is to use it to tee your ball up on in the rough. Or the beginner purchases some new weapon that promises to counteract the lifted head, the dropped shoulder, the ballerina swoop, the one-inch pivot, or the right-hand smash.

Because he is lazy, impatient, over-ambitious, and has no real love for the game as a fascinating study in self-discipline, from the day he gets his first driver in his itching fingers he is a sucker for anything that promises to improve his game or add distance to his drive or cure his slice. A new ball is put on the market with a honey center that is supposed to go farther. He buys it. He would buy a ball with a maraschino cherry center or a splinter off the Taj Mahal if he were told that it is a faster and longer ball. He invests in books and magazines, special clubs, special shoes, and a special kind of underwear that woos him with the assurance that crotch comfort can be translated into a saving of four strokes a round. He buys jiggers and approach putters and things that look as though Rube Goldberg had drawn them, because the lusty verbiage of the advertising copy announcing these miracles gives him hope. And nothing ever really helps him or ever will.

From the point of view of strict truth, none of these promises made in national golf advertising are false. The clubs and the golf balls will do exactly what their manufacturers say they will do—when in the hands of an expert. If they tell you that their ball will outfly by fifteen yards or more any other ball manufactured, it will. It has been tested against other standard balls on a driving machine. But the sucker doesn't hit his ball the way a driving machine does. The ball won't give the average golf chump more than an extra yard or two on *his* drive, which in a way is fortunate, because if it were otherwise it would only mean that the duffer would just get fifteen yards deeper into the woods or the rough than he would with an ordinary ball. No, golf advertising can be accused of no more than opportunism.

The golf professional is essentially an honest, hard-working fellow up against a tough proposition. If he has taken refuge behind the wearisome and eternally repeated: "Keep your head down. Look at the ball. You looked up," as the explanation of all dubbed shots, it is because it is about the only thing the duffer can understand. Of the thirty wrong things he did on a shot, it is a cinch that the first one was that he lifted his head. Keeping his head down is also one of the most difficult things he is called upon to do. It is a sort of panacea to him to be allowed to think that if he ever *does* manage to look at the ball, he will be able to play. He doesn't know that it is also quite possible to look a ball right square on the label while hitting it and still make a mess of it.

If I went to Tommy Armour, or Mac Smith, or Bobby Cruickshank, or any of the great golf teachers and said: "Look here, I've got a little time and I really want to improve my game," the first thing they would say to me would be: "Are you willing to stay off the course for six months and practice?"

Some of those men could teach golf to a wooden Indian if given half a chance.

But their pupils don't give them any chance at all. They are helping to pay the professional's salary at the club and a nice additional fee for a half-hour's lesson as well and they want miracles. Half a dozen lessons and away they go, hacking, stabbing, lunging, gouging, shanking, topping and fluffing. Three months of that and they come back for a session or two with the pro to "get straightened out." You hear them every day in the locker-room: "There's something wrong with my irons. I think I'll get Mac to straighten me out." And by that time they cannot be straightened out with a two-ton plate roller. It is too late. They have formed bad habits that are unbreakable. The best the pro can do is to look over the mess and try to give a few hints that will enable his client to hit a ball more frequently in his own cockeyed way.

Certainly the pro kids him, or lies to him, but no more than does a smart and fashionable doctor to a wealthy hypochondriac. He knows that if he tells the duffer the truth he will simply lose a customer, and later a job. The dub will go to another professional to get straightened out. The other professional is smarter. He has a magic. He says: "Try to think that at the finish of your drive you will be in such a position that if you then take a step, off your left foot and onto your right, you will have started to walk straight in the direction of the hole." The dub tries it. Lo! A miracle! It works! Look at that straight drive, and more than two hundred yards. Wonderful! Marvelous! The cure-all! He rushes off and immediately tells all his friends what the eminent doctor has prescribed. "See? Here's the way you do it! Just a simple little thing like that makes all the difference in the world." A week later either he forgets it, or it doesn't work any more because he is doing something else that is wrong. But another Voodoo specialist has written a treatise on how not to look at the ball, but the ground immediately behind the ball, or still a third exorcist has achieved magnificent results by making his patients repeat the first verse of the Lord's Prayer after hitting a shot before looking up to see where the ball went, or someone has invented and marketed a new club with a grip like that of an automobile steering wheel, and off he goes again in the eternal quest for the short cut to the magic figures—79, 81, 82. . . .

And because these things are so, the golf industry turns over some fifty million dollars annually, and championship tournament golf is no longer sport, but business. The United States Open Golf Championship, which used to be strictly a sporting proposition, has now, willy-nilly, been taken over by the manufacturers of golf equipment as the annual commercial and advertising sweepstakes, much in the manner that the results of the Indianapolis Speedway automobile race are important to the advertisers of motor-industry products. Golf championships today are played and won, not so much for the individual glory of the individual competing professionals, but for that of the golf-equipment and sporting-goods houses they represent. The companies gamble with their professionals, invest in them, speculate with them, and support them by paying them retainers and sustaining salaries. It is a much safer existence for the professional because his contract assures him a living, win or lose (though he must not lose too consistently), but it isn't nearly so much fun.

The Open Championship today, for instance, has become a rout of golf salesmen, company scouts, spies and cut-throat competitors for the services of unknown players who look as though they might have a chance to win. It is as important to Spalding or Wilson or Hagen or Croydon or McGregor that the winner of the Open Championship should have played their clubs or balls as it used to be to the Steinway or Knabe piano companies to have the great concert artists use one of their products when performing. More so in fact. Because, remember, in the background is that vast army of dub golfers waiting for its talisman.

Its very eagerness makes it the biggest sucker public in the whole world for aggressive advertising. Its resistance to sales-manship is practically zero. If the Spalding ball wins the Open Championship, that is the ball it will want. If Sarazen finishes first playing Wilson clubs with some trick, patented dooflicker in the head or at the neck of the shaft, the company can sell thousands of sets of those clubs. Perhaps the whole thing is summed up in the following example of the difference in attack upon the English buying public and our own. Some English golf professional had won an important tournament, playing the True Temper shaft, and the company had taken a page in an English sporting periodical to tell about it. They did it by smashing big, black type: "HE WOULD HAVE WON WITHOUT OUR SHAFTS. BUT HE WAS TAKING NO CHANCES!" The American version would have been: "TRUE TEMPER WINS AGAIN."

After all, too much emphasis on the skill of the player might have a discouraging effect upon the duffer. If some famous professor comes stumbling down in front playing Ace irons, the professor may be briefly mentioned as the person who had something to do with guiding the clubs to their ultimate triumph, but the advertising more than likely will read: "Ace Irons Won the Open Championships! An Ace in the Bag Is an Ace in the Hole! 'I play Ace Irons by preference,' says Angus McPar, nineteen thirty-umpth Open Champion. Ace Irons, with their 'Metronome Rhythm Balance,' will take strokes off YOUR game too. Play the irons the champions play." Nor is there any particular harm done by this. Certainly, the duffer is no worse off with Ace Irons than he was without them. They will be well-made clubs, probably not one whit better than any other club of similar price; but if the purchaser thinks they are, if he believes that the winner's magic lies within them and can kid himself into improving his game, he has not been swindled.

Selling golf balls is a relatively simple matter since the American golfer is the world's biggest wastrel and has no patience with looking for a lost ball. He plays the way he does everything else, in a fever, in a hurry, and in fear. He is afraid the foursome behind will catch up and want to go through, he is afraid of being thought cheap by his own foursome if he spends too much time looking, he is afraid that he will be thrown off his game if he delays, and very often he is also afraid of finding it—in an impossible lie. And he likes the look and feel of a new ball just out of the wrapper. He never acquires an affection for an old and battered pellet that has served him well. He buys a new ball practically every time he starts a round, or a box of three. And he asks only one thing of a ball—distance. More than sixteen million golf balls are sold annually in the United States. No wonder it is important to have the winning ball.

Selling golf clubs is a little more difficult because actually a well-made, well-balanced set of golf clubs, particularly irons, ought to last a man a lifetime. I have already owned three different sets, and so have most poor or average players. I consider myself reasonably intelligent, and certainly I have been on the inside of the golf racket for years. I cannot play the game well nor ever will because I haven't the proper co-ordination or time for practice, and I know its requirements and my limitations. But I have been, and will some day again be, a sucker for a cleverly devised sales campaign based on some new discovery in construction, a quarter of an inch of metal, placed in some new spot on the head of the iron, a change in the center of gravity, a new twist to the grip, that, according to the manufacturers, will render it impossible for me to make a really bad shot. I know perfectly well that there is nothing that can be done to a golf stick to make it foolproof, that once the weapon has been given proper balance, good feel, and good craftsmanship, there is nothing further that will insure a straight shot. But I say to myself: "Just supposing they *have* discovered something. Sometimes I play a series of good shots and hook up two or three holes in par with a birdie thrown in. With these new clubs they're talking about I might play more good shots and fewer bad ones." And I take a set out onto the practice tee and try them.

There is one curious psychological quirk to golf that is of

inestimable value to the manufacturer in aiding him to secure a turnover in golf clubs instead of selling a customer a set once and for all. No matter how badly you may play, a new, trial set of clubs on the practice tee works like magic. You hit a series of the sweetest, straightest, longest shots ever in all your life. And that settles it. You take them back to the shop and say: "Put 'em in my bag! Never hit such shots before. That's what's been the matter with my game." And you never hit such shots again, either. When you take them out to play them, the spell is off. You are worse than ever. You are used to your old clubs. The new ones are utter strangers.

Most of the star golfers—that is, the top-flight professionals who meet annually for the most dramatic and best-advertised of all tournaments, the National Open, as well as playing on the winter circuit in the South—are under contract to manufacturers to play their products, clubs and balls, etc. In addition they may have been paid retainers for the golf shoes they wear, the hose, the underwear, and the shirts. That takes care of the stars, or many of them. Some of the companies have four and five under contract, the number varying with their importance and standing. It's a lot like playing the horses. The more nags you bet on in a race, the better your chance of cashing a winning ticket. It's expensive, but more certain.

But in the field of from sixty to seventy golfers that tee off on the first day of the Open, there are a great many guys named Joe of no particular past reputation or record. And there is no telling when some hitherto unknown will suddenly go crazy, get hot, hook up four low rounds, and win the tournament. Almost invariably one of these unknowns is leading the field at the end of the first or second day. Someone playing with little or no gallery shoots a 69 for the first round, or hooks up a 69–73 for the first two days and is leading the nearest big name by two or three strokes.

Now commence the excitement, the trouble, the conferences, the scurrying about the locker-rooms, the attempts to segregate the guy named Joe and get him to sign. And this much is fairly reliable about a big golf tournament. It is better than an even-money bet that the unknown who has set fire to the course in those early rounds will blow himself to an eighty, or a seventy-nine on the third trip around the lay-out and ease himself right out of the party while one of the veterans will come from behind. But then again there is always the chance that the unknown will *not* fade and prove to be just another morning glory. Anything may happen in those mad, nervous, final eighteen holes, when jittery nerve-racked players crack and begin to toss the title around to one another.

The golf company must make up its mind what it will do. There is still time, the evening of the second day (the Open is played over a three-day period, eighteen holes each the first two, and thirty-six the last), to grab the unknown, if someone else hasn't grabbed him first, and sign him up. Nobody has been paying any attention to what ball or clubs he has been using. The boys don't like to change sticks in the middle of a tournament, but with the right price it can be done, especially if our friend Joe is broke, and in nine cases out of ten he is. The average professional doesn't much care with what make of clubs he plays if they are well balanced, well weighted, and the right length and feel for him. They all swing alike, and if you will leave him his favorite putter he will score just about the same with one set as with another.

The trick, of course, is to sign him *before* he has won, or at least to purchase an option for negotiations at reasonable terms if he does win. The price is cheap on the first or second day of the tourney, and, as has been noted, it is a hundred to one that Joe Unknown has thumbed his way to the show and is living from hand to mouth in some cheap rooming-house downtown, and a hundred and fifty dollars, or even fifty, sound like a million to him—maybe. For there is also the chance that Joseph will elect to gamble a little on himself. They are all sportsmen and gamblers, these professionals. If he signs now, it is a hundred and fifty dollars, or perhaps even two hundred, in ready cash. But, on the other hand, if he doesn't sign, and wins the tournament and the title, he can get anywhere from two thousand to five thousand for joining up, depending on the situation. If he takes the ready-cash offer before he has won and then blows up, as perhaps he fully expects to do, the joke is on the company. On the other hand, if he signs for chicken feed and then goes on to win, the joke is on him.

Of late, many of the large golf-equipment companies have tried to escape from the trials and uncertainties of the Open Championship by basing their sales drives not so much on the winner of that particular title but on the records of the leading professionals over the winter and summer circuits, because over the longer period the stars and regular circuit tournament players will run more to class and form and will show a good winning and low-stroke average. The Open Championship has been a sort of graveyard for professional reputations anyway, because of the attendant publicity, and when a widely heralded shaman treats himself to an eighty-three or an eighty-four, the public wants to know about *that*, too, and finds therein some balm for its own sufferings with the cursed game. But it won't work. At least not yet. There is a glamour that hangs around that Open Championship dating from the time that Jones was high priest, and to date nothing has been found to replace it. The Professional Championship is a much more difficult tournament to win, and the winner is probably the best golfer in the country, but nobody cares about it or pays any attention to it. The rank-and-file golfer is intensely interested in the annual amateur championship, but the Open has captured his imagination. He buys on the strength of it.

Sometimes the bitter commercial rivalry of the manufacturers, which is merely amusing to the spectator as long as it confines its assaults to the wallet of the great genus Goof, is not quite so happy, when it works, as it is liable to do, against the prospects of some capable professional who is signed with the wrong company or with no company at all, when the time comes to make the selection of the team for some foreign or international competition, such as that for the Ryder Cup. If the majority of the selection committee happened to be making a nice living out of an affiliation with the—ah—Tru-Flight Company, the crack golfer who garners his pars and birdies for the glory of Midwestern might find himself left out in the cold. Business ramifications sometimes take queer twists.

Well, there is the setting, then—the great Open Championship, with the handsome and beautifully attired professionals cracking their fine, clean, crisp shots, splitting the fairway, or hitting a green from 230 yards away as accurately almost as a man could with a rifle. There are the galloping galleries, the panting press, the messenger boys rushing copy, the broadcasters with their back packs and short-wave transmitting sets, the pretty girls, and the pure green, beautifully manicured countryside laced with white bunkers. The colored flags flutter gayly from the pins, the pretty girls are in bright summer clothing, the porch and lawn of the magnificent clubhouse gay with colored tables. Around the huge black scoreboards the crowd stands ten deep, reading the results of the struggle out on the links, and the handsome lay-out is alive with spectators, and well-groomed U.S.G.A. officials with their neat little badges, worried marshals wearing colored armbands and scurrying about the course bearing ropes and bamboo poles, and all the mixed, colorful crowd of golfers, caddies, police, officials, waiters, newspapermen, photographers, celebrities. . . .

It is exciting, stimulating, gay, healthy, good to look at, and in many ways sport—if one did not know that the driving force, the *raison d'être*, the cause of it all, was John Q. Sap, a little, slightly paunchy, testy, fussy squirt of a man who, when he plays golf, cannot manage to keep his head down, and that the whole great show somehow is called into being because when he stands on a tee and takes a cut at the ball with his driver, it winds up with a gorblimey slice, out of bounds, or in the brook or lake, or behind a tree in a thicket, and in his dull, stodgy way he wonders whether there ever will be anything that can be done about it —without too much, or any, effort on his part.

XVI

LAST STRONGHOLD

OF HYPOCRISY

COLLEGE FOOTBALL today is one of the last great strongholds of genuine old-fashioned American hypocrisy. During Prohibition, naturally, it ran second, but with the coming of repeal and the legalization of betting on the horses in most of the states of the Union, it easily took the lead. Its nearest competitor is the Amateur Athletic Union, and that isn't even close. It is highly discouraging that, one by one, all of our fine and worshipped institutions based upon the American precept of saying one thing and doing another, writing laws and then breaking them, have been crumbling. But football has stepped into the breach nobly and seems only to be beginning to come into its own as the leader in the field of double-dealing, deception, sham, cant, humbug, and organized hypocrisy. There are occasionally abortive attempts to turn football into an honest woman, but, to date, the fine old game that interests and entertains literally millions of people has managed to withstand these insidious attacks. Like the chronic drunk, it has its moments of remorse, but equally like the inveterate souse, the benders following the periods of repentance are that much bigger and better. The future looks rosy.

The idea has dwelt with me for some time that in some ways football was even dirtier than prizefighting, because it insists, every so often in proclaiming and harping upon its virtues, which prizefighting does not. The ring, as has been noted, is strictly a business proposition and is quite engagingly candid and shameless in the manner in which it goes about that business. The same golden rain that hoisted the manly art of self-defense into the surtax brackets likewise turned college football into a huge and highly profitable business. The college gang has been raking in the dough with both hands, but it still likes to pretend that the game is the same innocent college sport that it was back in the days when your father was posing for his picture against a corner of the quad fence, wearing a big turtle-neck sweater with his varsity letter a foot high on the chest. But it isn't—for which reason I say farewell and also good riddance to a game riddled with hypocrites, liars, perjurers, and sophists. It is a game which also holds the distinction of turning loose annually into the already turbid stream of national life a fresh collection of the world's greatest bores—ex-football-players.

An insight into why it is that the game prefers to go along as it is, shamming and faking, fraudulent and frequently mealy-mouthed, hiding beneath the sacred academic cloak, is interesting. The background is purely economic. We meet again our old friends cheap labor and the law of supply and demand.

The original premise upon which college sport, including football, is founded is that play and exercise are healthful and helpful to young men engaged in studies. Participants in inter-collegiate competition are supposed to be bona-fide registered students, paying their own way, or recipients of scholarships for excellence in their academic work. Scholastic standards are to be maintained up to a predetermined grade, a grade as nearly alike as possible in all the universities participating in extra-mural agreements.

Before the post-war sports hysteria, all this worked beautifully except for minor infractions. The tramp athlete and occasional semi-professional football-player existed back in the good old days of the turned-up hat-brim and the Gibson girl. And then suddenly football began to hit the high spots financially and collared its share of the loot that was flung about with such munificent abandon during the rich, spendthrift days of the Golden Decade; whereupon it was discovered that there just weren't enough good football-players to go round. The law of supply and demand entered into the picture and threw the whole system haywire. The puzzle still remains as to why the universities, reputedly the fountain-head of the country's ethics, brains, and culture, were unable to meet these new conditions as honestly and successfully as they have met other not dissimilar problems.

This much became immediately patent—that only winning football teams could hope to cut in on the melon, the big two-hundred-thousand-dollar week-end gates, the publicity, and the kudos and prestige that not only brought in ready cash at the turnstiles, but also upped the entrance applications and, best of all, attracted heavy donations of money from wealthy alumni, which last item is the one that is most liable to cause Prexy to shut his educated eye when the athletic board is up to shenanigans.

The universities tossed their football teams into the public entertainment markets to pick up their share of the swag, and the academicians immediately learned that, unlike the colleges and their staffs, trained and taught to appreciate beauty for beauty's sake, the spending public was not content with the spectacle of eleven men in handsome colored uniforms running around on the field, the band, the cheer-leaders, and the fair co-ed sponsors. It wanted to look at winners, or at least teams that had a fair and even chance of beating the other teams on the schedule. It was quite willing to spend freely, even at the high tariffs imposed by the universities, but it wanted to see something for its money.

These facts were painful to the colleges, but they had to be faced, especially after these same deep wells of learning had made the identical error of judgment that the rest of us made about the good times. They, too, thought that prosperity would last forever, and, as a result, dipped into their treasuries, or floated bonds, or mortgaged the statue of Alma Mater, to erect bigger and roomier stadiums to accommodate the ever-increasing throngs of customers who were parting with three and four dollars apiece each Saturday during the season for a look at football teams that cost the colleges nothing but maintenance, equipment, and the salary of the football professor engaged to instruct them. Old-world, retiring, and pedantic as they were, it didn't take the colleges long to experience acute pain and discomfort in the same regions where it is experienced by professional promoters when they are compelled to turn people and good money away because there is no more room inside. It makes good reading to be able to say that ten thousand applications for tickets had to be refused, but translated into the thirty or forty thousand dollars that might have been paid into the athletic association till, it hurts. Oh, how it hurts!

The next discovery made by the universities, to which knowledge they were for the most part assisted by their high-salaried football pedagogues and their ever-growing staffs, is really the crux and the kernel of the whole business. They learned that it takes football-players to play football—that is to say, high-pressure, modern, four-dollar-a-throw, stadium-packing football. And you cannot get enough of them out of the ranks of the students.

You may, to take a simple, analogous example, collect a tennis team of four or five men out of any student body. Some will be better than others, but none of them could compete as a Davis Cup team or even last beyond the first round in a big-time National Championship. None of them would draw a dime at the gate. Every big college has a baseball team, but nobody goes to see the games, because the players and the teams aren't good enough. It will do for Old Home Week, or Alumni Day, when the Old Boys come back and dress up in funny suits and hats, but any Class C professional team plays better ball, and the public knows it.

Large enrollments are frequently misleading. Out of a student body of one thousand, 750 must be discarded immediately because of the physical requirements of the game—perhaps more. The six-foot hundred-and-eighty- or ninety-pounder is an exception. Occasionally a good hundred-and-fifty or even hundred-and-forty-pound back is developed for football, but he is even more of an exception and is useful only for his speed and elusiveness. Of the 250 remaining, 150 will be eliminated for one reason or another, either physical or mental. Some don't like football and are more interested in other sports, some may have bad hearts or some other defect, and still others lack, not the courage, but the temperament to appreciate and render service in a hard body-contact sport. That leaves a squad of a hundred or so, out of which forty perhaps have had a thorough football training in prep school or elsewhere. And out of that hundred may be developed one or two stars and perhaps four or five other first-class players. But that isn't enough for the modern game, which requires a specialist in every position and from two to three complete teams.

Football is definitely a specialized sport—much more so than golf or tennis or swimming. The average life of a college football-player in his game is from five to six years, two of those spent in prep school and three or four in college. Thereafter —that is, after graduation—he never plays again, unless, of course, he goes into professional football. It has no social value whatsoever beyond the scars and the insignia that remain. It is no accomplishment in after life to be an ex-football-player.

Nearly every boy can run, jump, swim, play a passable game of tennis, or hit a golf ball, but not every boy can play football. The game calls for an extraordinary amount of physical courage and combativeness. If you do not think so, picture yourself hurling yourself into the path of a two-hundred-pounder who is charging at you full speed, picking his knees up to his chin as he runs. He is wearing heavy, cleated boots, a certain amount of protective body armor, and a stiff, hard leather helmet on his head, technically for the protection of his skull, but today developed to the point where it is a dangerous and powerful offensive weapon that can well smash a man's nose level with his face, split his eye, or break his jaw. The prospect to the average man is not too attractive. The game demands, too, a great deal of skill, skill that afterwards, as has been pointed out, will be useless to the player. The body movements needed to carry out the requirements of the technical problems of offense and defense—offense, attack without the use of hands; defense, with the use of them—call for long practice, drill, and training. Kicking is an art in itself, and so is the throwing and receiving of forward passes. And definitely the strategy of the modern game, its complicated running and passing plays and deception, demands a certain type of intelligence, or if not intelligence, then adaptability to regimentation and the formation of habits.

Yes, you must have football-players to play football. There are not enough of them in the average student body. Where to get them, then? And that is the problem that is making liars and hypocrites out of ninety per cent of the American universities and colleges. Because one curious development of the game has been that the intelligence that enables a boy to learn signals and master the art of riding an end or a tackle out of a play just long enough to let the man with the ball slip past him is not the same kind that enables him to master calculus or learn to read Goethe or Ronsard at sight.

Where to get them? The faculty, the dean, and the president suggest the ranks of the regularly matriculated scholars. The coaches and the athletic directors and the alumni laugh at them and yank players off trucks or out of boiler factories or the steel mills or prep-school farms. The faculty is asked to be its age or else. "Else" means having to support a losing football team and sacrifice rich-alumni backing, with a general financial shrinkage all around. And the faculty, generally courageous, honest, open and above-board in all other matters pertaining to university life, dogs this one, in a manner that is cowardly and craven and can hardly be called honest. It tries to get the football-players and the dough and yet maintain face by apparent strict adherence to academic and scholastic standards.

Any ten-year-old child knows that in eight out of ten universities or colleges entrance requirements and scholastic standards as far as good football-players are concerned are strictly phony and that few teachers any longer care to risk their popularity by benching the star halfback on the eve of an important game for a weakness in Virgil. It simply isn't done. Two schools, to my knowledge, are on the level with their scholastic ineligibility lists: the Military Academy at West Point and the Naval Academy at Annapolis. A few of the other larger and more ancient institutions of learning remain within the letter of the scholastic-requirements contract, but the spirit has been known to stretch.

Briefly, the publicized tenets of the universities are that (a) their football-players are all bona-fide students in good standing, and (b) they are all amateurs who do not receive any fee, emoluments, or honorariums for their services on the football field. In nine cases out of ten, one or the other or neither of these will stand up. Somewhere along the line there has been an evasion, a half-truth, or just a plain downright falsehood.

The evasions are almost too many to enumerate or remember. The scholarship racket is the best known, with a few colleges turning sufficiently square to list frankly a certain sum to be set aside for athletic scholarships—in other words, to pay a young man's tuition through college in return for his services on the team, an exchange of education for football, which is a pretty good bargain for the university. Then of course there is the phony job swindle worked by nearly every school that needs good football-players. It appears to be strangely axiomatic that only the sons of the poor seem to have real talent for football. This dodge is handled by the athletic office or the prominent alumnus. And the prominent alumnus is himself an important cog in the machinery of supplying football-players. Frequently he buys one or two and presents them to his grateful Alma Mammy, or constitutes himself a scout to look for promising material and import it to his college much as a baseball scout combs the bush leagues for fresh ivory. The new football coach generally brings a few transfers with him, boys who can play his system and who will be useful in breaking in the machine. Many up-to-date colleges maintain prep-school farms (in exactly the same manner that the major-league base-ball teams own minor-league franchises and use the teams to train and season promising material), and a couple of the Southern colleges even went so far as to stage pre-season foot-ball try-outs. Boys who made the grade in the opinion of the examining coach were given scholarships. Those who didn't had to postpone their thirst for knowledge and a college degree. In their search for first-class, winning football material the colleges have had to use every method found useful and practical by the organizers of professional sport in other branches.

The thing that is so inexplicable is that there is nothing actually wrong with what the colleges are doing to promote good football teams for themselves except their stubborn and dishonest insistence that they are still playing the game under the old standards. They haven't done that for the last ten or fifteen years. The old standards no longer exist and, for that matter, are probably no longer useful or valid. But by refusing to admit this the colleges have managed to get themselves involved in a dirty and subversive business.

In the first place, there is a bad economic balance, or rather unbalance. In the old days participation in a college sport conferred a favor on the boy. He received, free of charge, the benefit of expert teaching and coaching in a sport, the pleasure of winning a place on a team and earning a distinguishing mark in the form of insignia or a letter, occasional trips away from the school, and the joys of competing against his equals as a member of a team representing his college.

Today it is just reversed. It is the boy who confers the favor upon the college. The casual and frequently pleasurable practice periods of a couple of hours an afternoon have been supplanted by long, hard, daily grinds that are continued under floodlights long after darkness has set in, tedious spring practice, and perhaps a three-week training session at a football camp before the beginning of the fall school term. The long hours on the field are further supplemented by night blackboard lectures and early-morning skull practice. He is directly responsible, if he becomes a star, for earning thousands upon thousands of dollars for his college. Yale recently sold the broadcasting rights for Yale football games to an oil-refining company for twenty thousand dollars. And because of the attendant publicity, the boy comes under a terrific nervous strain as he acquires responsibility for victory or defeat.

Whether or not he reaps any benefit from the glare of publicity to which he is subjected is debatable, but that he is definitely injured by harsh public criticism to which he is subjected is not. He is in physical danger if he is a good player, since it is considered a part of good strategy on the part of opposing teams to put him out of action if they can. This may not be aimed for deliberately, but often deliberation is not necessary. If a player is known as a dangerous ball-carrier, kicker, or passer, he is a marked man on the field and his opponents concentrate on stopping him. If they can get him off the field, so much the better for their chances. If he is a key man on his team, an injury is often insufficient to keep him on the sidelines. The university is not particularly scrupulous about inquiring into the health of its football-players and the morals and ethics of its football coach. Kids have no sense, anyway, and the coach lives only by his victories. An injured star is liable to be baked, boiled, taped, and strapped and sent into the game in no condition adequately to protect himself, with the result that what might have been a minor injury is aggravated into a permanent disability which handicaps him all through later life. There is very little joy left in modern intercollegiate football. It has become hard, specialized work.

Economically, the principles under which the colleges work are sound. Ethically and morally, they smell to high heaven. There is only one conclusion that can be drawn from their stubborn adherence to outmoded principles, and that is that as long as they stick to them they can continue to get football-players for next to nothing—cheap labor.

At best, an amateur football-player under present conditions rarely earns more than fifty dollars a week besides tuition and board. If the universities were to turn square and actually pay their players what they were worth in box-office draw and services rendered, the profits from the football racket would be cut down tremendously. The boys are being just a little dumb about it all. But then, after all, they are just boys.

The colleges sell them a free education, a living pittance, and a phony glamour. It is a question just how attractive is the first bait. I doubt whether more than five per cent of the boys who shop for colleges to which they hope to sell their football wares are actuated by a desire to acquire an education, a degree, and a profession without paying for it. But the principle of exchange at least is a decent one, and would be more decent still if the schools would drop all pretense and state frankly: "Trade! For services on our football team, young men, eighteen to twenty-one years of age, will be given four years' free board, lodging, books, pocket money, and permission to attend such university classes as they may desire. Degrees granted if necessary work therefor is completed with passing grades."

From there it might be an easy step, especially if the boys woke up, to arrange to pay them a wage commensurate with their services and ability, time and a half for overtime, and adequate disability and death compensation. Also, if the colleges were paying their football stars a decent salary they might not be quite so reckless of their health. One is inclined to be much more restrained and careful of a property that costs five hundred dollars a week than of one that can be had for fifty.

Such a system might lead to other evils, but they could not well be any worse than those that exist now with the game organized on a one-way basis, ninety per cent for the colleges and ten per cent for the player. Play the professional game sub rosa, but keep that pure amateur countenance on the surface. It whipsaws the kids neatly and keeps the dough rolling in. It must also give the eighteen- or nineteen-year-old boy starting out on a college career a charming picture of what honesty, integrity, and truth are worth on the market, when the whole college athletic system is founded upon falsehood and double-dealing. Kids, goodness knows, are dumb, but not so dumb that they don't know what is going on. It is a curious thing that the college to which a boy goes, not only for an education, but for the set of morals, ethics, and ideals with which to carry on in later life, is the first place where he learns beyond any question of doubt that you can get away with murder if you don't get caught at it or if you know the right people when you do get nabbed. His university is playing a dirty, lying game and it doesn't take him very long to find it out. The non-athlete, with more brains usually than the football-player, who has little to offer his school in the way of immediate headlines or victories or gate receipts, sees the football-player receiving favors, free tuition and pocket money, that are denied himself. The football-player discovers early in his career that rules are made only for them as hasn't. Them as has can make up their own rules.

Perhaps it is a good thing for a boy to make these discoveries early in life so that the world as he finds it will not be too great a shock to him. But there are many who believe that in strong idealism and high ethical sense backed by courage and action lies the only salvation for this wretched globe, and that the last stronghold of such idealism is to be found only in the independent university. Perhaps it is, but in the meantime the fact remains that, seduced by that nice, crisp, shiny football money, Alma Mammy has become something of a tramp. I have no more respect for her than I have for any other racketeer.

The colleges are apparently rigged to try any way out of their dilemma except the obviously decent and honest one. They brought the dilemma—that of the huge, unpaid-for stadiums and athletic plants—upon themselves by greed, but they will not admit it or change to meet new conditions. One large Southern university, disgusted with the obvious hypocrisy of the double-barreled eligibility rules, put the screws on. No more tramp athletes. Only students of good scholastic standing wanted. But in the meantime there was still that steel and concrete bowl and the new field-house to be paid for. And so it still schedules games with the big high-pressure semi-professional teams, teams from colleges that are not handicapped by such niceties of feelings, and the kids take a mauling—to pay for the stadium. That does not strike me as being exactly high-minded either.

Another great and powerful university in the heart of a great city built its stadium out of bonds purchased by the small investors of that city, the tailor, the carpenter, the plumber, and the delicatessen-store owner. To default on those bonds would be a civic catastrophe and scandal. The university must fill that great arena two or three times a year. To do so it must put on the field a football team capable of competing on even terms and winning against the best in the country. There is only one way of getting such a team together today. In one way or another, you go out into the market and buy it. The boys, who in the old days had to die but once for dear old Rutgers, are now called upon first to perish for the mortgage- and bond-holders, or the First National Bank, before they get round to giving up the ghost for the beloved college.

The system is rotten from top to bottom. While the colleges close one eye to the methods used to acquire winning football teams, they haul down the other lid to the underground work, trickery, double-dealing, and questionable politics of their graduate managers and athletic boards in setting up fat money schedules. Before football became a national blight, a college would play a normal schedule of games with teams from the immediate vicinity, winding up on Thanksgiving Day with the big game with a traditional rival. Today every game must be a big game, and no schedule is worth anything without the carding of two or three intersectional games. Boys are expected to play through eight consecutive Saturdays against powerful elevens of semi-professional caliber and maintain a winning average or a clean slate, always with an eye cocked to that Rose Bowl invitation that awaits the stand-out team at the end of a season and the fat check that goes with it, a check in which they do not in any way share. They are supposed to take a week in proximity to the Hollywood movie queens for their end and like it. Well, some of the kids have done all right on that score too. The chiseling, petty politics, back-scratching, and maneuvering required to land a Rose Bowl invitation rivals that necessary to bag a nomination for the presidency.

The other alternative to playing a solid schedule of strong teams with a national ranking entails the scheduling of weak or set-up or "breather" teams. The school supplying the set-up team gets a nice little guarantee, a free trip, a look at a big-time football stadium; and their boys take a licking—a good licking, too. Coaches play politics and swap favors with the booking of these weak teams. The player is never consulted. He goes where he is sent and plays whom he is told. The fact that he has no possible interest in common with the rival he is meeting is unimportant. Traditional rivalry is no longer concerned. The boys know that they must play for the record and not for the fun of it. Each week the newspapers list the number of teams remaining unbeaten. The graduate manager knows that ivy-steeped tradition will sell plenty of seats in a football stadium—Yale and Harvard would come close to selling out if they had lost every previous game of the season—but he also knows that a "natural" meeting between two top-notch unbeaten teams such as Notre Dame and Ohio State in 1935 will pack it to its last cranny.

The football coach is usually not a regular member of the faculty. He is hired for but one purpose—to produce results. When he signs, there is usually a good deal of tripe peddled about the fine influence he will have upon the sterling young manhood in his charge, but it doesn't fool anyone, not even the coach. He knows his college employers and how much they are to be trusted. He knows that if he doesn't produce a winning team his shrift will be short and he will be fired. How he produces it is of no particular concern to his employers unless they are exceptional. He hires his own assistants and uses his own methods. Not even a graduate of the college that hires him, he owes the school nothing but the services for which he is paid, and has no loyalties except to himself. He has absolute power over the boys on the squad as long as they care to compete for places on the team. He can wreck a boy physically or with a careless or deliberately vengeful and malicious word about the boy's willingness or courage destroy him.

But the dirtiest of all angles of the football racket, perhaps, is the occasional face-saving indulged in by a college, by way of pointing up the fact that it is clean and pure in its conduct of the sport. Some poor, stupid youngster who is dumber than usual about covering up his tracks, or who has been so foolish as to take a check, or even, to relax from the nerve strain of playing high-pressure football, has gone off on a bender or smoked a cigarette, is turned up and immediately publicly disclaimed and then pilloried by his university. High-salaried coaches inflate their egos by firing kids who have been caught breaking training, off the team, and snitching to the press about it. With three or four such victims a year, or more, the self-respect of the colleges of the country is sufficiently restored to enable them to wade into another season of skullduggery.

If there is anything good about college football it is the fact that it seems to bring entertainment, distraction, and pleasure to many millions of people. But the price, the sacrifice to decency, I maintain, is too high. As far as I am concerned, it is good-by to college football and good riddance.

XVII

WITHIN

THERE SITS

A MAN

WITH A rush and a roar, a stink of gasoline and burning oil, orange flame and black smoke, the contraption thunders by. On wheels, or hull, or wings, the mechanized racers made of steel and metal alloys, wood and wire and canvas, hurl themselves deafeningly around the course, pioneering in speed, speed, and more speed. The fastest car, the fastest boat, the fastest plane of today is too slow for tomorrow. Yesterday's top speed is cruising speed today. The racecourse is the laboratory for the blue-print designs of the days to come.

The multiple-engined thunderboat will do a hundred and thirty miles an hour, the racing car will rocket down the straightaway at a hundred and fifty, and the incredible flying bullet has reached four hundred miles an hour. These machines are things at which to marvel, with their hundreds of delicate heat- and friction-resisting parts, turning, sliding, rocking, thrusting, interlocking, geared to generate unheard-of power and built to withstand the shock of their own passage over land, air, or water.

And in them sits a man.

Marvelous as are these modern monsters, I hold that the men who drive them are more marvelous still. I used to go to all the mechanized races, the Indianapolis Speedway, the Harmsworth Trophy races for the fastest thing afloat, the Thompson Trophy races for speedplanes, and I never could see the machines for the men who would pilot them. There never yet was a contraption for locomotion made, from the mathematically calculated products of the greatest engineering brains to the bench-made nightmares of crackpot inventors, that some man could not be found who would climb inside, strap himself fast, sing out: "All clear?" and give her the gun.

Who wins the race, the man or the machine? Over the long pull, the machine, they will tell you. In those final minutes when for hours or miles every moving and static part has been subjected to every shock, strain, torque, and force of mechanics, when the molecules of wood, metal, and fabric have been outraged beyond nature, it is the best drafting-room brain, the most careful and painstaking shop-workmanship that wins. But there is still that man in there, straining, steering, braking, hauling open the throttle, thinking. . . .

It is true that when something goes wrong, the man is helpless. A machine is a machine and no better than the brains of the man who designed it and the craftsmen who carried out those designs. There is no spirit in it to give that extra champion's ounce to go on and win when the breaking-point of stress and strain has been reached. The juggernaut fizzes, or flares, or sighs, or spouts flame and black fumes, or belches oil, grinds, clanks, hisses, or clatters, depending upon its nature and its indisposition, and then stops. The motor boat drifts helplessly until the patrol boat comes and tows her home. The car rolls into the pits and stays there. The airplane comes back to earth, whole if lucky, otherwise in splinters. And there ends the race and the story. Somebody in the laboratory was wrong or didn't have enough money or didn't use the right materials. When that happens there is nothing the pilot can do but save his skin—if he can.

But while that tachometer needle is still showing more revs to the minute than were ever dreamed of, the men who race, fly, drive, pilot, and run these high-speed thunder-wagons are the greatest athletes and the greatest heroes in all sport— or the biggest fools. But if so, they are blessed fools and belong to the last of the great adventurers on earth. I hero-worship them frankly, these men who can drive boats over the water at 130 miles an hour, belching flame and gas and shaking and roaring like a thousand demons, or fly the snub-nosed kiwi-winged, bullet-shaped Thompson Trophy racers that are nothing better than death traps when they take off or land, or ride the racing automobiles at Indianapolis that for four and a half hours rumble, shriek, and clatter around the two-and-a-half-mile brick track at top speed.

No one who has not had the experience of a fast ride—anything over 120 on land or water and 250 in the air—can have the faintest conception of the nervous and physical beating taken by 500 mile race drivers like Lou Meyer, Wild Bill Cummings, Kelly Petillo, or Cliff Bergere, or measured-mile drivers like Sir Malcolm Campbell (the only man ever to do 300 miles an hour with an automobile), Kaye Don, or the late Major Segrave, speedboat drivers like Gar Wood or Hubert Scott-Payne, or fliers of the caliber of Benny Howard, Roscoe Turner, Jimmy Doolittle, Harold Neuman, not to mention the fastest human in the world, Lieutenant Francesco Agello of Italy, who flew a Schneider Cup seaplane one lap at 430 miles per hour.

Every particle that goes into the speed wagons is laboratory-tested for three and four times the strain it will be called upon to endure. New and stronger alloys replace ones that have outlived their usefulness. Bigger and better combustion engines are built, carrier bodies are streamlined and friction-proofed. But flesh and blood still remain flesh and blood, and somehow the men who sit inside these machines can do things that mere flesh and blood, brains, sinews, and muscles, were never, by nature or any other agency, meant to endure.

There is a definite hypnotism about high speed, a transmu-

tation of the senses, an almost complete disembodiment sometimes. At sixty or seventy or even ninety miles an hour, it is
you who are rushing through space like a comet. But at veloci-
ties beyond that it is exactly the opposite. You are suspended,
shaken, rattled, and half choked in a static object that is the
center of an utterly mad and terrifying attack by ordinarily
immovable objects. Trees, houses, walls, bridges, roads, grandstands, leap at you with incredible ferocity.

At 130 miles an hour on the Indianapolis Speedway, it is
a world gone insane. Objects in the distance first seem to
crouch as you start the drive down the straightaway, then begin to creep forward, and suddenly spring at you with a terrifying "PAH!" as the air waves are thrown against them, like
something lurking in the dark trying to frighten little children. It has leaped straight for your throat, apparently, missed,
and immediately another and another and another object have
charged at you, an incessant barrage upon your nerves.

In the air this is not so noticeable until you approach such
incredible speeds as the Schneider Cup racers have achieved,
averaging 400 miles an hour, but on the ground or the water
it comes close to being unbearable, because man is not yet
geared to pass from one object to another at such a pace. If
you are an athlete, you can run to an object a hundred yards
away from you in ten seconds. But traveling at two miles a
minute in a car or boat, that same tree or house or rock is upon
you in two seconds, and in the case of Lieutenant Agello, who
fired himself through the air at 430 miles an hour, in four tenths
of a second. A miracle, if you will, this self-actuated bullet traveling at the rate of six and two thirds miles per minute, but
what, then, would you call the man who sits inside this shell of
metal, cloth, wood, wire, and varnish and runs it?

If you have ever had a vibrator held for too long at the base
of your skull by a careless operator, you will remember that suddenly you began to feel as though you were swelling up inside
and about to burst from your head. The race driver, no matter
what his machine, feels that way all the time. Vibration shakes

and rattles him until he has the sensation of his skin, from head to foot, turned hard and stiff, as though covered with dried clay. He feels all swollen and distorted, numbed and thickish about the hands and feet and lips. It is under those conditions that, to save his machine and save his own life with it, he must perform operations so fast and delicate and gauged to such accuracy that there is hardly a split-second watch made today fine enough to measure or time them.

A man driving a racing car at 120 miles an hour, and slowing down to 95 or 98 miles for a sharp curve to the left, can brace his external body, his head, arms, shoulders, legs, to meet the new conditions. He leans into them, bends towards the curve. But his innards don't. His heart, stomach, liver, and lights have no way of knowing they are coming to a corner. They have been traveling straight ahead at a rate at which they were never by nature intended to travel, and when suddenly the curve is taken, they keep on going straight ahead for a brief second of exquisite agony. Race drivers tape and strap their bodies from neck to legs to keep their organs in place through the grind.

Added to these strains upon the system are the choking and sickening fumes from exploded gasoline, and smoke from overheated oil, the thundering roar of the engine, and the ceaseless pluck of the rushing air upon the body. Ride at 130 miles an hour in the open, and it is almost impossible to keep your mouth closed. The wind of your projectile-like passage tears at your lips, forcing them apart, at your arms and shoulders, with what seems to be a living and deliberate malignancy. And the best springs or most powerful shock-absorbers made by man still cannot dissipate or even much minimize the shock of the slightest bump, the smallest unevenness in the surface over which you are traveling. The speed of your passage, as a matter of fact, magnifies each one of these beyond imagining. A ride in a speedboat or racing car is a constant physical beating.

A man who is running or competing in some physical sport knows instinctively, almost automatically, when he is begin-

ning to approach the end of his strength, endurance, and re-
sources. But the man at the wheel and the throttle must at all
times strain every one of his senses to help him detect and avoid
trouble that may put him out of the race, or in some instance
very quickly put him to death as well. He must try to feel his
machine and its behavior with and through his whole body.
He must see, he must listen, and he must smell, to try to detect the first sign of failure in one or more of a hundred moving
parts. He must not alone catch the first sign of trouble, with
one of his senses; he must, if he wants to go on living, antici-
pate it most of the time, because those speed carts, be they on
land, on water, or in air, when something that is an integral part
of their operation lets go, can and will kill you more quickly
than you can say Jack Robinson. And as a matter of strict and
accurate timing, the saying of Jack Robinson, clearly enunci-
ated, won't do any more as an old, stand-by cliché for rapidity,
because it takes approximately a second to say. In that time the
Schneider Cup seaplane has traveled exactly one hundred and
ninety-five yards, and Sir Malcolm Campbell would have been
into, or one hundred and forty yards beyond, whatever was
threatening him.

But not alone must this marvelous human being keep watch
over his own juggernaut, prepared for anything, but at the
same time he is racing other machines guided by other beings
with brains. The years of work, study, and cerebration in the
laboratory will be worthless if through his own stupidity or even
actual cowardice he permits his opponents to trick him or out-
smart him. The engineers may, at the conclusion of the race,
no matter in what position their product finished, chortle and
crow over the success of one tiny bolt or spring that came out
of the engine or the chassis as strong and useful as when it was
put in, but the world only recognizes a winner, and so does the
official entrusted with handing out the capital prize.

There were many who believed that the Silver Bullet, *Miss
England II*, brought over from England by Kaye Don to race
for the Harmsworth speedboat trophy against Gar Wood, was

a better and faster boat than Wood's *Miss America VIII*. Indeed, the Englishman won the first heat of the best two out of three heats, beating Wood by more than a mile. He had but one more heat to win and the Harmsworth Trophy would have gone back to England, and Mr. Wood's boat-building business would have suffered a loss of prestige.

And so when the second heat was run, Wood, who probably knew that his boat was slower that year, risked everything on a trick. He shot over the line some twenty seconds before the starting gun. Don had a stop watch in his hand, ticking off the seconds. He was a brave man, but he wasn't a bright man. He lost his head and chose to believe Gar Wood rather than his watch, and followed him over the line. Both Wood and Don were disqualified and Gar's brother George won the race, loafing around the course in a slower Miss America. To add to this ignominy, Gar flipped his wash under Don's bow on a turn and sank him, *Miss England II* leaping into the air and then diving nose-first under the water. Inasmuch as the challenger for the trophy then lay cosily on the bottom of the Detroit River, there could be no third and final heat, the race was called no contest, and the trophy and the speedboat supremacy remained in the United States. Gar Wood was universally condemned for having perpetrated a mean, Yankee trick upon an innocent foreigner, but in the meantime, with the English boat admitted to Davy Jones's locker, the question as to whether it *would* have won that second heat and the trophy remained a matter of conjecture. The machine might have been there, but the man wasn't.

The sharpest memory of the great mechanized sports meetings that I take away with me is Dead Man's Meeting, which takes place annually at the Indianapolis Speedway the afternoon before the famous five-hundred-mile race. They don't call it Dead Man's Meeting—drivers are not that macabre—but it is as good a name as any for the quiet, ordinary gathering that takes place year in, year out, a routine affair in which the race drivers and mechanics who are to take part in the race the next day meet the officials of the contest and listen to the same speeches, the same warnings, and the same explanations that they heard the year before and the year before that.

They meet on the lawn, inside the track, just to the left of the big control tower, and between the tower and the car pits. There is a small covered stand there on which are grouped the race officials, presided over by Eddie Rickenbacker, himself a former driver and now president of the racetrack, and usually three or four celebrities who have flown in for the event.

Sitting or reclining on the lawn in front of this small stand are some fifty or sixty men in white monkey suits, grease-stained, or just plain trousers and white shirts, with perhaps paper sun-helmets to protect their heads, because it is always broiling hot at Indianapolis at race time, hot, close, sticky, humid, and depressing. You cannot move about very much without suddenly finding yourself damp with perspiration. There is a mingled smell of gasoline and frying grease in the heavy air because close by there is a large, four-sided refreshment booth doing advance business before the big day. Many of the drivers are munching hamburgers and pickle, or tilting the contents of iced Coca-Cola bottles down their throats. They are all young, these men, of no particular type, stature, or build. They appear on the surface to be neither athletes nor heroes. They look like a group of ordinary workmen, if anything, lying about on the lawn, sleeves rolled up, arms and faces smudged with oil and grease. But these are the men who are to drive the thunder-wagons the next day, and the mechanics that sit beside them—who are perhaps even braver.

The routine is fairly interesting. They are shown various colored flags—this one means all clear, that one to slow down, the race is temporarily suspended; another to get over and let a faster car go by. Celebrities are introduced. Questions of procedure are asked. Rick makes his annual speech and plea for caution and begs the boys to forget that heavy foot on the accelerator and to drive safely and sanely as well as fast. Other officials talk on procedure in the pit, the amount of gasoline

permitted, technicalities; and then prizes for the winner of the
American Speed Championships for the past year are presented.

The young men smile and laugh at the well-known jokes,
smoke their interminable cigarettes, munch their hamburgers,
suck at their pop bottles, or mop their hot faces and necks. You
lie on the grass too, trying to get into the shade of the little
stand. You look and listen complacently because Rick has told
you that this annual meeting is an interesting affair and that
you ought to attend, and so you smoke too, and take an occasional note, looking into the crowd of the fastest, most daring
group of automobile race drivers in America and wondering
which one of those faces will be grinning into the cameras tomorrow after having been flagged the winner with the famous
black and white checkered flag.

And then suddenly, with a shock that turns you quite cold
in spite of the heat, you find yourself also wondering which one
of those gay, interested, alive young faces will be missing from
the group the next night. Because the odds are twenty to one
that sitting or lying somewhere on that bright green carpet before you is a condemned man, perhaps two, and if the luck is
very bad, even more. But one of the group, almost surely, has
barely twenty-four more hours to live. Among the living sits
a dead man. You close your eyes and fancy you can hear the
count going on as the Finger moves from figure to figure—
"Eeny-meeny-miney-mo, catch a nigger by the toe. . . ."

One of the men is on his feet nominating one of their number to serve on a committee to determine when a car is sufficiently disabled to be called out of the race. Will the finger
come to rest on the speaker? "If he hollers, let him go. . . ."
Another arises with a technical question having to do with time
in the pits. He is a good-looking kid, young, slight. "Eeny-
meeny-miney-mo!" Someone is "it"; the finger is on him. He is
marked irrevocably. But who? You find yourself shuddering.
Is it that sandy-haired man with the long jaw and the green eyes
over there? Should you be saying to him: "Go wind up your
affairs, brother. Feel the soft, smooth texture of the grass be-

tween your fingers for the last time. When you leave for the track tomorrow, say good-by with an extra measure of tenderness. If you love, love well tonight. Or better still, escape while there is yet time. You need not die. Walk out of the gates. Go home. Pack your bag. Step on a train for anywhere. And you will live. But climb into that slim, shiny red wagon tomorrow afternoon and you are a dead man"?

None of them would believe you. They all know that someone is pretty certain to die out there tomorrow, or be dragged off severely injured, but it is always the other fellow—until it happens. They get used to it, I suppose, the way men in war get used to the idea that of those setting out for an attack, only one third of their number will come back. But this is a peacetime pursuit, and there is horror in the knowledge that on the morrow one of these men will suddenly sicken as he realizes that he has come into a treacherous curve at the wrong place, that he has been a fraction of a second too late with his reaction, and that his life and that of his helpless mechanic at his side is spun on a thread no thicker or more secure than the line reeled out by a falling spider. A desperate twist of the wheel, a lurch to first one side and then the other, and then the stone wall of the high-banked curve leaps at him with all the speed and terrible malignity of an animal of prey and in one awful, tearing, crash bludgeons him into oblivion.

The mechanic dies even more terribly. The driver at least goes down fighting for control, cursing and wrestling with a wheel that has suddenly gone venomously alive in his fingers. But the crash comes upon him still fighting, still trying to save his car. The mechanic sits completely helpless and watches death spring at him. There is nothing he can do. He is entirely in the hands of his driver. There is nothing for him to yank, or twist, or open, or close, that will help stave off the disaster of a blow-out, a skid in an oily patch, or an error of judgment at more than a hundred miles an hour. Wedged in the narrow car, he cannot jump, nor would he, because he would jump to instant death. There is nothing to do but take it.

Some freak of high-speed auto collisions may save his life. But he looks the crash, the shock, the flash-streaked blackness, the wrenching pains, and then the end of all things squarely in the eye during the dreadful split seconds in which they happen.

They are great athletes, all of these men, in spite of the fact that they sit in a seat and pull levers and twist wheels, because their bodies must be as tough and hard as tanned rawhide, and their nerves wound tighter than the gut on an arbalest. One slip and it's game and rubber. Only the spectators hear the chilling, anguished scream of the siren on the meat wagon as it careens over to the dusty steaming wreck of what was once perfection in man and machinery.

I used to think a great deal about those men, Gar Wood grinning like a demon at the wheel of his Miss America X, jounced and bounced, a nerveless fearless hellion on water; Roscoe Turner, bringing his Thompson Trophy racing plane to earth when an oil line broke and for thirty seconds he was as good as dead, walking away from his ship smiling; the cool, laughing Bill Cummings, and comical Kelly Petillo, race drivers. I used to think of them especially when I would see a white-flanneled tennis-player in a tournament make a little moue of annoyance or deliver himself of a great big pout when during play a sports-writer or telegraph-operator in the press marquee went "ticketyite-tick-tickey-tick" on his typewriter or sending key.

XVIII

FAREWELL TO

MUSCLE MOLLS,

TOO

FOR ALL her occasional beauty and unquestioned courage, there has always been something faintly ridiculous about the big-time lady athletes. They never manage entirely to escape a vague hint of burlesque about the entire business. A generation ago they were funny in a mild way because they tried to play competitive games and at the same time retain their maidenly modesty. Today they manage to be amusing for exactly the opposite reason; they play with complete abandon and exposure, and as if that were not enough, the mores and morals of the times have made possible deliciously frank and biological discussions in the columns of the newspapers as to whether this or that famous woman athlete should be addressed as "Miss," "Mrs.," "Mr.," or "It."

Miss Helen Stephens, a big, rangy schoolgirl from Mississippi, out-galloped all the best women sprinters of the world in the hundred meters at the late Olympic Games in Berlin, including Poland's favorite, Stella Walsh. The Poles, with that sterling if peculiar sportsmanship for which Europe is famous, immediately accused Miss Stephens of being Mr. Stephens.

There had been two cases, one in Czechoslovakia and one in England, where a masculine lady had, with the aid of a surgeon, succeeded in transforming herself into a not too feminine gentleman. The Poles thought they had spotted number three.

The situation was already full of laughter, but it remained for the awe-inspiring papas of the Amateur Athletic Union to supply the topper to it. Were they caught unprepared? They were not. They revealed solemnly that before being permitted to board the boat to uphold the honor of the U.S.A. as a member of its Olympic team the Olympic Committee had had La Stephens frisked for sex and had checked her in as one hundred per cent female. With no thought whatsoever for the feelings of the young lady in question, these findings were triumphantly if ungallantly aired in the press. The laugh which had previously been confined to the squawking Poles now rippled far and wide to include the A.A.U. and, I am afraid, lady athletes in general. Somehow there seems to be a rather far-reaching and complete criticism of the muscle moll per se when, immediately a lady succeeds in sprinting a hundred meters in 11.4 seconds, a world's record for girls, she is suspected of being a man. The men do the same distance in 10.3.

But laughter or no laughter, the girls have always made good copy and I am duly grateful. For the last time, a little sentimental and regretful, I take the reviewing stand and watch pass the parade of the lady athletes.

Here come the golf gals in their rough, tweedy clothes, with a sturdy stride, hips and shoulders a-swing. Their faces are weathered, their skin tanned and dried by sun and wind, and most of them have little tiny lines around the eyes from squinting down glaring fairways and measuring and calculating distances. Some of the huskier ones can wallop the ball 230 yards on the drive, but the woman's game is played on or around the greens. They are usually short on their second shots and have to rely upon chipping close to the hole for their pars. Listen closely and you will hear their marching song: "Meow. . . . Meow!" Golf is a funny game. If there is any larceny in a man, golf will bring it out. The game is a natural reagent for the cattiness that is in woman.

Next the tennis ladies, some in shorts, a garment that, anatomically, they were never meant to wear; smarter ones in short, graceful, pleated half-skirts. Yes, they have those eye lines too, from peering steadfastly across the net, awaiting service, and they have a little forward lean as they walk, stepping on the balls of their feet. Look at the shoulders on them, the forearms and the legs. Those legs! The quick stops and starts and the running do knot up the muscles and make them hard and lumpy and do something to the knees, too.

Ah, the beauty chorus of women in sport, the swimmers and divers. Those close-fitting black swim-suits! And see that high-tower diver with the yellow hair in the pure white bathing-suit. Powerful shoulders they all have, those water maidens, but their muscles are long, smooth, and flat. Some of the older ones are a little broad in the beam, a trifle hippy, but it makes them more buoyant. Too bad about those dogs. Refrain—all little swimmers have big feet. Never saw a good lady swimmer with small feet. There are some lovely faces in the ranks, though. A lot of them are merely children too. They catch them young. Somehow I am enormously tickled by the thought of a yellow-haired tadpole by the name of Mary Hoerger who at the age of eleven was national springboard champion, but who when she had attained the ripe and passé age of twelve suffered from an attack of nerves and failed even to place on the 1936 Olympic team. But at that, the event in Berlin turned out to be a triumph for veterans. It was won by a Marjorie Gestring, also of the United States, aged thirteen.

Oh, oh! The female track athletes, the runners, leapers, hurdlers, and throwers. Flat-chested, most of them with close-cropped hair. Not much on looks either. Most of them have hard faces. And those legs! Talk about your tennis girls, take a look at those sprinters. The track girls can wear those bias-cut shorts and shirts because they are not built or muscled like women, most of them. Only a man can wear a running-suit to advantage—or a woman constructed like a man.

Here is the minor sports division, the skaters, the fencers, the squash-players, the skiers, the field-hockey players, and the oars-women. What lovely legs and bodies those figure-skaters have! And how well those graceful skating-costumes show them off! Pity so many of those girl fencers *will* wear bloomers or knickers. But ski-clothes and flying-togs were made for women. There are those knotty muscles on the squash-players again. And what is it that could possibly want to make a girl sit in an eight-oared shell or barge and row?

The freaks bring up the rear guard. A pitiful crew, the female boxers, wrestlers, and ball-players. Most of them are toughies and exhibitionists. For the most part they have ugly bodies, hard faces, cheap minds. . . .

A strange, almost fantastic crew, all right, these muscle molls, especially the pretty ones. But sexless and unattractive, all of them? Not a bit of it. They have a definite glamour, these top-flight swimmers, divers, skaters, fencers, tennis-players, golfers, and fliers, a strong physical attraction.

As people, most of them are poor specimens, jealous, petty, spiteful, often bad-mannered, spoiled, frequently stupid, wretched sports, dull and self-centered, and yet withal gay and exciting, brave and absolutely game. They are, for that matter, gamer than most men, bear pain and discomfort better; and when they get their teeth into any kind of match, it is something to see.

The greatest girl or woman athlete that ever lived, certainly the greatest of our time, was an exceptional person as well as a great performer. She is Gertrude Ederle, the daughter of a German-American delicatessen-store proprietor, who on August 6, 1926 swam the English Channel from France to England, in 14 hours and 31 minutes, and was the first woman ever to accomplish this feat. She had made an attempt the year before and failed. She went back to it again and succeeded. No other woman athlete in any line of sport has ever come close to this performance as a demonstration of skill, stamina, courage, and indomitable will. Seven British girls have since swum the Channel, but none of them within an hour of Miss Ederle's time. And it must always be remembered that Trudy was the first. She softened it up for the others.

There is perhaps no athletic effort quite so useless and pointless as the swimming of the English Channel, and perhaps, too, no gesture in all sports equally gallant with the one made by this simple, brown-haired, round-faced storekeeper's daughter who learned her swimming in the tiny, tiled indoor pool of the Women's Swimming Association on the East Side. She made up her mind to do something that no girl had ever done before —beat the rip tides, cross-currents, and bruising, chopping waves of the world's stormiest, trickiest channel. It was also, I suspect, one of the few purely unselfish acts in the history of feminine sport. The girl wanted to do something for her Swimming Association—to make it famous.

And furthermore, she accomplished this feat alone. There were no cheering crowds to stimulate her, nothing but an accompanying tugboat carrying her sister, a few friends and newspaper reporters, and a hostile French captain who would have been glad to see the girl fail because she was an American. Her opponent was an insensate body of water that could be expected neither to tire nor to quit. Her opponent was also herself. The entire measure of difference between failure and success lay within herself. She had only to call out and she would have been lifted out of the water immediately.

Once, during the darkest hour, when the nasty, gray, choppy waves had battered her apparently to the limit of human endurance, when, for a time, for every yard she gained with her threshing crawl the tide and the cross-currents threw her back two, a friend on the escorting tug leaned over the side and asked her whether she wanted to quit. The girl rolled over on her side, lifted her face, quite blue with cold, out of the water, and called back: "What for?" She was just that simple and earnest. As long as she was conscious she would go on. She won her bitter fight, and paid for the winning of it. The battering she took about the head from the waves permanently affected her hearing.

Her backers implored her to return immediately. Instead she went to pay a visit to her grandmother in a little village in Germany. New York was sports mad at the time she accomplished her feat, and no woman in modern times was ever accorded the hero's welcome that this girl received when she finally did return from the other side. Thousands of harbor craft tied their whistles down when her liner came steaming up the bay, where she was met and taken off by the Mayor's Welcoming Committee boat, with Grover Whalen in charge, plug hat, gardenia, and all. She was paraded up Broadway then through miles of cheering crowds and showered from the canyon walls of the skpscrapers with Broadway confetti,—ticker tape and shredded telephone books and newspapers.

And yet of all the hundreds of girl athletes who have attained fame and publicity she was the only one I knew who remained completely unspoiled by publicity, adulation, and flattery. Her financial affairs upon her return to the United States were badly handled. She might have acquired a small fortune in personal appearances, indorsements, newspaper articles, and so on. The opportunities were wasted and lost, and besides, while she was in Germany, another woman swam the Channel, an English mother, and it took some of the edge off Trudy's performance. She was never bitter. She never complained. She was never rude or snobbish. She clung, almost pathetically, to the friends of the days before she was famous. She was never at any time anything but a simple, unassuming, wholly lovable person. She had become a professional as the result of her swim. She stuck to it and took a job as a swimming instructress and is working at it today. She never trades upon her past reputation or expects anything because of what she did. Deafness and other injuries suffered during her swimming career—she hurt her back and spent eight months in a plaster cast—have only sweetened her temper. There never has been a girl athlete like her.

The best all-around woman performer the country has ever known, was a hard-bitten, hawk-nosed, thin-mouthed little hoyden from Texas by the name of Mildred Didrikson, but her nickname was Babe. She was the sensation of the 1932 Olympic Games at Los Angeles, in which she won two events, the hurdle race and the javelin throw, and she should have won a third, the high jump, but was heckled out of it by officials who objected to her style. But in addition to being able to run, jump, and throw the javelin better than any other girl in the world at that time, Mildred could also play basketball, tennis, pool and billiards, swim, golf in the eighties, throw a baseball and a football, and also be pretty handy with her mitts when the occasion presented itself. Actually, there was no sport at which she could not perform better than average for a girl. She was the muscle moll to end all muscle molls, the complete girl athlete. Apparently she didn't have another thought in her head but sport. She was a tomboy who never wore make-up, who shingled her hair until it was as short as a boy's and never bothered to comb it, who didn't care about clothes and who despised silk underthings as being sissy. She had a boy's body, slim, straight, curveless, and she looked her best in a track suit. She hated women and loved to beat them. She was not, at that time, pretty. Her lips were thin and bloodless, with down showing on the upper one, and she had a prominent Adam's apple. She had good, clear, gray-green eyes, but she was what is commonly described as hatchet-faced. She looked and acted more like a boy than a girl, but she was in every respect a wholesome, normal female. She was as tough as rawhide leather. And yet, too, she was one of the loneliest and most appealing characters of all the more prominent girl athletes and perhaps one of the easiest to understand. I always thought that she became the greatest all-around athlete in the country simply because she would not or could not compete with women at their own and best game—man-snatching. It was an escape, a compensation. She would beat them at everything else they tried to do. And she did. You could see what was driving her in her intense dislike and contempt for all things feminine, rouge and powder, hairdressers, pretty clothes, silks and satins, and the women who made use of them. She lumped them all as sissy. Beyond her ability in sports she had no personal vanity whatsoever. And nothing pleased her so much as to walk up to a girl against whom she was scheduled to compete and state succinctly: "Ah'm gonna lick yuh tomorrow." And then deliver.

A curious but quite understandable change came over Babe Didrikson. Shortly after the Olympic Games in '32 she ran afoul of one of the trick amateur rules and was declared a professional. And as a professional she made considerable money touring the country, giving exhibitions. She acquired a manager and became even more of a celebrity than she had ever been before. And being a famous person suddenly, she began to attract men a little more. Ugly duckling that she was, she had acquired that strange and inexplicable glamour that apparently is a part of every great woman athlete.

And the last time I saw Mildred, the Texas Babe, she was an ugly duckling no longer. It was at the Men's National Open Golf Championship at Pittsburgh. The tomboy had vanished. Her hair had grown out and it had a stylish permanent wave. There was a touch of rouge on her cheeks and red at her lips. She wore an attractive sports ensemble and had a purse to match, with her initials on it. Inside the purse were compact and lipstick, tiny lace handkerchief and comb and all the rest of the first-aid kit to repair feminine ravages. I looked at her and grinned and she knew what I was grinning at. She said: "Yeah, and Ah got silk on underneath and Ah like it." She had come into her woman's birthright by a curiously devious route, but she had got there, which, I imagine, was more than she ever expected.

With but few exceptions, lady athletes are wretched sports. This is generally admitted throughout the sports world, even by the girls themselves, and cited as an example of just going to show. But the girls are not deliberately bad sports, nor can it be said that they do not know what good sportsmanship is. It is just that at all times they are women and no woman ever plays fair in any kind of competition against another woman if she can help it, and usually she cannot. It isn't instinctive with them, and above all it isn't practical. Man's competitive spirit derives from a desire to play, to be gregarious, to show off, perhaps to express himself. Woman's competitive instincts are rooted much deeper than that. They spring from the necessity to survive, to perpetuate herself. Women simply are psychologically unable to approach a contest of any kind from the same angle that a man does. Whether it happens to be golf, tennis, or squash makes no particular difference. It is still competition and the girls are not geared to take it. You can, with patience and training, teach some of them to lose with good grace, but you can never make them like it. It is quite true that nobody really likes to lose and that men as well as women often have to swallow something and set their faces into the prescribed cheerful masks of the good loser before they trot over to shake hands. But the ladies bear grudges afterwards, have alibis, and make remarks. No man ever takes a game as seriously as a woman does. And a man views his opponent with complete personal detachment. He represents a temporary problem and nothing more. A man will brood upon the forthcoming contest if it is of sufficient importance, but once it is over, win or lose, he forgets it, and the man against whom he has played is no longer an opponent, but simply another person to be liked or disliked for his social qualities. It is only an exceptional woman athlete who is able to be that impersonal about someone against whom she has played. The unspoken enmity between Helen Hull Jacobs and Helen Wills Moody is an interesting case in point. It is common knowledge that there is no love lost between them. For years Mrs. Moody barred Miss Jacobs's path to the championship and the fame that goes with it, such as it is. And for the same years Miss Jacobs was Mrs. Moody's most dangerous rival. Sport and the love of both for the game of tennis have failed completely to bring them close together. Neither has been able to see in the other anything but a danger to ambition—in short, an enemy from whom no quarter was to be expected at any time. The girls don't forget and they don't forgive.

As has been suggested, women golfers seem to be the worst sports and the cattiest of all the strenuous sisters, but they are run neck and neck for honors by the figure-skaters, with tennis-players in third place. The girl swimmers seem to be the best-mannered and the best sportswomen of the lot. I have seen a girl swimmer awarded first place in a meet—it was an Olympic trial, and the place meant a lot—march up to the referee and heard her say: "I'm sorry, but I know I wasn't third. I saw Joan touch me out. I came in fourth." And she meant it. As much cannot be said for the male coaches of the female swimmers, and the mothers of the girls.

Unattractive girls are usually comparatively good sports. Pretty girls are not. This might be simply enough explained. An attractive woman hates to be made to look bad, and no one looks his or her best taking a licking at anything. The ugly ducklings, having taken to sport as an escape and to compensate for whatever it is they lack, sex appeal, charm, ready-made beauty, usually are too grateful to be up there in the championship flight to resent losing so much. The pretty ones go into high-pressure sports competition because—because—well, I'm damned if I know why they do.

The figure-skaters in their lovely ballet costumes and the swimmers in their bathing-suits manage to look attractive at all times, but there is no girl living who can manage to look anything but awful during the process of some strenuous game played on a hot day, particularly when she is tired, winded, perspiring, and losing. The tennis ladies bend over double, trying to catch their breaths and blow out of O-shaped mouths like netted fish. Their wet blouses cling damply and stickily to them, their faces get beet-red and glow like incandescent lamps. Their hair invariably escapes from the bandeau and looks frowsy.

If there is anything more dreadful æsthetically or more depressing than the fatigue-distorted face of a girl runner at the finish line, I have never seen it unless it was a little lady I watched once in a series of prizefights arranged for ambitious girl pugilists in a New York taxi dance-hall. The girl had been rapped on her chin a little harder than was good for her and she proceeded to come all apart at the seams and stagger glassy-eyed, with sagging jaw and wispy, drooping hair, like an old charwoman on a bender. And then there were the two lady wrestlers who started out to give a refined exhibition, forgot their lines, lost their tempers, and went at it in real earnest, two viragos in a filthy brawl. And once, too, I saw what was left of a girl after she had spattered her red airplane and herself all over a potato patch during an air race. The girl golfers should see themselves when they squat down on the green and screw up their faces into a series of corrugations to study a putt, or when they waggle before a drive. They are imitating men and they just look silly. Not that men ever were any bargains æsthetically while at play and in the last stages of exhaustion. But that doesn't alter the fact that women, because of their sex, look twice as bad and ought to know better.

But courage? Not the courage it takes to accept a beating gracefully and finally, but physical courage and ability to overcome pain and physical discomfort and carry on. Nothing can beat them on two or four legs. When it comes to gameness they can look any man in the eye—and very often pass him. I seem to remember a girl diver in a springboard competition. The dive was being held in water that was too shallow for the purpose. Before the start, one of the men went off in a practice dive. The water began to turn red before he came up, and when he did, one hand was crimson where he had gashed it on a piece of broken bottle. The girl diver was standing on the board waiting to do her practice dive. The man swam in and was taken away for first aid. The girl did her dive and so did the rest of them. I have seen a girl skater in a mile race trip and fall on the first lap, gash her leg on a skate, get up, set out after the pack, and win. There was the high-tower diver who had hurt herself. A physician told her that if she did another dive before allowing the injury time to heal, there was every chance that she would break her neck. She thanked him and then went on up the thirty-foot tower and took off because it was in the middle of a competition and she couldn't think of stopping. When you find a real fighter in a girl, it is something to see if only as an exhibition and demonstration of pure bull-dog tenacity. Molla Mallory used to be like that. She would get her teeth into a tennis match and refuse to let go.

It is a pity, with all the effort, the publicity, and the acclaim, that actually, none of the girls can be taken seriously at their games, because, always excepting the amazing Miss Joyce Wethered, the English golf star, who could keep pace with the men and was the only woman I ever knew who could, they are at best second-rate imitations of the gentlemen. Miss Didrikson was unquestionably a great all-around girl athlete, the best in the world in her day, but any first-class high-school track man could easily have beaten her at any of her events. Mrs. Moody would be lucky to take two games from a player like Ellsworth Vines or Tilden. A man has swum a hundred yards in fifty-two seconds. A girl takes one minute and three seconds for the same distance, and so it goes. No matter how good they are, they can never be good enough, quite, to matter.

XIX

S. A.

THE BEST-KNOWN group of girl athletes in the whole United States is not made up of tennis-players, golfers, runners, or jumpers, but of swimmers. This is due to Miss Annette Kellermann and the various gentlemen responsible for the art of the camera obscura and photo-engraving; it is axiomatic that nothing so gladdens the heart of a rotogravure or Sunday page editor as the picture of a pretty girl or a group of pretty girls in one-piece bathing-suits. There have been many theories and explanations for the sudden rise of women's swimming to the tremendous popularity that it enjoys in America today. The simplest and most valid of all is that it has sex appeal.

The newspaper editor and publisher for many years has been aware of the value of s.a. in his pages as a sales stimulus. Incoming cuties and movie actresses on transatlantic liners cross their legs for the camera man. Follies girls and fan dancers make elegant page lay-outs. Society girls sunning themselves at the social beaches, bathing beauties on parade, the female figure in any form of exposure, sell papers.

But there is a definite limitation imposed upon the editor. The use of these figures and exposures must be legitimate, otherwise it will prove a boomerang and cost him more in sales and class advertising than it will win for him. He cannot afford to turn his paper into a form of *Police Gazette*, with nudity displayed merely for the sake of nudity, or he will offend the solid-citizen background of his circulation, the "family." This family is the buying power of his circulation, the class that responds most heavily to advertising. Lose them through displays of bad taste or too much nudity and bang goes your respectable national and local advertising along with them and there remains nothing but to open your columns to the sale of shady postcards, love-philters, mail-order pistols, and what every young married woman should know.

Thus, the crossed legs that decorate Page One all belong to prominent people whose arrival or departure is news; the full-length portraits of scantily clad professional beauties, actresses and night-club cuties, when removed from the theatrical pages where they belong are likewise legitimate news when they have pistoled a husband or lover or sued for divorce or are blackmailing for alimony or breach of promise.

But semi-legitimate as are these uses, nothing of late years has been able to approach in sweet innocence, coupled with undeniable sex appeal, photographs of handsome young girls in revealing bathing-suits lined up on the edge of a pool, waiting for the starting gun, or poised on the end of a springboard or diving-tower, or caught in mid-air in full flight. It is news—sports, decent, completely privileged, in good taste and at the same time arresting and stimulating as all get-out. These pictures may be used ad lib on the sports pages—a section that appeals chiefly to men, anyway—occasionally on page one when a championship is at stake, and at all times to dress up the Sunday or rotogravure sections. Whether or not the girls and their parents and the swimming authorities and the prissily proper A.A.U. know it, the newspapers have been using the swimmers as circulation-pullers just as the real-estate promoting corporations in Florida, California, and New York have been using them for bait for years—ever since, due to the great missionary work of La Kellermann, who first wore the bathing-suit to which eventually she gave her name, the one-piece silk swimsuit supplanted the bloused, skirted, stockinged bathing-clothing of the early and late nineties.

However, sports have had some strange bedfellows before,

and this set-up is by no means the strangest. And to date it has been pretty much of an even swap. The newspapers got their exciting pictures. The girls got their necessary publicity. And on this publicity women's swimming, in itself not a particularly exciting spectacle, built itself up from semi-private meets held in tiny indoor pools to a huge and successful sports attraction that upon several occasions has drawn more spectators than a heavyweight prizefight or a baseball match for the world's championship.

None but a very few would know offhand if you were to ask who Jean Shiley and Nan Gindele are. Because I have a record-book available I am able to tell you that they are two American girls who hold the world's records in the high jump and the javelin throw, respectively. But, comparatively, no one ever heard of them. Ask any kid in the street who Eleanor Holm is, however, and the betting is ten to one you will be told that she is the back-stroke champion, with like as not additional infor-mation that she is married to Art Jarrett, the band-leader and crooner, that she can croon herself, and that she was fired off the Olympic team for drinking too much champagne at one time. It all depends, you see, on how you look, what you wear, and how many times a year they print your picture in the papers.

The photographs that have appeared of such athletic geniuses as the Shiley, Gindele, Stella Walsh, Evelyn Hall, Lillian Cope-land, Helen Stephens, et aliæ, our greatest women track and field stars, have represented them in track shorts or sweat-suits, a sort of a baggy overall pajama, with a mop of hair over their eyes, their leg muscles standing out like object lessons on an anatomy chart. They have been interesting as studies of lady athletes and personalities, but their æsthetic value has been nil. When Ellie Holm or any of her colleagues stepped before the camera lens, it was six, two, and even that she was wearing a one-piece rubber bathing-suit, backless, a burst of orchids at one shoulder large enough to choke a heifer, lips carmined, teeth flashing, hair neatly parted, combed, waved, and brilliantined. The caption-writer would take one look at the hand-some head, the shapely figure, the smooth, well-turned limbs, and write "Water Queen." The country worships the pretty girl. And when she is a champion besides—wow!

The newspapers had merely to advertise or announce that this *lecker-bissen* was to be on view in person and in action at a certain place at a certain time, and the beach or pool conducting the meet had to call out the reserves to hold back the crowd. Father might hesitate at being caught at a burlesque show or demanding seats too far down front for the new musical extravaganza, but no one thinks any the worse of him if he takes the kiddies to see an afternoon of good, clean sporting competition. Sport for sport's sake is all right, but even the most case-hardened athletics enthusiast realizes that it is more than a help when a couple of the participants look like something off of a magazine cover.

There was great sorrow among the slaves of the lens and their assignment editors, I remember, when Eleanor temporarily withdrew from competition, to travel and sing with her husband's band. The crop of swimmers and divers at the time, with the exception of the blonde and shapely Dorothy Poynton Hill, the Los Angeles high-tower diver, had gone off a bit. And then suddenly, like manna from heaven, into their little black camera boxes fell the two Kompa sisters, Erna and Elizabeth, members of the famous Women's Swimming Association of New York, back-stroke swimmers, and not one pippin, but two, almost as alike as twins. With a whoop and a holler the boys descended upon them. Assistants had to stand by pouring cold water on the red-hot fast-clicking camera shutters to cool them off. Sunday and roto editors dropped ten years off their lives. And business around the swimming meets, which had fallen off a little, began to pick up wonderfully. And the girls were good enough to be news. The newspapers do stick by their guns and their code of ethics. Just being pretty isn't enough. A girl must be a winner too. La Jarrett (Miss Holm) stood just so much of that and then in a great hurry got back into training and drove the Kompa sisters smack off the Sunday pages by whipping them in the back-stroke swims every time she started against them. There was no complaint from the press. Eleanor redonned her white gum bathing-suit, buried her brown left shoulder in orchids, shined up her chestnut locks, and flashed the smile. All was right with the world again.

What used to be a healthful and pleasant pastime for young ladies, as well as a safety measure—"everybody ought to be able to swim"—has in the past ten or twelve years practically taken on the aspects of a career. Girls are trained to become swimming and diving stars almost the way ballet dancers are trained —from infancy. Go to any popular pool around New York, or Miami, or Los Angeles, and you will see a host of precocious water babies, four, five, and six years old, swimming the racing crawl or doing dives off the ten-foot board and even higher, watched over by ambitious and doting mothers. The swimming mother is becoming almost as much of a nuisance as the child-actress mother. Victory, a national championship, or a berth on the Olympic squad reaps a terrific harvest of publicity, and publicity, in our mad land, has become synonymous with success and a foothold to wealth and social advancement. What becomes of these girls as human beings, when their heads are turned at an age when they cannot possibly assimilate or evaluate the flattery or attention they get, never seems to be of much concern to their parents. The 1936 Olympic women's springboard diving champion, Marjorie Gestring, is thirteen. Eleanor Holm was fourteen when she made her first Olympic team. Mary Hoerger was a stringy tow-headed frog of eleven when she won the national springboard championship, and she was competing when she was eight. Katherine Rawls was a national swim champion at the age of fourteen, and her entire life —her dress, her routine, the cut of her hair—was regulated by her swimming coach—to keep her a champion. The fatter the clipping book, the greater the success of the swimmer.

There is an amiable fiction among the swimming fraternity that the world is actually interested in speed swimming to the extent that it is necessary to hang out the S.R.O. signs wherever a bevy of water nymphs is performing in the pool or off the springboards. The fact remains, however, that the gentlemen swim much faster, smoother, and better than the ladies and are much more capable and graceful off the springboard or the high platform, but nobody, comparatively, ever bothers to go to see the gentlemen at their swimming meets. It is true the public does like to see records broken, but it likes to see the girls break them, and not the men. Why? The men's national swimming and diving championships are a drug on the market annually as a production or a promotion, but old Mr. John I. Day, the Long Island auctioneer and real-estate promoter, will pay as high as ten thousand dollars, if necessary, to bid in the women's championships for his Manhattan Beach as a free attraction, and the News, New York's most successful tabloid, has spent as high as seventeen thousand dollars staging swimming meets with women predominating, likewise as free entertainment for its readers, has brought girls to New York from the Pacific Coast and from Europe, while it would not spend a dime to bring the fastest male swimmer down from the Bronx. And yet Johnny Weissmuller (who later became famous as Tarzan) swam the 100-yard course in 52 seconds flat and it took Helene Madison 1:03 to negotiate the same distance; Jack Medica's time for the 440-yard or quarter-mile swim is 4:50.9; Lenore Kight's for the same, 5:32.5. The men's championships might get three quarters of a column in the newspapers. The girls splashed all over the page. They had something.

This beauty chorus of the sports world had an amazing development during the wild days after the war, the era of gold, coincident with the great Florida boom. The real-estate promoters of that happy land were not dumb. They had the sunny skies and the Spanish architecture and the palm trees and the tiled swimming-pools, but they needed publicity and something warm, lovely, and living for their settings—bait. They imported whole troupes and circuses of women swimming stars, all expenses paid, suitably chaperoned and properly attested to by the A.A.U., always glad to aid a worthy cause. Meet after meet was staged, with the promise of broken records as the announced lure. Swimming for women had been backwards for years. In their races the girls used to have to drag yards of heavy, sodden cloth along with them, and the records then standing were particularly fragile and ready to be wiped off the books. The modern swimming girls, equipped with the light, silk, one-piece swim-suits and, above all, the modern technique in the crawl-stroke, could and did crack them by the dozens. In one afternoon at the Miami-Biltmore pool they created twenty-five new records. Every time an old record fell, there was free publicity in the newspapers, with the pool or development, Coral Gables, Roney Plaza, Miami-Biltmore, or Palm Beach, mentioned prominently. The crowds packed the pools and beaches to see the latest athletic phenomena—which didn't hurt the pictures or the advertisements any. But no one lost sight of the fact that the girls who were competing were most of them damned good-looking.

There was Helen Wainwright, a blue-eyed, raven-haired little beauty, one of the loveliest girls ever to climb into a bathing-suit; Sibyl Bauer, a graceful, fine-looking girl; Helen Meany, another dark-haired, blue-eyed diver with a stunning figure; Josephine McKim, a tall, slim girl with a soft mouth and eyes like a doe; Martha Norelius, a handsome German type; Aileen Riggen, a little beauty with tremendous personal charm and style; Agnes Geraghty, a gay, sunny girl; Doris O'Mara; Adelaide Lambert; Ethelda Bleibtrey, a handsome blonde; Ethel McGary, a stunning brunette; and other heroines of the original troupe who in their way became almost as famous as the original Floradora Sextette.

Not one of their names remain in the record-books of today, only a few years later. New beauties replaced the ones who got married and left the scene, Georgia Coleman, Dotty Poynton, Ellie Holm, the Kompa sisters. A strange thing, the fascination of these swimming girls, because many of them were and are fascinating. Probably they are the only group of girl athletes who have ever been able to couple complete femininity with real athletic achievement. True, a lot of their records were cooked-up ones at trick distances. There are American records, world's records, Olympic records, and records that again fall into classifications depending upon the type of pool or body of water in which they were made, a twenty-yard course, short course, long course, salt or sweet water. The shorter the pool, the better the time, the swimmer getting the benefit of more turns and added speed from the kick-off at each turn. Nevertheless, those girls could swim, and some of them could swim faster than any other girls in the world, and did. And what is more, after climbing out of the pool where they had been fighting like terriers for winning positions, they could put on evening dress without looking like the first-string halfback playing the feminine lead in the varsity show, and dance at night, hold their liquor like gentlemen, most of them, smoke a cigarette if they felt like it, and spoon a little, or be gay and wholly feminine.

Probably just because their costumes while at work were so revealing, you had the feeling that these were really girls, women who were not trying to be imitations of men. All their traits and mannerisms at the poolside were feminine, and most of them had crushes or beauxs or young men who hung around the pool and adored them and waited to take them away in cars as soon as they had done their work. They were good girls too, honest and not at all promiscuous although they lived in a promiscuous age. Few of them were of a high level of intelligence or had a thought beyond winning a race or getting a movie contract or cadging enough from an expense account to get a new dress, but, if anything, that added to the complete normality which made them stand-outs among women in sport. If you had a girl who was also a swimming champion you found somehow that she had two distinct personalities. She was your girl, and too, when the chips were down and the starter's gun went off she was all champion. Most of the women in other lines of athletics are sportswomen twenty-four hours a day and therefore almost as great a bore as the complete male athlete.

Gertrude Ederle was the great all-around waterwoman of fifteen years ago. Her counterpart of today in all-around ability is a little chit from Florida named Katherine Rawls, who almost from the time that she was able to walk was tossed into a pool and trained to become a champion waterwoman. She is. She can swim free style, back-stroke, and breast-stroke and win championships off the ten-foot springboard. She once took part in a swimming and diving decathlon against seven of the best girl swimmers in the country and won every one of the ten events, which is some sort of all-time record for decathlon performance. She is an ingenuous child with a birdlike face and manner and doesn't look big or strong enough to win anything. This is another pleasing feature of swimming. Size and muscle are not especially essential. Helene Madison, who set up a sensational string of records around 1931–2, happened to be a big Brunhilde of a girl. But later swimmers who wiped every one of her records off the books, Lenore Kight Wingard, Rawls, Olive McKean, and others, were small and slim. The swimming muscle is a long, flat, smooth one that never bulges or shows. Speed in the water is acquired with efficiency more than strength, although the Dutch girls who cleaned up in the last Olympic Games in Berlin, Mastenbroek, Willie den Ouden, and Wagner, were all a little on the beefy side.

The most famous of the modern girl swimmers is the already mentioned Eleanor Holm Jarrett, who was sufficiently beautiful to be tapped by the late Dr. Ziegfeld for one of his *Follies* where he intended, in one of the most dreadful words that has come into common use, to glorify her. Ellie passed it up because inside a more than luscious arrangement of flesh there was a level head. She was the daughter of a Brooklyn fire captain, and she became one of the most renowned girls in the United States by swimming on her back. She could swim on her back faster than any other female in the world, and faster, too, than most people could swim on their faces. It was in a way a great blessing that Eleanor elected to swim in the dorsal

position, because her face deserved to be seen at all times, especially when in the green or blue waters she framed it in the
white, curling foam created by the swiftness of her own passage.
She was a product of the Women's Swimming Association of
New York City, taught and coached by Lou B. De Handley,
probably the greatest swimming coach in the country. Eleanor
was neither a large nor a husky girl, although she had a good pair
of shoulders, but she swam with such beautiful rhythm, efficiency, and smoothness and apparent lack of effort that she always seemed more to be swimming a water waltz than a race.
She was one of those rare athletes like Bill Tilden, or Bob Jones
or Babe Ruth who had the artistry of perfection. She swam on
her first Olympic team in 1928.

Madame Jarrett, the only married lady on the squad, won
herself some sort of undying fame by getting herself sacked
from the 1936 Olympic team en route to Berlin for adhering too
closely to the bar of the S.S. *Manhattan*, and for a time even
threatened to become the Harry Greb of the lady swimmers.
She won her place on the Olympic squad fresh from two solid
years of trouping with her husband's band, during which time
she sang nightly, never went to bed before three or four in the
morning, and carried her share of the burden of the traveling
cabaret show business by drinking with the local big shots and
helping her husband sit up with them until the waiters whipped
the cloths from the tables and turned out the lights. Like Greb
and Grover Cleveland Alexander and a few others, she punctured the cherished illusion of the virtuous that a lady or a gentleman cannot smoke cigarettes, drink wine or whisky, and still
win. The campaign of vindictiveness against the little lady was
inspired not so much by the fact that she drank champagne,
but that she could drink and still win. That was and always is
the unforgivable sin. Her performance at the *Manhattan's* bar,
where admittedly she got tight on champagne, was merely
routine and a quite usual way of living for her. It seems no
more normal to take a girl who has been living a professionally
high-pressure night life for two or more years chaperoned by an

adoring husband and suddenly decree that she shall say "No, thanks," when the corks begin to pop, or climb into bed at ten p.m. than it would be suddenly to require a Baptist preacher to sit up from ten every night to four the next morning drinking Scotch and soda and puffing at cigarettes.

The A.A.U. and Olympic officials threw her out anyway, which smacked a little of cold ingratitude, I thought, because the former Miss Holm's contributions to the development and popularizing of swimming by means of her white caoutchouc bathing-suits, her face, her figure, her nosegay of shoulder orchids, and her strict adherence to every absurdity of their amateur rules can hardly be overestimated. The Amateur fathers were always delighted to avail themselves of the girl's services—gratis, of course—at their swimming meets and cash in on her attractions; but when she punctured an illusion for them, they repaid her with public disgrace. It was a noble ganging-up.

Well, so much for swimming. Just how good the modern girl performers are remains to be seen. It must be remembered that, as far as we know, the modern technique is of comparatively recent development, within the last thirty years or so. On the strength of the smashed records of those years, the swimming times of today cannot be expected to stand up for very long, but the foundation of the success of the women's swimming racket in the U.S.A.—sex appeal—looks as though it is due for a good long run of popularity.

XX

UNDER THE

GUNS

THE CROWD is still roaring and rustling with excitement. There are policemen in the ring, and seconds and attendants are dragging the fallen and unconscious champion to his stool and beginning the work of resuscitation. The victorious fighter and new champion is still jigging deliriously around the ring, waving one arm aloft and with the other holding his bathrobe about him, bowing and smirking and dancing. His manager is trying to kiss him, his seconds are pounding his back, his friends are attempting to climb through the ropes and are being pushed back by the men in uniform. The announcer is making a circuit of the ring, leaning through the ropes and bawling the time of the knockout to the reporters, his face purple with the effort of making himself heard above the hubbub. Photographers are everywhere, their flash bulbs winking and flashing continuously.

You yourself are still trembling and thoroughly shaken as the result of what you have just seen, the stunning knockdowns, the staggering, helpless champion trying to save himself, a tragically broken caricature of what was once a man, the relentless doom-laden pursuit of the challenger with the sweet scent of victory flaring his nostrils, the vision of triumph and wealth dilating his eyes, the soft, thup-chuck-thup of blows driven home, and the hard, savage breathing, the tight, tense hand

256

duel between two men that suddenly exploded into raw and brutal drama. . . .

At this point your telegraph operator, sitting at your right, goes "Ticky-tick-tickety-de-tick-tick," with his bug, as he calls his transmitter, and looks at you expectantly. He isn't excited. Excitable telegraph operators are never sent to serve red-hot sports wires if it can be avoided. The other end of the copper strand runs right into the composing-room of your newspaper where another telegrapher sits at the receiving instrument with a typewriter and little half-books of copy paper and carbons, waiting to translate the incoming dots and dashes into copy. An editor sits at his shoulder waiting to snatch the sheets as they come out of the typewriter and make a swift stab at copy-reading them and marking them for the compositor. At his side waits a copy boy to rush the sheets to the linotype machines. The make-up editors stand impatiently at their forms and yell for type. They aren't excited, either. They don't care who has won or lost, or how. Some of the drama from the far-off stadium may have come filtering through to them, but not enough to matter. There are more important things to hold their attention. They have already sent away the flash edition replate, with the round-by-round account of the fight, and the big black headline naming the winner. Now they want that story. They don't want it fancy, they want it quickly. Every second counts in getting on the street with the complete story of the fight, to beat the opposition. Trucks are waiting at the delivery-room. There are trains to be made at the big terminals. To hell with pulling a Joe Conrad or a Kipling. They want type. They must have type. If it is any good, so much the better for the man covering the story. But you cannot put beautiful but unwritten thoughts into a paper. You need that type. . . .

And so when the ringside telegraph operator gives you that expectant look, it means that the wire is clear and the boys down at the office are waiting to get out a newspaper. You draw a deep breath, try to quiet the pounding of your heart, run a sheet of copy paper into your mill, rap out your by-line automatically, and begin to write. Before the bell on your carriage has indicated the end of the first line, the operator's bug is clicking away furiously, mingling with the hurried tapping of the typewriter keys. No X-ing out, please, or throwing the beginning away and starting the lead all over again. That first line is in the office already. Keep it coming. Tell what happened in that first paragraph, and tell it quickly—who won, the time, the round, the fatal punch, the crowd, the gate—and get emotional and literary afterwards. Tell the yarn dramatically if you can, and make it live, but above all, *tell* it and feed those machines. You cannot sell papers that aren't on the street even if you are Bernard Shaw, Ring Lardner, and Tolstoi all rolled into one. This is sports-writing at its most exciting—under the guns. I used to like that.

Or perhaps you are working in the narrow press coop built along the roof ridge of a baseball park at world-series time, fighting that first-edition deadline. Hundreds of things worthy of note happened in that nine-inning ball game that has just ended. The players have hardly dived down into the dugout passageway to their dressing-rooms, the inevitable knot of curious spectators has already gathered around home plate and the pitching mound, the crowd is not yet through the center-field gates, and your story is already begun—or should be if you don't want a pleasant but sarcastic little note to come clicking over your wire from the boys back on the desk, inquiring solicitously whether you think they are getting out a weekly magazine, or what.

You are editor there as well as reporter. You must make up your mind instantly as to the news and dramatic value of the things that have occurred, which happenings to play up as the turning-points of the struggle, which to give secondary place, which to mention briefly, and which to leave out. And you must be right. There are some three hundred other baseball-writers and reporters at work on the same job, as well as from fifty to sixty thousand spectators. No two people will look at any game exactly alike, but in the main you must have seen it just about as the spectator and the other reporters have. And the space for your story is limited too, at least on a tabloid.

But that final story, slugged at the top of your page in the upper left-hand corner: "New Lead All," is the least of your jobs on a big baseball show. Sometimes you have only one thing to do—look at the game, estimate it, and report it when it is all over. And at others—notably, when your paper is enjoying the throes of a periodic economy wave—you may be called upon to do four or five. A pleasant and exciting afternoon working a world series during a period of press parsimony will go something like this:

Arrive at the ball yard an hour or so before game-time, go down on the field, mingle with the ball-players and managers of both teams during their warm-up periods, and pick up stray bits of news, gossip, advance dope on choice of pitchers, human-interest touches, injuries, news. Climb up to the press box about thirty minutes before game-time and slap out two pages of notes on what you have just picked up, little, short, three- or four-line paragraphs, and likewise a page or two of solid filler, sometimes called "A" matter, on the crowd, the situation according to the games already played, or the prospects if it is the first game of the series, or anything in the news or feature line that you can think of. This is to hold up the first edition with your flash lead and fill space that will later be occupied by your detailed story of the game. Just before the game starts, you make certain to shoot in the corrected line-up with the starting pitchers and catchers, for the kid in the office who will make up the box score from your play-by-play account.

The first batter approaches the plate at last, swinging his two bats, tosses one away, and takes up his position. The pitcher regards him long and earnestly, the crowd settles back, buzzing with tension and excitement, and the fun begins—especially if it happens that you have to work two wires.

On the narrow bit of planking in front of you is your portable typewriter; just to one side, your score-book, a pair of field

glasses, sharpened pencils, copy paper, and a package of cigarettes. A telegraph operator sits at your left, another at your
right. The chap on your left is going to send your written copy,
the other one will take your play-by-play dictation.

The pitcher winds up and lets go. Strike! You make a nota-
tion in your score-book. You do that for every ball pitched, because when a hit is made, especially an important one that con-
tributes to the final outcome of the game, the reader will want
to know what the count was on the batter and whether the
pitcher or the hitter was in a hole. It adds interest and zest to
the dramatic story of the game. Suddenly there is a sharp crack,
the ball is a white streak against the green and tan surface of
the infield, the runner is dashing for first base, an infielder
moves smoothly forward, swoops, and makes a quick throw.
You note a baseball shorthand hieroglyphic in your score-book,
turn to the operator on your right, and begin to dictate: "With
the count two and two, Smith, the first batter up, hit a sizzling
grounder towards short. Jones made a great running one-hand
stop and threw him out by a step." Then you run a sheet of
paper into your typewriter, slug it: "Add Notes," and if it is
the first game of the series, usually try to bat out a string of
"firsts" for the edification of the reader: the first ball pitched,
the first strike, the first out, the first hit, the first squawk, etc.,
etc. And in the meantime your game is going on, and going on
rapidly. Every move made on the diamond far below must be
dictated to that play-by-play operator. Then a run or two is
scored. You rip out the sheet marked: "Add Notes," insert
a fresh one, headed: "Add Bulletin Lead—1," and write the
details of the scoring in story form, with comment and color.

As the game progresses, you try to keep all three things moving along, the dictation, the notes, and the Add Bulletin Lead.
In the notes you retail spicy little items that are of themselves
interesting or outstanding, but which may have no direct bearing on the outcome of the game—sensational catches, arguments, injuries, behavior and reactions of individual members
of the teams and the crowd. In the Add Bulletin Lead you are

trying to tell the story of the game as though it had been written after the game was over, which means that you cannot commit yourself too strongly. One inning is sufficient to change the
complexion of the game entirely. It may switch three, four,
and five times before the last man is out. This material will be
used above the filler material or "A" matter that you have sent
before the game started, and just under the one-paragraph bulletin lead that you rap out when the game is over.

How do you manage to do three things at the same time? I
don't know. You just do, and try not to get rattled or fall too
far behind on any one job. You get used to it after a while.
You can always write a paragraph or two while the sides are
changing. Arguments, injuries, time out, and change of pitchers represent invaluable minutes in which you can catch up.

And then the game comes to an end. You check the total of
hits, runs, and errors and the time of the game and shoot those
over the play-by-play wire. You head a sheet: "Bulletin Lead"
and bat out a quick, fifty-word paragraph on who won the game
and why, and shove it at the operator on your left. You head
another: "Lead All Notes," and tap out another forty to fifty
words of feature lead, including the score, that will tie your
notes together, and pass it to the operator on your right, who
by this time has cleared his wire. Then you sigh, light a fresh
cigarette, head a new piece of paper: "Sports, *Daily Blah*, New
Lead All," add your precious by-line, glare at it for a moment,
and begin, hoping vaguely that this time it will be literature,
but not feeling any too certain about it.

The blow-by-blow description of a big prizefight is, I think,
the most difficult of all sports-reporting work on which to do a
decent and accurate job, and the next is a one-man coverage of
a big football game. A fight is simple enough to describe as
long as the boys are enjoying a pleasant little boxing match or
are spending most of their time embracing one another, but
when one of those million-dollar heavyweight matches suddenly goes berserk, it is something else again.

In the first place, you come to your working press seat at the ringside, abutting on the canvas-covered platform, in a fine state of nerves. One trouble is that in nine cases out of ten, you have sold yourself on your own ballyhoo, and the struggle you are about to witness seems important and epic out of all proportion. Fifty or sixty thousand people, or even a hundred thousand, will be witnessing what takes place in the ring, but close to a million or more are depending on you for an accurate description as well as a colorful picture. Many sports-writers are as nervous and keyed up and on edge as are the fighters shortly before the fatal hour of ten p.m. They all want desperately to do a fine story on the big fight and they don't know whether they can or will.

By the nature of your work, too, you know both men involved intimately. You have lived with them at their camps, eaten with them, played cards with them, been in their homes, played with their children, and in a way you are fond of them, perhaps fonder of one than of the other, which is another handicap. It is a dangerous business on which they are about to embark. It may result in disfigurement, blindness, even death, not to mention the financial importance to both parties. It is a good deal like having an appointment to go to see a friend have an accident. Then, also, because you are supposed to be an expert and the readers demand it, more or less, you have committed yourself by making a positive prediction as to the eventual winner, the manner of winning, decision or knockout, and if you are exceptionally brash, the round in which the knockout may be expected.

This is no help either to your state of nerves or to your subsequent judgment, and realizing that, it worries you. Your reputation as someone knowing something about the prize-ring (nobody really knows very much—vide the Louis-Schmeling debacle for the press) is at stake, and you would prefer the next day to be among those who called the turn even if they are the obvious majority. But having made a selection—and often it is the fighter you happen to like best personally—you are worried that the one thing will happen that no newspaperman wants or can afford to have happen: a bias of judgment in recording the winner of the various rounds of the fight.

You are aware that a hundred people can look at a prizefight and each come away having seen a totally different fight from any of the others. And besides, there is an official verdict to be rendered at the end of the contest by two judges and a referee, a bad one or a downright larcenous one, frequently, but official nevertheless. You do not look any too good awarding twelve rounds to White and three to Black and then have Black adjudged the official winner, especially if in your forecast you picked White to win. Fight decisions were so bad around New York for a time that a current gag was to imitate a fight broadcaster at a big match with: "Oooooh, White is down again. He is up and staggering around the ring. He is bleeding. Oh, there goes White down again. He gets up again, but is helpless and Black batters him all over the ring. White is helpless. He is bleeding from cuts over both eyes and the nose. He goes down again. He won't get up this time. White is out. No, the bell ending the final round saved him. The bell rang at the count of six. Poor White never stirred. Well, folks, here comes the official decision. Flash! White wins!"

But that doesn't help your job. You've got to call them as you see them, but you've also got to see them as they happen. A smart reporter will call the close rounds even and give himself a margin against the astigmatism, poor digestion, or downright burglary of the officials. And as the two heroes sit leaning forward on their stools, their hands on the rope strands, glaring at one another and ready to leap forth at the call of the gong, your heart is thumping right up in your neck, your hands are trembling, and you are scared sick. But this passes when the bell rings and the first leads are exchanged, and you go to work, at first in a queer, choky sort of voice, but later steadying down fairly close to normal.

With a fast, experienced, cool telegraph operator, it is possible to dictate three or four hundred words a round. But that won't do. Not only is space limited, but this is copy for a flash edition. If everybody on the mechanical end down at the news-paper—the editors, the composing-room, the press and stereo-type men—is on his toes, the papers will begin rolling from the presses and start tearing around town in trucks almost before the two men involved have quit the ring. Wasted words cost time and money. You must edit out the light and useless blows and the clinches as you go along—in other words, select your material and send only punches that have an effect or might have an effect later.

Your office is depending on you not only for a curt, swift, ac-curate description of what is going on, but also for reliable tips on which way the fight is turning so that the editors and make-up men in the composing-room can slap the already prepared heads and office-written short leads naming the winner into the open forms, and wait only with a little hole for the last inch and a half of agate type describing the last round and the official flash from the ringside. To lock up the form and roll it away to the steam tables where the mats are made is only a matter of ten or fifteen seconds then. If your eyes are sharp and you see a man suddenly wince and fall forward a little from a punch that wasn't hurting him earlier in the fight, you interrupt your flow of dictation with a quick: "White looks bad. Tell 'em to get ready for a knockout," and gain precious minutes.

On the other hand, if your judgment is wrong and you have inadvisedly telegraphed along towards the fourteenth round: "White can't lose," and it turns out when the slips are handed in that, according to the official verdict, White not only can, but has lost, you have cost your paper thousands of dollars in wasted time, lost sales, and prestige. The "White Wins!" headline, bulletin leads, and picture captions must be ripped out from front and inside pages and correct ones substituted. The delay snowballs as the paper progresses from composing-room through all the various operations until it reaches the street. The opposition gets out first and grabs the bulk of the quick street sales, and the circulation manager raises hell. When you get back to the office, the managing editor is comparing your faulty round-by-round decisions with those of the other newspapermen covering the fight, as well as the official round tabulations of the judges and referee, released by the Boxing Commission, and wants to know how come. Two or three of those, and you don't cover fights any more, no matter how expert or literary you are.

And so you go along, tense and cautious, dictating your series of left jabs, varied by an occasional right cross or left hook or right swing, until suddenly there is a quick flash of an arm, a blur of red leather, and a body crashes to the floor, rolls over twitching, or lies quite still for a moment. Then, all hell lets loose.

Seventy thousand odd people are on their feet, screaming. Seconds in the corners are losing their heads, and you suddenly find that at a moment when you too are choking with excitement and the blood is ringing in your ears, you have need of a thousand eyes and the cool detachment of a visiting surgeon looking in on an operation.

White is down! Get that over first. Which hand did it? Left or right? Hook or cross? No time to think back. You must know instantly and trust that knowledge. There is too much else to be done for any reflection. Watch the stricken fighter. Is he out cold—in which case you can beat the flash by nine seconds—or is he stirring and likely to get up? Yes, he has rolled over and is going to try to climb to his feet. But can he make it? Pick up the count. You should have started to count to yourself with the timekeeper as soon as the man hit the floor, because in the thunder of noise that is in your ears you can hear neither the referee nor the man with the ten-second stopwatch, but merely see their arms rising and falling. Note the corners quickly for chances of disqualification due to a hysterical second. See what Black, the other fighter, is doing, whether he has retired promptly to a neutral corner. Take in the attitude of the referee as the fallen man begins his attempt to rise. Does he look as though he were going to stop the fight immediately or let it go on? Most of the time he doesn't know himself, and

that is no help. But you can observe quickly whether he is
keeping his head in the crises. Some referees don't. And all
the time keep that wire hot. Keep on dictating. Note the condition of the man getting up: ". . . rolled over at the count of
four and got to one knee at seven; he's up at nine, but in bad
shape. . . ."

He gets up, his opponent rushes in for the kill, and now the
fun really starts. The roar from the hysterical crowd redoubles,
and in the terrific swing and rush of movement in the ring
above you, it is almost impossible to sit still. You feel impelled
to give way to the impulse to rise to your feet, to join in the
movement.

Another knockdown! Another count! Another decision as to
what punch did it, and now the victory-scenting Black is throwing them so fast and indiscriminately that it defies the eye to
tell whether a single blow or a series sent White down again.
And any moment now the referee is liable to step in and end
the fight to save the loser from further punishment and you
must be razor-keen to detect the first move in that direction
and send your technical knockout flash. Sometimes they fool
you. The night that Max Baer knocked out Primo Carnera, the
referee stepped between the men just as Baer cocked a right
that would have knocked Primo clear down to the Battery. To
all intents and purposes, the fight was over. But the referee,
after taking a long look at Carnera, suddenly stepped back
again and motioned the men to continue fighting. Many a
flash had gone in.

But the referee is not to be blamed. He, too, has a tremendous responsibility at the moment. A man's life may depend
upon his quick action, but so too may his own entire future.
The fighter may be able to get up, hang on, survive the blast,
land a lucky punch, escape by running, even win. Tunney did
it with Dempsey, and Dempsey with Firpo and Sharkey. You
try then to keep well on top of the third man in the ring, to
fathom his mind: ". . . the referee looks as though he were
going to stop it. Get ready. He's going over—no—he's letting

it go on. White is down again in his own corner from a series of rights and lefts to the head [good old series of rights and lefts to the head], his seconds are screaming at him to take the full nine seconds. . . . There's less than a minute of the round left to go [you are supposed to be aware of that, too]. . . . He's up again at nine in very bad shape . . . his legs are gone. . . . Here comes Black with his right cocked. . . ." And finally the winner and the flash. And when it is done you cannot remember a single thing that you have said, whether you missed any knockdowns and their locations or the duration of the counts.

Or there has been a foul, or a questionable blow, or one of those curious happenings of the ring, a referee's error, a foul seen only by one judge, a man knocked from the platform, a man quitting, or the bell ringing to end the round just as the referee is in the process of stopping a fight; and the ring is immediately filled with shouting, gesticulating, semi-hysterical men and officials who have quite lost their heads, and you must try desperately among two hundred other yelling newspapermen to try to find out what is the final and official decision that will stand, and flash it, and have it stick. There was the night, for instance, when Schmeling won his championship from Sharkey on a foul, and the referee didn't make up his mind for more than a minute, while seconds yelled and argued; or the night that Dempsey knocked Sharkey out after first fouling him; or the evening in Boston when the fans rioted after Sharkey had knocked out one Unknown Winston in a questionable bout and the officials decided to make them fight the whole fight over again, starting from the beginning.

And then before you can cool off a little and catch your breath, there is always, as I have suggested before, the impassive operator looking at you expectantly. The office wants your new lead with all the correct information, and they want it right away. It's swell.

Of all the sports-reporting jobs, modern football is the biggest mess and the most difficult to write accurately. And it is quite true that except for descriptive passages that come to you through viewing the scene on the field, or the manner in which the scoring plays are executed, the football reporter might just as well sit at home by his radio and prepare his report. It would greatly shock his managing editor and his public if it ever became widely known, but to all intents and purposes, he does it anyway, except that his radio happens to be located high on the rim of some huge concrete bowl or horseshoe, in a glass-inclosed press box if the game is in the Middle or Far West, or exposed to the elements if it is in the East.

True, if you look at the field, you may see twenty-two tiny figures, so small that you cannot distinguish their faces, moiling and grubbing on the gridiron below, and before the rain sets in, you are able to distinguish which university is which by the colors of the jerseys, but that is all. For the details of who does what and to whom, you depend almost entirely upon the observer in the press box serving the public address system, or in the more primitive plants in the East, where they do not care particularly whether the press is served or not, yowling it through megaphones, said yowling being promptly drowned out by the noise of the excited crowd. I seem even to remember one important football game in which I couldn't even see the figures on the field. It was at Michie Stadium at West Point, and the cadet corps was seated immediately in front of the press box. Every time a man took the ball and began to run with it, the entire corps jumped to its feet. We didn't see a play all day long.

Considering the importance of football and football news to the newspaper-readers, it is amazing to see how little the football reporter has to go on in an important game, the results of which will interest literally millions of people. The game between Army and Notre Dame, for instance, is played annually at New York's Yankee Stadium, a park built for baseball. Narrow strips of pine planking are tacked up across the backs of the seats in front of each row in the press box, barely large enough to hold the typewriters, and posts and pillars obscure and obliterate certain parts of the field completely. A Notre

Dame and an Army spotter are provided each with a big megaphone.

The line-ups are provided for the press before the start of the game. Then the two teams come trotting onto the field wearing nice white numbers on their backs—and what a fight it was to get the colleges to number their players!—the figures supposedly corresponding to those in the printed program. You immediately discover that the line-up you were given has been switched, or is all wrong, and you begin frantically to write down the numbers of the twenty-two men as they warm up, tumbling, or throwing passes, or jogging about, to check them with the names on your program. There is one player, however, Bull Smith, whom you can always tell by his build, even without his number 13. You check quickly, and there is Bull Smith all right, only he is wearing number 43. Then it gets good. You discover that in a brilliant attempt to confuse the opposing players, the Notre Dame coach has switched all the numbers so that nobody will know who is playing. The Notre Dame spotter in a desperate attempt to help the floundering press has got as far as: ". . . I think Wocjhiwooski, number 8, is wearing Flanagan's number, 39. Flanagan isn't playing. He is sitting on the bench wearing Goldstein's number, 24. Goldstein is now 34, but he's playing end instead of tackle . . ." when the whistle blows and the game starts. And now you are in for it.

If you are serving a play-by-play wire for an early edition, the same as in baseball, and keep on dictating: "Notre Dame gained eight yards through tackle. Notre Dame ran the left end for six yards. Notre Dame completed a fourteen-yard pass . . ." your wire will begin to steam pretty soon with caustic messages from the chap on the desk in the office, wanting to know if by any chance there are any football players on the field and who they might be. And it won't do you any good to say that you cannot tell who is who, because he will only say, and with considerable justice: "What the hell are you up there for? You don't expect me to tell down here, do you?"

Here is a job that calls for a real expert in reporting, a man who knows football plays as well as football-players, and even if he cannot recognize a player covered with muck and slime from head to foot, can still hazard a fairly accurate guess as to who it should be from the position into which he has shifted, the way he took the ball, and where he ran with it. But left half, right half, quarterback, and fullback mean nothing any more, the way coaches arrange and shift and shuffle their backfields, and really to be an accurate and competent football reporter today, you must and should be thoroughly familiar with the strategy and campaign plans of every coach whose teams you plan to see in action. Since coaches are rather silent fellows and chary with their information, that is manifestly difficult.

And so the mad scramble goes on in the press box. The ball is snapped. There is a pile-up and a man loose for fifteen yards. A tackler cuts him down. The spotter calls out: 'Smith, tackled by Warskiwicz." A sharp-eyed reporter yells: "It wasn't Smith, it was Harkins. Smith never takes the ball from that side." The spotter shrieks: "Correction! Not Smith. Plasnik. Plasnik, tackled by Grunauer." You get up out of your seat hot-eyed and howl at the poor spotter: "For God's sake, make up your mind. Who was it, Smith, Plasnik, or Harkins?" A colleague tugs you by the sleeve and says: "It was Smeekers, the end. I saw him come around." By that time another play has taken place which you have missed completely. You take your choice and say that it was Plasnik. "Tickety-tick-tick," goes your wire, and your telegraph operator shifts the chaw in his cheek, leans over, and says: "Note from your office. They say the Associated Press says it was Harkins. What do you want to make it?" And this is supposed to be reporting.

When the game is over, the loudspeakers supply you with the statistics of the game, you check your notes, knock the cover off your portable typewriter, and wax as lyrical as you can over something you have partly seen, partly heard described to you, and partly guessed, and hope that you are not too far away from the facts. On the train home that night, you will, if you are lucky, find yourself in the same car with one of the officials, who tells you what actually happened. Well, you can still get back to your office and do a new piece, or, if too far away, file it from the hotel.

Tennis matches are comparatively simple to cover if you can survive the atmosphere and a good glaring at, but golf tournaments are poison unless you have good legs, and an absolute instinct and nose for news, and colossal luck. The play is scattered over a couple of square miles of landscape, and in an open championship there are some ten or fifteen players to be watched, any one of whom may win.

You may be following the man who seems to have the title in his bag, when word comes flashing over that curious golf-course grapevine that just over the hill someone is burning up the course and needs but to finish in par to win the championship. Shall you abandon the man you are following and cast in your lot with the new sensation? It's your guess, and you had better be right. If you are, you get a good story. If you are wrong, your account the next morning is a rehash of what some colleague has told you.

One of the best golf reporters I know, whose descriptive accounts of the thrilling duels on the links are really literary achievements, never leaves the press tent during the entire tournament. He sits and watches the scoreboards and listens to what his co-workers have to say as they come in off the course. And no individual can equal or beat the news-gathering system of the Associated Press, which puts units of men bearing short-wave radio transmitters lashed to their backs into the field at strategic points. They radio their eyewitness accounts back to the editor in the press tent.

In the old days it used to be easy. You just followed Bob Jones. But when the master retired, his crown was liable to land on any one of thirty heads. It was merely a question of who was likely to get hot on that last round. If you were lucky enough to smell him out and bring him home, your account would be alive, the next day. If you were in the wrong place, you might fool the readers, but your editor would know, and make remarks.

You've simply got to be lucky. I will never forget one tournament where luck and a hunch saved my skin. It was the Augusta National Open, two years ago, better known as the Master's Tourney, the only one in which Bob Jones still competes, and therefore big news. To all intents and purposes, Craig Wood had it cinched, posting a score that looked like a certain winner. There was a good story in Wood. It was a birthday or a first wedding-anniversary, or something, and he needed that money. I brought him home to the eighteenth green, went to the press tent, wrote my story, filed it, and was through for the day. Nobody else had a chance. There was nothing more to do that day but hang around the crying-room, drink corn whisky, and listen to the boys tell lies and weep over lost shots. There was only Sarazen still out on the back nine, needing to come in three under par, even to tie. And that back nine at Augusta wasn't giving anything away.

A reporter came in and I asked him where Sarazen was and how he stood. He said: "Gene's out of it. He's even par coming up to fifteen and he needs three under to tie." That meant that Sarazen needed three birdies on four holes. They were a par five, a par three, and two long, hard fours. Sarazen was out of it all right. At that point I had the hunch. Well, perhaps I knew Sarazen, too. He was a tough man on a golf course, that little Italian. He never quit. Once I saw him play a shot off the concrete floor of a little four-sided refreshment booth into which he had hooked, and get his three. Supposing something impossible *should* happen. I got up and walked out down the eighteenth fairway, to find Sarazen and bring him in, passing through the gallery that had abandoned him and was headed for the clubhouse. I came upon Gene as he was marching up the sixteenth fairway to his drive. This was the long par-five hole. The green was a distant little emerald island, 240 yards away, with a winding creek in front of it. Sarazen said: "Hi, kid! Coming to bury the body? Well, it isn't dead yet."

I said: "Now what?"

He said: "I'm gonna lay this ball close enough to that hole to blow it in. You never can tell what a ball will decide to do in this cockeyed game. Watch this one." With that he drew a spoon out of his bag, a flat-headed thing, sighted on the distant flag, and let fly. The ball hissed away in a low, slightly rising trajectory, hit on the bank just over the creek, bounced, bounced again, rolled onto the green, and headed for the pin. I got my field glasses on it just before it disappeared from sight into the cup, and a mighty shout from those gathered around the green confirmed what was probably the greatest single shot ever made under fire and in competition for a major prize. Sarazen had holed out a two, a double eagle, on a par-five hole. With one shot he had robbed the course of three strokes, the three he needed. Then I watched him play the next three holes in even par and come in with a tie. The next day he beat Wood in the play-off and won the title. There would have been no particular blame attached to me had I not seen that shot, because nothing but a miracle could have put Sarazen back into the running. But if I hadn't seen that miracle, I should have been a bad reporter.

There was once a golf tournament at Lido, near Long Beach, for the Metropolitan Championship, in which the reporters, all of them, filed their stories about the leading scores for the day and went away because as dusk arrived there were only a couple of unknowns still struggling out on the back nine. But one of those unknowns came in just before darkness, the last player into the eighteenth green, carding a sixty-eight, a new record for a tough course. A lone telegraph operator packing up for the night covered the papers on the sensational score. It was made by a gentleman by the name of Potter, who had never done anything extraordinary in golf. Nobody had the story, and there was hell to pay. Mr. Potter became an overnight sensation and there had been no one there to receive him and properly strum the lyre. But there was even more hell to pay two days later when it developed that Mr. Potter had scored his great round with his pencil and not his golf clubs, with the connivance of his partner and their caddies, who later peached. A couple of good golf-writers on the spot would probably have turned up the fake that night.

There is no hard and fast rule for being in on the big stories that I can think of except to come early, stay late, and be lucky. I have seen a football game in which three touchdowns were scored in the first four plays, two by one side, one by the other; after which there was no further scoring all afternoon. Late comers to Forest Hills by five minutes one afternoon were shocked to find by looking at the scoreboard that Helen Wills Moody had lost the first set of a match to Betty Nuthall, an English girl, by 6–1. And reporters strolling to their seats for the Terris-McLarnin fight in Madison Square Garden who lingered to light a cigarette or chat with a friend never saw a lick of the fight, because Terris was being carried out by the time they got there. The second punch got him. That is what makes it exciting under the guns.

XXI

YOUNG MEN

OF

MANHATTAN

OF ALL the queer animals in the newspaper zoo, the sports-writer is the strangest of the lot. He is reporter, critic, editorial writer, special investigator, press agent, cynic, and hero-worshipper all in one. He is, today, essentially honest. He has a tremendous amount of power and rarely misuses it. He has more editorial liberty and freedom from interference than any other employee on the paper with the possible exception of the columnist. Whereas the news-writer is confined rigidly to fact, a sports story is considered dull, drab, and almost worthless unless colored by the personal opinion of the writer.

There is an ancient scandal that adheres to the sports-writer, a hangover from the days when no professional sport was in especially good repute, and when the sports pages were less important and well considered than they are today, when the salaries of sports-writers were lower even than those paid the leg-men or the copy-readers on the local side. Today the sports-writer is the aristocrat of the newspaper, but laymen still inquire frequently: "What about the payroll?" and when a writer, carried away by his own enthusiasm, concocts a particularly effulgent article praising an athlete or a promotional concern, he still gets letters, usually anonymous, the general trend of which are: "How much were you paid for *that?*" But, except in isolated cases, the sub-rosa hand-out to the sports-writer for favorable publicity is a thing of the past. The boys prefer their independence, and on their present salaries and in present living-conditions can afford to maintain it.

The basis of the payroll scandal was economic, and the blame in most cases lay with the publishers who paid starvation wages in the sports department and were satisfied to have the editor and his staff make up the difference—on tips, like a waiter. The sports pages in those days had no powerful circulation-pull or value and were considered a necessary evil. A young man elevated to the job of sports editor might find his salary fixed at fifteen or twenty dollars a week, not a very attractive stipend. But the outgoing sports editor would soon straighten him out. Before departing he might say: "The job's good for fifty or sixty a week more, son. The bi-monthly boxing show is good for a hundred dollars a month, the wrestling promoter will always kick in with fifty, and the local ball club will take care of you if you treat 'em right. It's okay; it goes with the job. Good luck." There was nothing particularly dishonest about it. It was merely short-sighted on the part of the publisher who was willing to have the professional promoter pay his sports editor's and sports-writers' salaries for him instead of collecting it from them in the form of paid advertising. By so doing he laid the foundation of a custom and usage which eventually cost him millions of dollars in free advertising. He could stop the graft to sports-writers—indeed, that situation practically corrected itself with the coming of decent and even large salaries to members of sports staffs. But he couldn't close his columns to free publicity given daily to baseball, boxing, bicycle-riding, football, horseracing, track meets, and all the rest of the gate-producing sports ventures. The most he has ever been able to get out of the baseball magnates in revenue has been a three-line agate reader, daily: "Baseball today—Yankees vs. Boston,

Yankee Stadium, 3.00 p.m. Grandstand seats, $1.65," and usually not even that, as the ball games are listed anyway in the schedule of current sports events as a service to readers. But if a newspaper tried to leave out all sports publicity, it would very quickly lose half to two thirds of its readers. If in the early days the publishers found it cheaper to let promoters pay their sports-writers, when the big times came, the promoters likewise found it cheaper to pay the sports-writers than the publishers. And when the new generation of sports-writers appeared, college-bred, many of them, well paid and independent, the promoters made the pleasing discovery that they didn't have to pay anyone for publicity. In any crowd of one hundred men there will always be one thief, one liar, and one grafter. But on the whole, sports-writing today is clean and honest.

There are, roughly, three classes of sports-writer: the specialist who is assigned chiefly to one sport, baseball, boxing, golf, turf, or what not, and who is able to double in other sports during the off seasons; the general sports-writer who specializes in none, but is a sort of Jack-of-all-sports; and the feature writer or columnist.

By the very nature of his work, the specialist very often becomes a poor reporter, and whenever there is any important news breaking about an athletic celebrity, the wise sports editor usually yanks the specialist off the yarn and assigns another chap, either from the news side, borrowed from the city editor, or another member of his own staff. He does this because the expert and specialist is so close to his sport and the athlete that he is always the last to get any real news break from him; and even if he does come upon an unusual story, if it is an unfavorable one or liable to cause the hero some trouble or embarrassment, he is liable to withhold it or try to kill it because he likes the man and knows him too well. It is not easy to break bread with a person, play golf with him, be received in his home as a friend and sometimes as a trusted adviser, and then go down to the office and write a signed story to the effect that the athlete is temporarily useless at bat or will lose a scheduled prizefight because he is suffering from a recurrence of an unfortunate social disease contracted during some extra-marital shenanigans on the road, or to report that he is upset, ill at ease, and not putting his heart into his work because he has suddenly discovered that his little wife has been chasing around with some gentleman who doesn't live by his muscles and therefore isn't tired most of the time.

Reporters are reputedly cynical and hard-boiled, but actually they are not. They are soft-hearted and frequently sentimental and their code of honor is often more rigid than might be found in many other industries, much more stern and reliable, for instance, than that of the people about whom they write. Because, no matter how friendly, an athlete will lie to a reporter or sports-writer until Ananias gets vertigo in his grave from sheer jealousy. He will give him quotes and then deny them baldly the next day when he finds out they have led him into trouble. Gratitude the athlete knows not, and justice is not in his vocabulary. As long as the sports-writer is praising him, he is a sweet pal. The first line of criticism, no matter how honest or well deserved, and the writer becomes a rat and an ingrate.

But the sports-writer in the recent past has had another reason for protecting his athlete and keeping him reasonably human, decent, and heroic in the eyes of the reader. There is only a certain limited audience for the class of sports-writing that has been termed the "Oh, nuts!" variety as opposed to the "Gee whiz" type, and by far the greater percentage of readers prefers the boost to the knock. It is human to hero-worship provided the hero is human too. The reader wants his too godlike heroes humbled sometimes, not being overfond of supermen, but he still wants them heroes. The sports celebrity is the sports-writer's meal ticket. If the writer knocks him down or bends his efforts to destroying the game about which he is writing for a living, he may some day find himself out of a job. There is a use for boxing-writers only as long as there is regular legalized boxing and the public takes an interest in the sport.

And there you see immediately the horns of the dilemma—to be honest with, let us say, a thoroughly crooked and swinish game such as boxing, and yet not destroy it and with it the opportunity of earning a living.

The sports-writers, especially the feature writers and columnists, soon discover that they can have no friends except among their own craft and among non-athletes, if they are at all interested in their own integrity and conscience, and most of them are. I remember one time when I was covering one of Max Schmeling's training camps. Max was a friend of mine. Of all the prizefighters I have known, the German seemed to have come the closest to being a sportsman and a decent fellow. I gave him his first publicity break when he came to America, and we liked each other, probably the more because I spoke his language.

The feature of that particular period of Max's training was that he was knocking out his spar boys regularly. This is an important news item in any training-camp story. It has a powerful influence on the betting odds and certainly is an indication that a fighter is right in his timing and hitting. Because I was a friend and at that time also Schmeling's ghost—we were running a signed series by him in our paper, which I was writing—I was permitted in his dressing-room after his workout, to chat with him while he was getting a rub-down. Talking idly, I happened to pick up one of the soggy gloves that he had just discarded, and suddenly, through their lightness, became aware of something that had escaped all of us during the workout, and that, incidentally, we should have noticed, but didn't. They were six-ounce fighting gloves with very little padding in them. His spar-mates were using the big fourteen-ounce pillows. No wonder he had been knocking them bow-legged. It was a good story, news, and belonged in the paper. What to do? If it hadn't been for being close to Schmeling, I never would have been in the position to find out. Which way should loyalties take me? An unimportant item, but sports-writers face similar questions all the time. I ran the story and felt like a louse. I didn't even have the courage to write it myself, but gave the tip to our boxing-writer to write up as though he had discovered it himself. Nobody was fooled. The fighter learned a lesson about having newspapermen too close to him, and the newspaperman learned one about making friends with prize-fighters.

Another time I had a boxing-writer who was a great pal of Jack Dempsey's. He was covering Dempsey's camp on the eve of his important come-back fight with Sharkey. Because he was a friend, he was admitted to the inner circle that gathered in Dempsey's cottage when the day's work was done and supper was over. Somebody turned on the phonograph, and Dempsey grabbed the writer and began to waltz him around. The writer rested his hand on Dempsey's right forearm and suddenly and unexpectedly discovered something. Under Dempsey's shirt-sleeve there was something that came before the skin. It was a bandage. The fighter's arm was taped from wrist to elbow. Something was wrong with it, a strain or a sprain, something obviously necessitating treatment, and the fight was just two days away. Again, what to do? The writer chose to be loyal to his paper and, incidentally, his bread and butter, and wrote the story. It raised hob with the betting odds. A Dempsey with an injured arm was not so good a risk. As it turned out, it was only a minor strain that did not particularly bother him, and he won the fight. But it might well have been otherwise and the public might have lost a good deal of money wagering on a cripple, because a fighter will never reveal an injury before go-ing into the ring. His interest rarely goes beyond getting through the ropes so that he may collect his money. And yet if Dempsey had taken that man aside and told him confiden-tially that he had strained his arm, but that it was a minor mat-ter, and not to print it, the story would have been safe, because there is one faith that no sports-writer or newspaperman worth his salt and a job will ever break, and that is to repeat a story told in confidence.

The story given in confidence to the sports-writer is sealed.
And usually it is a dangerous and awkward thing. The writer's
curiosity and his desire for exclusive information that will some
day be useful to him, as well as his instincts of self-protection,
prompt him to listen to these confidential stories, but in nine
cases out of ten he wishes that he hadn't, because they put him
right in the bag and keep him there. He is now firmly impaled
on the horns of another dilemma. He is in honor bound not to
break the story and nothing will make him do it and no editor
would try to coerce him into breaking his word. But he is also,
now that he has it right from the source, in a certain measure
bound to ignore all other possible sources of the same story.
And a red-hot yarn is worse to try to control than a leaky garden
hose. It is liable to pop at any one of a dozen places. A dozen
boxing-writers knew that Gene Tunney was going to retire from
the ring after defeating Dempsey the second time, and at least
three knew that he was going to marry an heiress, because he
had told them so—in confidence. Eventually one of the best
boxing stories as well as human-interest yarns of the year was
broken by a sports editor who had been told nothing and found
it out for himself. All that the rest of us could do was confirm
his beat. If you have not been tied by a smart athlete who has
deliberately given you a story to prevent you from using it, you
might detect the leads or symptoms of a good story, follow
them up, uncover and print it. But once your promise is given,
all you can do is sit back and take a good licking on the story
when it does break. And by the time it breaks, your exclusive
inside information is too late and useless. The veteran sports-
writer will run a mile when he hears the familiar: "Confiden-
tially, and don't print this until I give you the word. . . ." He
learns either to walk away or to say: "Brother, if you don't
want this printed, don't tell me." Just another reason for not
getting too friendly with the people about whom you must
write. Sometimes even meeting them is sufficient to handcuff
you. No man is wholly bad, and once you have shaken hands

with and smiled at a person, it is no longer easy to slide a knife into him and turn it in the wound, no matter how much it is deserved.

And yet the sports editor is bedeviled by the knowledge that certain members of his staff must be close to the athletes about whom they write if they are to present the intimate, colorful, personal stories that sell papers. The best writers in the world cannot make a character live by sitting at a desk in the office and rewriting clippings. I had a sports-writer once who quarreled with a baseball manager. The justice of the quarrel was unimportant. The important thing was that until the disagreement was patched up, that writer was useless to me on that assignment. He couldn't travel intimately with the team, he couldn't get into the dressing-rooms to write those sweat and liniment and post-game badinage stories that the reader loves. He was an outsider and therefore valueless.

There is no particular trick to sports-writing beyond knowing how to write, and that, I suspect, is not much more difficult, given any talent in that direction, than making an umbrella or painting a good portrait. You take your place in the press box. Pretty soon a group of athletes appear upon the scene and begin to contest against one another. When they have finished and are taking their showers, you run a sheet of copy paper through your typewriter rollers and report who won, what the game was, the score, who played and how, how many people were there, how much money they paid to get in, and what was the manner of the winning and the losing.

It is just as simple as that; but the size of the sports-writer's pay-check and his popularity are contingent upon whether he is able or not to make the struggle he has just witnessed live before the eyes of the readers who didn't see it, and relive for those who did. There simply is no excuse for not writing a good story about the average sports event, because something always happens, even when there is a draw or a tie. There is always a struggle, always, except in the case of a tie, a winner and a loser. You always have ready-made for you a hero and a villain—your side and theirs. A sense of the dramatic is necessary to evaluate the importance of what you have seen. A little originality of thought and expression does the rest.

It is not at all necessary to have played games or to be an expert to be a successful sports-writer, provided that you can write and have imagination. It merely makes it a little more difficult. I have always found that it helps to have played or at least attempted to play the games and do the things that the athletes and sportsmen do, because it gives you a better feel of the thing if you understand what the men and women are up against in the matter of speed, timing, and stamina and what they are trying to accomplish.

Earlier I wrote that a sports-writer cannot have bias in judging a prizefight, and here I am suggesting what appears to be a flat contradiction by intimating that there is always a hero and always a villain. I am about to go a step further and suggest that bias is absolutely vital to the successful sports-writer. The trick is to know when to have it and when not.

I have never had much respect for a sports-writer who can sit calmly and coldly in a press coop with no interest whatsoever in the outcome of the game or event he is watching. The bored sports-writer who doesn't root isn't a good one and never will be. It is human to take sides, to want to see someone win and his or her adversary lose. All the world roots. It merely requires tact and experience to know when to do it. The smart sports-writer always roots for the home team against the visiting firemen. Everything the home boys do is right, everything the visitors do is wrong, or laughable, provided due credit is given for good performances. If the home boys win they are marvels; if they lose, they had bad luck and were done out of a well-merited victory by foul fates.

It is in the long run a commercial proposition. Your job, after all, is to please people and sell papers. And you don't please readers by ridiculing their favorites. The sports-writer must feel the public pulse as delicately as the editorial writer. I remember in my early days as a sports editor and columnist I

had a terrific crush on the New York Yankee baseball club—
every writer eventually gets a favorite ball club, fighter, golfer,
tennis-player, football team. Well, the Yanks were my team,
and the Giants, the other New York major-league team, were
just nine other fellows. I rarely wrote about them, and gave the
colorful American League team much more space in the sports
pages. One afternoon J. M. Patterson, our publisher, dropped
by at my desk for a chat about this and that and said suddenly,
out of a clear sky: "You know, I always have to think about
something my father once told me in Chicago when I was a
violent Cub fan, and the Chicago *Tribune* as a result was full
of the Cubs and printed very little news about the White Sox.
He said he thought there were probably just as many readers of
the *Tribune* who liked and followed the Sox as the Cubs and
that they must be having lean days unless they took some other
paper." Thereafter the Giants got their share of enthusiasm.
After a while you learn to judge which way the sports wind
blows and sail with it. Once in a while it is salutary to get
tough and head into the breeze—but not too often. And the
smartest and most popular sports-writers are those who can admit that they have been wrong and change tacks. One of the
most valuable tricks in sports-writing is to pretend or admit
that you are just a little dumber and more befuddled than the
average reader. Some sports-writers build up a following by the
accuracy of their forecasts. I built mine up by being wrong
much more often than right. I didn't have to fake it. I just
was. And then admitted it, worried over it, and marveled that I
should not have seen what was apparently obvious to many
thousands of readers. It pleased the readers to see how much
smarter they were than the so-called expert and to come up behind me at the ringside and yell: "Hey, Gallico—wrong again,
eh?" and see me shake my head in despair. But it all helped to
sell papers, which is the first job of the sports-writer. A nice
blend of bias and enthusiasm for the favored party, coupled
with strict justice in giving the devil his due and a little bit
more, is a vital asset. I have never in all my years of sports-

reporting bet on anything but a horserace. It is harder to keep control of your judgment when you have money up.

One cannot live a certain kind of life for nearly a decade and a half and then abandon it without missing something. I think most of all in the days to come I shall hanker after that magic ticket of admission marked with the red letters: "W.P.," standing for "Working Press," the press inclosures themselves, and the men gathered in them to cover the big sports events. There are few people in any walk of life who are as alive and entertaining as sports-writers. I shall never forget how I used to look forward to that hour at the ringside before the first preliminary to a big fight. You went up to the Yankee Stadium or the Polo Grounds early, around six o'clock in the evening, to avoid the crowds and perhaps do an early filler story, but mostly to hang around and gossip with the gang.

You would find Mark Kelly from Los Angeles and Tommy Laird from San Francisco, Harry Salsinger from Detroit, Harvey Woodruff from Chicago, Havey Boyle from Pittsburgh, and Bill Cunningham from Boston, all of them wise men and leaders in their own territories. And for a wholly delectable hour you could sit around smoking cigarettes and exchanging shop talk. Each brought, as to market, inside stuff, tips, little news items from his city in return for information as to what was going on around New York and who was swindling whom. The red-headed saturnine Kelly would be touting a new lightweight on the Coast to be watched, or bring the inside story of a faked fight perpetrated there. Tom Laird might have news of a coming track phenom at Stanford, Salsinger would contribute vital and fascinating material about Joe Louis or the Detroit ball club and Mickey Cochrane, Cunningham always had reliable dope on the probable football heroes of New England the coming fall.

Your own gang would be there, all the prototypes of "Young Man of Manhattan," and variations: Damon Runyon, wise in the lore of ring iniquity; Grantland Rice, perhaps the best-informed sports-writer in the world; wise-cracking Bill Corum and giant Dan Parker; dry Alan Gould, sports editor of the United Press; big, bald Stu Cameron, also of the United Press; and his amusing henchman Hank McLemore. There would be the magnificently vindictive Pegler; and, before he died, the brilliant McGeehan, the greatest sports-writer who ever lived; and owlish little Hype Igoe, the boxing-writer and cartoonist, the only one I ever knew who could write as well as he could draw and vice versa; smart, whip-cracking Joe Williams; the crabby but brilliantly bitter Davis Walsh of I.N.S.; and a great host of others who were your friends, colleagues, and competitors. They were all keen, witty men, and never a dull word fell from their lips during those periods.

It was the same in the world-series press boxes, or the big golf and tennis tourneys, or great intersectional football matches. It seemed as if there was no place in the world as exciting, alluring, and entertaining as the press box, or the hotel rooms out of town, before or after a big show, when the gang gathered for a fanning bee. Most of the boys were even better conversationally than they were on paper. I shall miss them all like the very devil. . . .

XXII

THE

FEEL

A CHILD wandering through a department store with its mother, is admonished over and over again not to touch things. Mother is convinced that the child only does it to annoy or because it is a child, and usually hasn't the vaguest inkling of the fact that Junior is "touching" because he is a little blotter soaking up information and knowledge, and "feel" is an important adjunct to seeing. Adults are exactly the same, in a measure, as you may ascertain when some new gadget or article is produced for inspection. The average person says: "Here, let me see that," and holds out his hand. He doesn't mean "see," because he is already seeing it. What he means is that he wants to get it into his hands and feel it so as to become better acquainted.

As suggested in the foregoing chapter, I do not insist that a curiosity and capacity for feeling sports is necessary to be a successful writer, but it is fairly obvious that a man who has been tapped on the chin with five fingers wrapped up in a leather boxing glove and propelled by the arm of an expert knows more about that particular sensation than one who has not, always provided he has the gift of expressing himself. I once inquired of a heavyweight prizefighter by the name of King Levinsky, in a radio interview, what it felt like to be hit on the chin by Joe Louis, the King having just acquired that experience with rather disastrous results. Levinsky considered the matter for a moment and then reported: "It don't feel like nuttin'," but added that for a long while afterwards he felt as though he were "in a transom."

I was always a child who touched things and I have always had a tremendous curiosity with regard to sensation. If I knew what playing a game felt like, particularly against or in the company of experts, I was better equipped to write about the playing of it and the problems of the men and women who took part in it. And so, at one time or another, I have tried them all, football, baseball, boxing, riding, shooting, swimming, squash, handball, fencing, driving, flying, both land and sea planes, rowing, canoeing, skiing, riding a bicycle, ice-skating, roller-skating, tennis, golf, archery, basketball, running, both the hundred-yard dash and the mile, the high jump and shot put, badminton, angling, deep-sea, stream-, and surf-casting, billiards and bowling, motorboating and wrestling, besides riding as a passenger with the fastest men on land and water and in the air, to see what it felt like. Most of them I dabbled in as a youngster going through school and college, and others, like piloting a plane, squash, fencing, and skiing, I took up after I was old enough to know better, purely to get the feeling of what they were like.

None of these things can I do well, but I never cared about becoming an expert, and besides, there wasn't time. But there is only one way to find out accurately human sensations in a ship two or three thousand feet up when the motor quits, and that is actually to experience that gone feeling at the pit of the stomach and the sharp tingling of the skin from head to foot, followed by a sudden amazing sharpness of vision, clear-sightedness, and coolness that you never knew you possessed as you find the question of life or death completely in your own hands. It is not the "you" that you know, but somebody else, a stranger, who noses the ship down, circles, fastens upon the one best spot to sit down, pushes or pulls buttons to try to get her started again, and finally drops her in, safe and sound. And it is only by such experience that you learn likewise of the sudden weakness that hits you right at the back of the knees after you have climbed out and started to walk around her and that comes close to knocking you flat as for the first time since the engine quit its soothing drone you think of destruction and sudden death.

Often my courage has failed me and I have funked completely, such as the time I went up to the top of the thirty-foot Olympic diving-tower at Jones Beach, Long Island, during the competitions, to see what it was like to dive from that height, and wound up crawling away from the edge on hands and knees, dizzy, scared, and a little sick, but with a wholesome respect for the boys and girls who hurled themselves through the air and down through the tough skin of the water from that awful height. At other times sheer ignorance of what I was getting into has led me into tight spots such as the time I came down the Olympic ski run from the top of the Kreuzeck, six thousand feet above Garmisch-Partenkirchen, after having been on skis but once before in snow and for the rest had no more than a dozen lessons on an indoor artificial slide in a New York department store. At one point my legs, untrained, got so tired that I couldn't stem (brake) any more, and I lost control and went full tilt and all out, down a three-foot twisting path cut out of the side of the mountain, with a two-thousand-foot abyss on the left and the mountain itself on the right. That was probably the most scared I have ever been, and I scare fast and often. I remember giving myself up for lost and wondering how long it would take them to retrieve my body and whether I should be still alive. In the meantime the speed of the descent was increasing. Somehow I was keeping my feet and negotiating turns, how I will never know, until suddenly the narrow patch opened out into a wide, steep stretch of slope with a rise at the other end, and that part of the journey was over.

By some miracle I got to the bottom of the run uninjured, having made most of the trip down the icy, perpendicular slopes on the flat of my back. It was the thrill and scare of a lifetime, and to date no one has been able to persuade me to try a jump. I know when to stop. After all, I am entitled to rely upon my imagination for something. But when it was all over and I found myself still whole, it was also distinctly worth while to have learned what is required of a ski runner in the breakneck *Abfahrt* or downhill race, or the difficult *slalom*. Five days later, when I climbed laboriously (still on skis) half-way up that Alp and watched the Olympic downhill racers hurtling down the perilous, ice-covered, and nearly perpendicular *Steilhang*, I knew that I was looking at a great group of athletes who, for one thing, did not know the meaning of the word "fear." The slope was studded with small pine trees and rocks, but half of the field gained precious seconds by hitting that slope all out, with complete contempt for disaster rushing up at them at a speed often better than sixty miles an hour. And when an unfortunate Czech skidded off the course at the bottom of the slope and into a pile of rope and got himself snarled up as helpless as a fly in a spider's web, it was a story that I could write from the heart. I had spent ten minutes getting myself untangled after a fall, *without* any rope to add to the difficulties. It seems that I couldn't find where my left leg ended and one more ski than I had originally donned seemed to be involved somehow. Only a person who has been on those fiendish runners knows the sensation.

It all began back in 1922 when I was a cub sports-writer and consumed with more curiosity than was good for my health. I had seen my first professional prizefights and wondered at the curious behavior of men under the stress of blows, the sudden checking and the beginning of a little fall forward after a hard punch, the glazing of the eyes and the loss of locomotor control, the strange actions of men on the canvas after a knock-down as they struggled to regain their senses and arise on legs that seemed to have turned into rubber. I had never been in any bad fist fights as a youngster, though I had taken a little physical punishment in football, but it was not enough to complete the picture. Could one think under those conditions?

I had been assigned to my first training-camp coverage, Dempsey's at Saratoga Springs, where he was preparing for his famous fight with Luis Firpo. For days I watched him sag a spar boy with what seemed to be no more than a light cuff on the neck, or pat his face with what looked like no more than a caressing stroke of his arm, and the fellow would come all apart at the seams and collapse in a useless heap, grinning vacuously or twitching strangely. My burning curiosity got the better of prudence and a certain reluctance to expose myself to physical pain. I asked Dempsey to permit me to box a round with him. I had never boxed before, but I was in good physical shape, having just completed a four-year stretch as a galley slave in the Columbia eight-oared shell.

When it was over and I escaped through the ropes, shaking, bleeding a little from the mouth, with rosin dust on my pants and a vicious throbbing in my head, I knew all that there was to know about being hit in the prize-ring. It seems that I had gone to an expert for tuition. I knew the sensation of being stalked and pursued by a relentless, truculent professional destroyer whose trade and business it was to injure men. I saw the quick flash of the brown forearm that precedes the stunning shock as a bony, leather-bound fist lands on cheek or mouth. I learned more (partly from photographs of the lesson, viewed afterwards, one of which shows me ducked under a vicious left hook, an act of which I never had the slightest recollection) about instinctive ducking and blocking than I could have in ten years of looking at prizefights, and I learned, too, that as the soldier never hears the bullet that kills him, so does the fighter rarely, if ever, see the punch that tumbles blackness over him like a mantle, with a tearing rip as though the roof of his skull were exploding, and robs him of his senses.

There was just that—a ripping in my head and then sudden blackness, and the next thing I knew, I was sitting on the canvas covering of the ring floor with my legs collapsed under me, grinning idiotically. How often since have I seen that same silly, goofy look on the faces of dropped fighters—and understood it. I held onto the floor with both hands, because the ring and the audience outside were making a complete clockwise revolution, came to a stop, and then went back again counter-clockwise. When I struggled to my feet, Jack Kearns, Dempsey's manager, was counting over me, but I neither saw nor heard him and was only conscious that I was in a ridiculous position and that the thing to do was to get up and try to fight back. The floor swayed and rocked beneath me like a fishing dory in an off-shore swell, and it was a welcome respite when Dempsey rushed into a clinch, held me up, and whispered into my ear: "Wrestle around a bit, son, until your head clears." And then it was that I learned what those little love-taps to the back of the neck and the short digs to the ribs can mean to the groggy pugilist more than half knocked out. It is a murderous game, and the fighter who can escape after having been felled by a lethal blow has my admiration. And there, too, I learned that there can be no sweeter sound than the bell that calls a halt to hostilities.

From that afternoon on, also, dated my antipathy for the spectator at prizefights who yells: "Come on, you bum, get up and fight! Oh, you big quitter! Yah yellow, yah yellow!" Yellow, eh? It is all a man can do to get up after being stunned by a blow, much less fight back. But they do it. And how a man is able to muster any further interest in a combat after being floored with a blow to the pit of the stomach will always remain to me a miracle of what the human animal is capable of under stress.

Further experiments were less painful, but equally illuminating. A couple of sets of tennis with Vinnie Richards taught me more about what is required of a top-flight tournament tennis-player than I could have got out of a dozen books or years of reporting tennis matches. It is one thing to sit in a press box and write caustically that Brown played uninspired tennis, or Black's court covering was faulty and that his frequent errors cost him the set. It is quite another to stand across the net at the back of a service court and try to get your racket on a service that is so fast that the ear can hardly detect the interval between the sound of the server's bat hitting the ball and the ball striking the court. Tournament tennis is a different game from week-end tennis. For one thing, in average tennis, after the first hard service has gone into the net or out, you breathe a sigh of relief, move up closer and wait for the cripple to come floating over. In big-time tennis second service is practically as hard as the first, with an additional twist on the ball.

It is impossible to judge or know anything about the speed of a forehand drive hit by a champion until you have had one fired at you, or, rather, away from you, and you have made an attempt to return it. It is then that you first realize that tennis is played more with the head than with the arms and the legs. The fastest player in the world cannot get to a drive to return it if he hasn't thought correctly, guessed its direction, and anticipated it by a fraction of a second.

There was golf with Bob Jones and Gene Sarazen and Tommy Armour, little Cruickshank and Johnny Farrell, and Diegel and other professionals; and experiments at trying to keep up in the water with Johnny Weissmuller, Helene Madison, and Eleanor Holm, attempts to catch football passes thrown by Benny Friedman. Nobody actually plays golf until he has acquired the technical perfection to be able to hit the ball accurately, high, low, hooked or faded and placed. And nobody knows what real golf is like until he has played around with a professional and seen him play, not the ball, but the course, the roll of the land, the hazards, the wind, and the texture of the greens and the fairways. It looks like showmanship when a top-flight golfer plucks a handful of grass and lets it flutter in the air, or abandons his drive to march two hundred yards down to the green and look over the situation. It isn't. It's golf. The average player never knows or cares whether he is putting with or across the grain of a green. The professional always knows. The same average player standing on the tee is concentrated on getting the ball somewhere on the fairway, two hundred yards out. The professional when preparing to drive is actually to all intents and purposes playing his second shot. He means to place his drive so as to open up the green for his approach. But you don't find that out until you have played around with them when they are relaxed and not competing, and listen to them talk and plan attacks on holes.

Major-league baseball is one of the most difficult and precise of all games, but you would never know it unless you went down on the field and got close to it and tried it yourself. For instance, the distance between pitcher and catcher is a matter of twenty paces, but it doesn't seem like enough when you don a catcher's mitt and try to hold a pitcher with the speed of Dizzy Dean or Dazzy Vance. Not even the sponge that catchers wear in the palm of the hand when working with fast-ball pitchers, and the bulky mitt are sufficient to rob the ball of shock and sting that lames your hand unless you know how to ride with the throw and kill some of its speed. The pitcher, standing on his little elevated mound, looms up enormously over you at that short distance, and when he ties himself into a coiled spring preparatory to letting fly, it requires all your self-control not to break and run for safety. And as for the things they can do with a baseball, those major-league pitchers . . . ! One way of finding out is to wander down on the field an hour or so before game-time when there is no pressure on them, pull on the catcher's glove, and try to hold them.

I still remember my complete surprise the first time I tried catching for a real curve-ball pitcher. He was a slim, spidery left-hander of the New York Yankees, many years ago, by the name of Herb Pennock. He called that he was going to throw a fast breaking curve and warned me to expect the ball at least two feet outside the plate. Then he wound up and let it go, and that ball came whistling right down the groove for the center of the plate. A novice, I chose to believe what I saw and not what I heard, and prepared to catch it where it was headed for, a spot which of course it never reached, because just in front of the rubber, it swerved sharply to the right and passed nearly a yard from my glove. I never had a chance to catch it. That way, you learn about the mysterious drop, the ball that sails down the alley chest high but which you must be prepared to catch around your ankles because of the sudden dip it takes at the end of its passage as though someone were pulling it down with a string. Also you find out about the queer fade-away, the slow curve, the fast in- and out-shoots that seem to be timed almost as delicately as shrapnel, to burst, or rather break, just when they will do the most harm—namely, at the moment when the batter is swinging.

Facing a big-league pitcher with a bat on your shoulder and trying to hit his delivery is another vital experience in gaining an understanding of the game about which you are trying to write vividly. It is one thing to sit in the stands and scream at a batsman: "Oh, you bum!" for striking out in a pinch, and another to stand twenty yards from that big pitcher and try to make up your mind in a hundredth of a second whether to hit at the offering or not, where to swing and when, not to mention worrying about protecting yourself from the consequences of being struck by the ball that seems to be heading straight for your skull at an appalling rate of speed. Because, if you are a big-league player, you cannot very well afford to be gun-shy and duck away in panic from a ball that swerves in the last moment and breaks perfectly over the plate, while the umpire calls: "Strike!" and the fans jeer. Nor can you afford to take a crack on the temple from the ball. Men have died from that. It calls for undreamed-of niceties of nerve and judgment, but you don't find that out until you have stepped to the plate cold a few times during batting practice or in training quarters, with nothing at stake but the acquisition of experience, and see what a fine case of the jumping jitters you get. Later on, when you are writing your story, your imagination, backed by the experience, will be able to supply a picture of what the batter is going through as he stands at the plate in the closing innings of an important game, with two or three men on base, two out, and his team behind in the scoring, and fifty thousand people screaming at him.

The catching and holding of a forward pass for a winning touchdown on a cold, wet day always make a good yarn, but you might get an even better one out of it if you happen to know from experience about the elusive qualities of a hard, soggy, mud-slimed football rifled through the air, as well as something about the exquisite timing, speed, and courage it takes to catch it on a dead run, with two or three 190-pound men reaching for it at the same time or waiting to crash you as soon as your fingers touch it.

Any football coach during a light practice will let you go down the field and try to catch punts, the long, fifty-yard spirals and the tricky, tumbling end-over-enders. Unless you have had some previous experience, you won't hang on to one out of ten, besides knocking your fingers out of joint. But if you have any imagination, thereafter you will know that it calls for more than negligible nerve to judge and hold that ball and even plan to run with it, when there are two husky ends bearing down at full speed, preparing for a head-on tackle.

In 1932 I covered my first set of National Air Races, in Cleveland, and immediately decided that I had to learn how to fly to find out what that felt like. Riding as a passenger isn't flying. Being up there all alone at the controls of a ship is. And at the same time began a series of investigations into the "feel" of the mechanized sports to see what they were all about and the qualities of mentality, nerve, and physique they called for from their participants. These included a ride with Gar Wood in his latest and fastest speedboat, *Miss America X*, in which for the first time he pulled the throttle wide open on the Detroit River straightaway; a trip with the Indianapolis Speedway driver Cliff Bergere, around the famous brick raceway; and a flip with Lieutenant Al Williams, one time U. S. Schneider Cup race pilot.

I was scared with Wood, who drove me at 127 miles an hour,

jounced, shaken, vibrated, choked with fumes from the exhausts, behind which I sat hanging on desperately to the throttle bar, which after a while got too hot to hold. I was on a plank between Wood and his mechanic, Johnson, and thought that my last moment had come. I was still more scared when Cliff Bergere hit 126 on the Indianapolis straightaways in the tiny racing car in which I was hopelessly wedged, and after the first couple of rounds quite resigned to die and convinced that I should. But I think the most scared I have ever been while moving fast was during a ride I took in the cab of a locomotive on the straight, level stretch between Fort Wayne, Indiana, and Chicago, where for a time we hit 90 miles per hour, which of course is no speed at all. But nobody who rides in the comfortable Pullman coaches has any idea of the didoes cut up by a locomotive in a hurry, or the thrill of pelting through a small town, all out and wide open, including the crossing of some thirty or forty frogs and switches, all of which must be set right. But that wasn't sport. That was just plain excitement.

I have never regretted these researches. Now that they are over, there isn't enough money to make me do them again. But they paid me dividends, I figured. During the great Thompson Speed Trophy race for land planes at Cleveland in 1935, Captain Roscoe Turner was some eight or nine miles in the lead in his big golden, low-wing, speed monoplane. Suddenly, coming into the straightaway in front of the grandstands, buzzing along at 280 miles an hour like an angry hornet, a streamer of thick, black smoke burst from the engine cowling and trailed back behind the ship. Turner pulled up immediately, using his forward speed to gain all the altitude possible, turned and got back to the edge of the field, still pouring out that evil black smoke. Then he cut his switch, dipped her nose down, landed with a bounce and a bump, and rolled up to the line in a perfect stop. The crowd gave him a great cheer as he climbed out of the oil-spattered machine, but it was a cheer of sympathy because he had lost the race after having been so far in the lead that had he continued he could not possibly have been overtaken.

There was that story, but there was a better one too. Only the pilots on the field, all of them white around the lips and wiping from their faces a sweat not due to the oppressive summer heat, knew that they were looking at a man who from that time on, to use their own expression, was living on borrowed time. It isn't often when a Thompson Trophy racer with a landing speed of around eighty to ninety miles an hour goes haywire in the air, that the pilot is able to climb out of the cockpit and walk away from his machine. From the time of that first burst of smoke until the wheels touched the ground and stayed there, he was a hundred-to-one shot to live. To the initiated, those dreadful moments were laden with suspense and horror. Inside that contraption was a human being who any moment might be burned to a horrible, twisted cinder, or smashed into the ground beyond all recognition, a human being who was cool, gallant, and fighting desperately. Every man and woman on the field who had ever been in trouble in the air was living those awful seconds with him in terror and suspense. I, too, was able to experience it. That is what makes getting the "feel" of things distinctly worth while.

XXIII

EIGHTBALL

WHEN THE colored brother is capable in sports or athletics of any kind, he is usually too capable for his own good. It is written, or, rather, unwritten, in our land that he may give, but that he should not ask to receive. When we need him for the track team or the boxing squad, for football or to take part in the Olympic Games, he is a full-fledged citizen, our dearly beloved equal, and a true American. At other times he remains just plain nigger, and we'd rather he weren't around, because he represents a problem. The North is free and enlightened, and the Negro is any white man's equal in franchise and liberties until we try to get him into the hotel with the rest of the team. Some hotels will take Negroes if they happen to need the money and want the business of the white members of the squad, but many more of them will not. And what are you going to do about it?

During the time I have been connected with sports, I have both reported the American Negro athlete as well as promoted him. I have traveled with amateur boxing teams a good percentage of which was African, and learned that the colored man is little more welcome in the North than he is in the South. Jim Crow is still boss. The Senegambian, if we are feeling kindly disposed towards him at the moment, may compete against us as an equal provided he uses the tradesman's entrance and is, in the vernacular, "a good nigger, who knows his place." Knowing his place consists of many things, chief of which is self-obliteration and cheerful willingness to accept the white man's ban as inevitable. The decision as to whether or not the price is too high always rests with the black man. After all, if he doesn't like it, he can remain in Harlem, or run elevators, or tote baggage, or hop bells. Often, his treatment, especially in boxing, is contingent upon how important the Negro vote happens to be at that particular time. I have known very few people in sport to give the tar baby a break unless they had to do so. On the other hand, they were always willing to use him.

In golf and tennis the Negro keeps to himself. He has his own clubs and his annual tournaments. Baseball he plays on all-colored teams. There is no place in any organized major- or minor-league baseball club for a colored man. There is nothing in their rules or charters which bars him. That would be un-American. But he just doesn't get into organized baseball. He isn't much of an aquatic star; in fact, I never heard of a great Negro swimmer, chiefly because speed swimming is learned in pools, and white pools will not admit Negro swimmers. They are not wealthy enough to support pools of their own, though I believe there is one in Harlem now. There are Negro exercise and stable boys, but, to my knowledge, no jockeys.

That leaves three fields in which the Negro may and does compete apparently on an equal footing with the white man. They are college sports, which are closed to no one, and include football; amateur track and field sports, controlled by the Amateur Athletic Union; and amateur and professional prizefighting. And in this last sport, until the astonishing advent and even more astonishing toleration of Joseph Louis Barrow, better known as Joe Louis, he has been relegated to the role of clown. His battles are fought to the chorus of: "Kill the eightball! Don't hit him in the head, you'll break your hands. Hit him in the body! Downstairs! Downstairs! He'll quit!" And competition in all of these sports is open to the Negro only provided that he is the aforementioned "good nigger" and doesn't insist upon staying in the same hostels with the white folks and coming into the dining-rooms to eat with them. If he will submit to segregation when it is demanded and use the basement entrance, he is welcome—at a distance. I have never liked seeing the Negro competing on the white man's teams, because I know something of his heart-aches. I have often found myself wishing that his racial pride carried him a few steps farther than it does. His greed for the white man's blessings and the white man's mode of living defeats him and makes him a set-up for exploitation.

Each year when I have taken my Golden Gloves amateur boxing teams to Chicago for the big Inter-City bouts, I have dreaded the moment on the train when I should have to take the six or seven colored members of the squad aside in a little group—we traveled as a mixed family, black and white, perfectly happy, because we always had an entire special train to ourselves—and to say to them: "Ah—boys, when we get to Chicago, why—ah—the *Tribune* has made arrangements for the team to be put up at a private club—you know how it is, and, ah—as we are guests of the *Tribune*, we must go where they put us" (it would have been even stricter in any Chicago hotel); "and so we have, ah—made arrangements for you all to live together in the colored Y.M.C.A. downtown, where you will be well looked after. You will come up to the club every afternoon and train with the team in the club gymnasium. They, ah—have set aside a special elevator which will bring you right up to the dressing-rooms. You get to it from the rear" (past the ash-cans and garbage-cans, the boiler-room, and sub-cellar passageways), "and of course we'll have someone looking out for you."

I have always been waiting for one of them to say: "Look here, Mr. Gallico. We're good enough to be on your team and fight for your paper against Chicago and make a lot of money for your Athletic Association. We were good enough to enter your tournament and win it. Then why aren't we good enough to live with the team?"

I shouldn't have had an answer. I suppose there is one, but

I doubt whether it would have satisfied either them or me. I never heard the direct question, with the implication that they were ready to quit unless granted rights equal to those they had enjoyed in the ring as members of the New York team, however. They took the half loaf. When there were indications of coming trouble they could usually be offset with an appeal to their never-failing good nature and an indication of my own helplessness in the situation, a helplessness no doubt born of wishing to get out of an unpleasant situation as quickly as possible with the least effort. There was little time or inclination to crusade. The main thing was to hold together a team of many races, get them into the ring in fighting shape, and fulfill the obligations to the ticket-holders and thus, indirectly, to my employers.

I do not bring any particular knowledge or incisive philosophy to this problem, beyond a frequently outraged sense of justice. To the Negro-hater's eternal question: "But do you want to sit down at table with a nigger and invite him into your home?" I have no particular answer. I have sat down to dinner with some very strange people and races without coming to grief. If it were a matter of compulsion, I might be upset, not by the company, but by the compulsion. As it is a matter of choice, I keep to the company of my own kind. But I have always felt that where we make demands upon the Negro and exploit him as we do in sport, there is no longer any choice possible. When I send a boy out to the amateur wars to fight —indirectly, for the glory and better condition of my wallet— he is an equal and entitled to the considerations of an equal, or, at the least, to the same treatment accorded to similarly exploited white brothers.

Once I saw a human heart broken. True, it was encased in a brown skin and therefore did not count, even though its owner walked, talked, and behaved like a man. I had a little café-au-lait-tinted lightweight on one of my Golden Gloves boxing teams. He had a Spanish name and was to all intents and purposes a Puerto Rican. In New York he was accepted as a white member of the team and lived with the white boys at the first-class hotel where we kept our squad in training for the Chicago bouts. When we reached Chicago, the Negro members of the team were as usual weeded out and with their colored trainer packed into a couple of cabs and shipped off to the colored Y. We took the rest of the team to the huge athletic club where we were scheduled to be put up. The boys registered, were assigned to their rooms, and we began to plan the routine of training and amusement up in the headquarters suite. The telephone bell rang. It was the manager of the club asking for me. He said: "I am sorry, Mr. Gallico, but one of the boys you have registered here is colored. You will have to get him out of here."

"But," I protested, "he's a Puerto Rican. He isn't a Negro. He was accepted with the white boys in the Blank Hotel in New York."

He said: "I'm very sorry, but we don't make any distinctions here. This is a private club" (it was a hotel-athletic club), "and all colored men are alike to us here in Chicago. That boy cannot remain here."

I still curl with shame when I look back upon the incident. I didn't have the backbone to yank the whole team out of the place and I didn't have the courage to break the news to the kid, but sent one of the trainers to do it. Eventually I got up the nerve to go downstairs and talk to the boy. It was like taking a bottle away from a carriage baby and then beating him over the head with it for good measure. He spent one night with the Negroes down at the Y. The next day I had to put him on a train and send him home. He could live neither with white man nor with black. The entire team was no good after that. Both white and black boys resented the incident bitterly, and with all justice. We grown-ups running the show must have looked a pretty sickly lot. We were, too. Whether in New York he had lived as white or as black and reached out for something he had had before, I never found out. He was a good fighter, too. I have never heard of him since.

The Negro football-player, if he is tough, hardy, and courageous, has little trouble, provided he is willing to pay the penalty for being a black man playing a white man's game. The chief punishment in this instance is to have to suffer the consequences of enthusiastic and determined efforts made by members of opposing teams to cripple him during the course of the afternoon. It is not always possible to determine whether this is racial prejudice or merely the lusty strategy of high-pressure American football which calls for the removal of an opposing player who seems to be doing too well, but the pains, bruises, and compound fractures are identical. The Negro player who wins a place on a big college team is usually exceptionally good and a great athlete. Luckily, he is also above the average in intelligence and therefore the white man's world can hold but few surprises for him. If he is playing for a school that schedules decent teams he is even likely to get a fair shake of the dice. If he is playing against high-pressure teams he will get hurt. And if a Southern team is scheduled he may be requested not to play at all on that particular day. There is something a little disgusting today in the venom displayed by some types of Southerners against the Negro. One feels the same sort of shameful distaste as when listening to a Nazi fulminating against Jews. But, on the other hand, the Southerner has a palatable frankness on his side. He doesn't, as we do, offer the simple jungle child or his descendant glittering Christmas-tree ornaments and then snatch them away. He offers him nothing.

The great University of Michigan found itself nicely pinned upon the prongs of the race dilemma not long ago when Willis Ward, a fine track athlete and football man, was a star of the eleven at one of the ends. He was a dream of an end too, and a pleasure to watch in action. But a famous Southern team was on Michigan's schedule at Ann Arbor, and the famous Southern team advised that it could not take the field to play if Mr. Ward was in his regular position on the Michigan team at game-time, or in any position at all.

Michigan was inclined to stand by its guns and play Ward.

The Negro was an enrolled student, a brilliant scholar; and he had earned his place on the team through ability. But it was pointed out that big games are scheduled several years in advance, and at the time this one was signed, Ward had not yet made his name, or the Southern school never would have signed to play in the first place. At the same time Michigan, as host to the visitors, was under some kind of obligation to respect the beliefs and customs of the guest. To insist that we are all one big happy family united under the name of Americans, a free and loving democracy where racial prejudice should not and does not exist, would have been sophistry and wouldn't have worked anyway. Michigan was in honor bound to let Ward play. The Southern team did not play against Negroes. And there it was.

There was a good deal of bickering in the newspaper sports columns as to which side had the right or wrong of the question, but the most important point was quite overlooked in the debating—namely, that the situation existed at all. It was, as I remember, solved finally by a Detroit sports editor, Harry Salsinger, who persuaded Ward voluntarily to withdraw from that game. He pointed out that if the Southerners did yield the point and take the field, there would be no football played until they had attended to the matter of crippling him so that he would have to be removed from the scene on a stretcher. He granted that this prospect held no terrors for Ward, but held that Ward must also grant that they would eventually accomplish this, no matter how much skill and courage he displayed. Inasmuch as Ward was expected to be of great service to his university on the track team, he would be showing poor college spirit by getting his leg or his shoulder or his ribs broken for a not too clearly defined principle. Nobody came out of the affair with any too much honor, but then, nobody ever does when the Negro question is raised in sports.

The Negro's greatest temptation has always been the prize-ring, with its quick, rich rewards (ostensibly) in exchange for a little pain and punishment. The black man has always shown great aptitude for boxing. He is generally a magnificent physical specimen, powerful, wiry, hard, and not nearly so sensible to pain as his white brother. He has a thick, hard skull, and good hands. He is crafty and tricky and, contrary to public opinion, as game as the white man when the cards are not stacked against him. But in eight out of ten cases when he enters the ring, the dice are loaded. He has agreed either to lose or to "carry" his white opponent and refrain from knocking him out; in the graphic language of the ring, he is handcuffed. Or if he is fighting without the manacles he must be far out in front to get the decision from the officials unless his manager has the right connections.

Our philosophy here is curiously akin to that of the modern German. We differ merely in our method. The Nazi declares: "The Negro is an *Untermensch*. We will not permit him to compete against the members of the Aryan race because he might win, and then we should not feel good." The American sportsman says: "The Negro is inferior to the white man. We will let him fight white men because it seems to amuse white audiences, but we won't let him win."

Fight managers, the most shameless, rapacious, and unmoral crew in the world anyway, lose practically every last vestige of decency when dealing with Negro fighters. The Negro is regarded as pure cattle to be exploited, swindled, and burgled for their own profits and never, if possible, for his. He is after all only a nigger, and so the ordinary rules of conduct applied to white fighters, which are in themselves none too sweet, don't go. He wouldn't know what to do with his money if he had any; therefore it is considered foolhardy to give him any if it can be prevented.

The Negro of course is a poor, misguided fool ever to go into the profession of prizefighting, because except in the rarest of instances the rich rewards are not for him, and from the point of view of sportsmanship and a square shake, he is whipped before ever the bell rings. The whole thing boils down simply enough to a question of showmanship. It is pleasing and enter-

taining to a fight audience consisting mainly of white sportsmen and women to see a white man beat a Negro, punch him
around the ring, cut him, bloody him, knock him down, and
knock him out. The stricken Negro fighter rolls his eyes in a
funny way; he looks and acts like a monkey. It is considered
a prime sally to yell: "Throw him a coconut," when one enters
the ring. He makes funny faces when he is hurt, and when he
is losing makes an excellent foil for a white hero.

It is displeasing to a white fight audience to see a white man
punch-drunk and groveling before a Negro, or flopping about
the canvas like a gaffed fish from the effects of a punch, or ab-
sorbing a cruel and systematic beating. Ergo, in the past the
smart promoter has avoided presenting such spectacles.

Joe Louis has enjoyed an extraordinary vogue, and the rules
that have applied to the general run of Negro fighters have not
been invoked in his case for several reasons. One is that he appeared at just the right time, when the public was sick and
tired of the clowns, fakes, phonies, and misfits they had been
looking at in the guise of white champions. And another is
that he was exceptionally well managed and handled by a hard
and capable crowd of people of his own race, a lawyer, an ex-
numbers man, and an ex-convict, an outfit just as tough as some
of the gangsters who have been acting as impresarios for some
of the white valiants, if not tougher. Louis is what is known
definitely as a "good nigger who knows his place." He has been
carefully trained in the sly servility that the white man accepts
as his due and he really had an exquisite skill at his trade and
a thrilling efficiency. Schmeling or no Schmeling, he once was
so good that it was an artistic pleasure to watch him work.
Following hard on the heels of the Sharkeys, Baers, Carneras,
Levinskys, et alii, he gave the fight audiences something for
their money—action and results. He had mastered the magic
of destruction. He also happened during an era of tolerance.
The white man's ego was still a little shaken by the depression.
The pale-faces patronized him and permitted him to ply his
profession unhampered, and preened themselves a little about

it. There is about the question of Joe Louis an attitude some-how of: "You see what fine people and sportsmen we are. We are letting a nigger earn a fortune in the ring just like any white man." It was the part of good showmanship to present Louis *au naturel.* He was a box-office draw. But a great and happy yell mounted into the evening skies the night that Aryan Max Schmeling set him on his panties in the fourth round of their famous fight, and an even lustier and more joyous one went up from the unpigmented spectators when the German knocked him rigid in the twelfth. The white brother is fickle and tires very quickly of seeing a Negro triumph too often. It is a curi-ous fact, but Louis won the heavyweight championship of the world when he was on the downgrade. He will not hold it long. The measure of his tolerance is always expressed at the box office, and the smart promoter is quick to take note and arrange for the type of exhibition he is craving at the particular time. Otherwise the Nordic, who has all the money to spend on prize-fights, will stop buying tickets and then nobody will make any money, not the manager, not the promoter, not the fighter. To the manager and the promoter this is unthinkable. What the fighter thinks doesn't count. He is there to do what he is told.

The economic principle as it has been expounded to the darky in the past and as it will be expounded to him again is very simple and can be understood even by a primitive child of the bush. It is, briefly, as follows: "You want to eat, don't you? And you can't eat unless you fight. And you can't get a fight with a good white man, one that will draw any money for your end, unless you agree to lay down or carry him. They don't want to see you win. They want to see you lose." The African is an obliging fellow and, above all, he wants to eat and maybe even acquire a shiny car. He is always hoping for a break, even though he rarely gets it. The success of Joe Louis will result in a perfect rash of colored fighters. The market will be glutted with them, the public will get sick of seeing them, and they will be right back where they started from.

But the Negro can always earn himself a little stake by pretending to be knocked out, or just boxing a nice ten-round bout and losing a close decision to a man he could knock out in two rounds if the shackles were off. He is only rarely tempted to do any double-crossing with the kindly white man who is enabling him to earn his pork chops by losing to him, because if he did there would be no more fights with white gentlemen, or they might even take the trouble to look him up and kill him. They have.

Seven out of the eleven track and field events won by the United States at the last carnival of sweat, the Olympic Games at Berlin, were taken by Negroes. Three of these were won by one individual, Jesse Owens, who also shared in winning a fourth, the 400-meter relay, in which he and Metcalfe, a brother Aframerican, put the team so far out in front on the first two legs that the white boys to whom they turned over the baton could have crawled in on their hands and knees. Even the Germans had to cheer Owens because he was such a poem in action. Some of the experts profess to see this triumph of the colored man in athletics as the beginning of a new era for the black athlete and the coming of the time when we shall have to send an all-sepia track squad to compete for us, but I do not believe it. Athletes go in cycles, and our next Olympic team may by natural processes have only one or two Negro stars. But if natural processes won't work, I have great faith in the white man's ability to keep the scales balanced in his own favor. He always has in the past.

XXIV

MISCELLANY—

RASSLIN', BIKE-RIDING,

FOOT-RUNNING

WRESTLING IN the boom days was an amusing comic hippodrome, and sometimes good theater as long as it kept within the bounds of decency and good taste and essayed no more than occasional flights of fantasy or too much imagination.

It was often even a joy, when Cheemy Londos, the Greek Adonis, was champion, and the promoters dug up an assortment of plug-uglies, greaseballs, chestnut-stabbers, spaghetti-benders, and goulash-champers for Jimmy to flatten monthly or bi-monthly in the pits at Madison Square Garden with his famous and dramatic "airplane spin." This was a maneuver which occurred always when things looked blackest for the champion and he seemed about to succumb heroically to some cruel torturing hold that could contort his handsome face in agony, but could not unseal his Spartan lips in protest or surrender. Susceptible ladies in the audience would come nigh to swooning at this point, but the boys in the press row would suddenly put aside their copies of the *American Mercury* or newspapers or whatever they were reading to pass the time, knock the lids off their portable typewriters, write their leads, hand them to their telegraph operators, and reach for their hats and coats. For by the time they had them on, Londos invariably would have escaped from the killing hold and, suddenly and dramatically turning upon his almost victorious opponent, would pass one arm under his crotch, the other around his neck, lift him high into the air—and he could hoist pigs weighing two hundred and seventy to three hundred pounds—whirl him around once, twice, thrice, and then crash him to the canvas exactly like a stevedore depositing your favorite trunk on the pier, and then flop on top of him to receive the victor's pat on the shoulder from the referee, who was also anxious to go home.

Jim Londos was another picture-book athlete, a genuine Greek and a fair-to-middling wrestler, but a fine actor, a brilliant showman, and a master at plastic poses. He had a beautifully developed body that was always bronzed and glistening, and a fine dark head, with crisp dark-brown curly hair and a gleaming set of even white teeth. Society ladies a little weary of the flat-chested, knock-kneed, spindle-legged, or paunchy figures off their mates would come just for the moment when Jimmy under those white lights slipped off his bathrobe and stood forth. Wow! He had only one fault. He was too short and stocky. But he remedied that in the same manner adopted by actors who are too short. He wouldn't play opposite anyone who was taller than he. His opponents were carefully selected for him. The shorter and fatter and uglier, the better. They showed up Cheemy's beauty all the more.

Those were pleasant days when one looked forward to the next barrel of lard that the promoters would dig up for Londos to toss, almost as one haunted the news-stand waiting for the copy of the magazine with one's favorite serial to appear, or went pelting off to the picture house because Valentino was appearing, never mind in what. Wrestling was organized very much like the theater, with heroes, or leading men, villains, or foils, secondary leads, clowns, and comic reliefs, but for a time it had even a wider appeal to the populace than the theater because it called for no particular intelligence or cerebration on the part of the audience. The plot was always the same. The handsome good man won. The fat, ugly man with the whiskers, who fouled and kicked and butted and snarled, and bared his teeth and sneered, and who seemed just upon the verge of an ill-deserved triumph, always received his just deserts in the nick of time and, mumbling into his beard, slunk from the premises accompanied by the hisses of the virtuous. It never varied. The characters merely changed. The spirit was one of good, clean, ingenuous fun. Nobody took wrestling or the so-called championship very seriously. But then neither, after leaving a mystery play on Broadway, did one rush off to police headquarters to lodge a complaint that a man had been shot and killed on the stage of the Cort Theater, and what were they going to do about it? It was all a part of the happy land of Make-Believe.

But even as the elegant Romans found the tap-tapping of faces and skulls with lightly bandaged hands a good deal of a bore, demanded blood, and got it, so the wrestling fan of today, turning his back upon fine art, demands brutality and realism and is getting it to the point where the wrestling show, to continue to pack them in, has had to overstep every limit of decency and good taste. The poor, great oafs who make a hazardous living out of the game are expected to assault one another rough-and-tumble, nothing barred, gouging, biting, kicking, punching, occasionally even beating one another over the head with spanners or blackjacks, and in the gentle southland, where this form of public mayhem and assault and battery is in a particularly flourishing state, one athlete in the attempt to introduce a little novelty wherewith to titivate a jaded public, managed somehow to secure a handkerchief heavily perfumed with $CHCl_3$, the same being chloroform. This he pressed over his opponent's face until he relaxed nicely in deep slumber, and then pinned him, to the great joy of all present. Another original left the wrestling platform and an astonished opponent, ran quickly to his dressing-room, returned bearing a monkey wrench, climbed back into the ring, applied the wrench to his opponent's skull, naturally quieting him so that he could pin his shoulders to the mat. The game would still be a pleasant memory and fair entertainment if its promoters and participants restricted themselves to such artless and even appealing pranks, but in order to dig still further coins out of the public's pockets and cater to a waning interest, wrestlers have been forced to resort to tactics in the ring that would have made the Marquis de Sade scream for smelling salts had he been a spectator.

It may all still be the same naïve and innocent pretending that it used to be during the great Londos renaissance when wrestling came back to popular favor after many long years in limbo, but when the men bleed, or perhaps only pretend to bleed, and kick one another in what nice nellyism has compromised upon calling the groin, or gouge at eyeballs, or bite ears, it is close to a degeneracy that ought to be reserved for private performances before the degenerates who enjoy them.

One hardly knows whether to blame the greed of the wrestling promoters and their wars over territory as jealously and bitterly contested, short of the killings, as any beer monopoly during the sainted days of prohibition, or the public for the exhibitions staged today in public places under the name of wrestling. It is usually safe to figure that most presentations are reflections of audience taste. But the chief wrestling trust, in which Londos in his day was a partner and large shareholder, found itself somewhat in the same position as a theatrical manager with an aging star whose repertoire has begun to pall and who is faced with the problem of replacing him with someone new. It is true, the public is tired of the old star, but it will continue to make invidious comparisons with the new offerings. Good as Londos was as a showman and performer—he coined an enormous fortune—he did wear out his welcome, because he was, like an old trouper, too set in his ways. He could play Jack the Giant-Killer with occasional variations, but it was still the same part. The trust decided that Londos must be replaced by a new leading man and hasn't found one yet who will stand up or draw crowds the way Londos did, and it has tried a dozen. Rival trusts have muscled in, and the result is complete confusion and lean days for promoters who present anything but sheer brutality. Wrestling is on its way back to limbo again until another combination Gable-Valentino-Taylor-Apollo-Sandow appears to lead it forth again, and back to the legitimate theater, where it belongs. What has this to do with sport? Nothing. It is merely catalogued as such. Did you ever see a real wrestling match? One night, in a fit of pique at the press and the public for complaining of his presentation, the late Jack Curley, the head of the big Eastern wrestling trust, staged a "shooting match," which is the wrestler's term for a bout that is on the level. Two of his biggest hippos tugged at one another for a solid hour and a half without ever going to the mat, and when they went there they remained reclining in damp embrace for another hour. They had to fire off cannon to wake up the spectators so they could go home, and a lot of them have never been the same since.

Six-day bicycle racing is another of the exhibition sports that are more of a show than a contest, but I always loved to go to it. Its social possibilities are simply unsurpassed. For one thing, I used to like to dine in the bike-riders' mess in the basement of Madison Square Garden, where one Charley Stein, a reformed motorcycle pacer, had the feeding concession and set up a vast kitchen which operated on a twenty-four-hour schedule and which tackled the considerable problem of refueling men who were engaged in exercising sixteen hours a day in such a manner that they would not get the stomach-ache. It is nothing for a bicycle-rider to be balancing the last morsel of a juicy steak on the end of his fork just as an S O S reaches him from the track that a jam is on and his partner is clamoring for assistance. Picture yourself jumping up from dinner-table just before dessert and coffee, leaping onto a bicycle, and riding twenty-five miles at top speed. Somehow, on Charley's grub, they managed not only to hop at all hours from provender to the saddle without tying up in bow knots inside, but actually showed a gain in their weight at the end of what is known as the six-day grind.

He fed them (and me) the most magnificent of thick sirloin steaks, lamb chops that would melt under a severe glance, broiled chickens that simply flew at your gullet, heaps of vegetables, plenty of bread and butter, tons of raw celery, and nothing but custards and fruit salads for sweets. Some of the boys would eat eight and nine meals a day, but I never heard of one of them having to leave the track owing to an attack of dyspepsia.

There would always be five or six bike-riders in their varicolored jerseys at the long, linoleum-covered trencher tables, stoking in food with both hands—bushy-haired Italians, small, bright-eyed Frenchmen, big, stolid Hollanders, Belgians, Germans, Americans—chattering away in their various languages and calling for food, food, and more food. There would also be present, usually, a handful of newspapermen and photographers covering the race, three or four nondescript, unidentifiable females, wives or sweethearts, chiseling a meal on the house, sweatered trainers, rubbers, handlers, hangers-on, et al., and over the stimulating aroma of sizzling steaks and broiling chickens there was always wafted the curious but arresting cocktail odor of liniment and rubbing lotion. White-coated servitors slammed down the grub on thick, white crockery and scurried back to the kitchen for more. Stein was always around, grinning and supervising with a "How's the steak? Tender? What do you want to follow, some chops or a chicken?"

Upstairs at the pine track built inside the arena, the press box was the village clearing-house for the six nights that the riders wove their endless colored patterns around the yellow-white oval. Sooner or later, but inevitably, everybody in town wandered through there, prizefighters, actors, jockeys, ballplayers, men about town, night-club crooners, comics, gangsters, fight managers, artists, writers; and if you couldn't pick up a dozen stories or items or news leads of an evening, in addition to the one you were trying to concoct on the bike-riders, why, your ears just weren't open.

Nobody really cares who wins the race or who is leading—that part is pretty well cut and dried and determined beforehand by the way the riders are paired—except the congenital bike fans packed on the top shelf, or standing around solemn and moon-eyed in the infield, the huge space on the floor inside the track given over to song-pluggers, hot-dog venders, and standees. The gentry in the side arena and loge seats are occasionally pleasantly stimulated by the swift colorful movement of a lap-stealing jam when every rider in the pack is on the track and partners relieve one another after every two or three laps of breakneck sprinting, or when four or five riders collide and tumble to the bottom of the track from the twelve-foot embankment at the turns in a welter of splintered machines and sometimes broken bones. But for the most part the high-tariff guests are more concerned with getting pleasantly tipsy with their box parties, visiting friends and renewing old acquaintances, exchanging gossip, or acquiring a little publicity by offering "preems," apparently the slang contraction of the word "premiums," a prize of twenty-five, fifty, or a hundred dollars for a five- or ten-lap sprint. The loudspeaker bellows: "Attention! . . . Attention, please! A Mr. Hyman Rosenzweig of Rosenzweig Fits-U-Tite Knit Underwear, sitting in box thirty-seven, has offered one hundred dollars for a ten-lap sprint. . . ." There is a buzz of excitement from the crowd, impressed with such munificence, a great craning of necks to see the Crœsus in box thirty-seven, and a pistol-shot to indicate that the sprint has started. Usually there is little return for the money but the momentary publicity, because the pack, if it is tired or wary, speeds up by no more than half when going after a preem, and finally one rider jumps the lead a little and holds it until the line has been crossed.

Nobody has to go home until five o'clock in the morning—the Americano has a perfect phobia against going home and therefore loves the six-day race like nothing else—and there is always something going on, always something to look at when conversation lags. But that, too, is a fascinating hour to the sports-writer when the cleaning women take over the arena and move like tired gray ghosts through the empty aisles of seats, mopping up the night's debris of paper cups, half-munched frankfurters, torn programs, and empty bottles, and there is no sound but the scraping of their ever-weary feet and the soft whir of the endless riders, proceeding around now, however, at tortoise pace. There is an unwritten agreement among them not to start any hostilities, lap-stealing jams, in those early morning hours when their partners are catching a few winks of quiet sleep. And besides, what would be the purpose of exercising too violently with nobody there to see them?

The race breaks down and relaxes pleasantly during those empty in-between hours. A couple of the newspaper boys on the late shift, working for the early editions of the afternoon papers that hit the street at ten o'clock in the morning, will mount bikes and ride around the track, clowning with the riders; or a sleeping drunk, not yet swept from the building with the rest of the garbage, will collar a machine and wobble about the saucer, to the cheers of the press and the edification of the charwomen, until a sleepy, short-tempered private gendarme arrives, picks him up between thumb and forefinger, and deposits him in the alley. The six-day race is definitely fun.

For real spectator thrill, a hot foot-race is still very close to tops, and of all the dashes, sprints, and runs, the mile still remains, for me, the classic distance, because it calls for brains and rare judgment as well as speed, condition, and courage. The dashes, the 100- and 220-yard sprints are terrific explosions of energy in which every ounce of strength is expended when the tape is reached—is being expended, as a matter of fact, every foot of the way, in a quick, desperate assault upon the fractional part of a second.

The mile run is a far different affair. Here is a really magnificent duel between man and time, every second of which may be seen and watched and weighed by the spectator in the stands, especially with the modern innovation of the giant Western Union split-second timing clock set up at one end of the track so that the actual bitter struggle against the finger moving relentlessly across the dial, and the inexorable processes of fatigue, become great and powerful drama.

Every runner down on the track has a bank-account with nature, of strength and energy. When that account is overdrawn, the runner must drop in his tracks. When the chemical poisons of fatigue have crippled his muscles, he cannot move another step, no matter how great his courage and will-power and desire to win. Experience and intelligence of high order are required to know how to husband this bank balance so that there will be something left for the rainy day—the last desperate sprint for the finish line.

And yet hoarding won't win races either, because the law of the mile run is immutable. It is run by quarters. If the athlete runs the first two quarters too fast, he is done. He must pay back to nature in the last two. And the processes of fatigue are accumulative, like a snowball rolling downhill. And if he loafs the first two quarters in an attempt to save his strength, then he must run the final ones, to make up, in faster time than is humanly possible for a man who has already traversed 880 yards, or a half-mile.

Thus the problem becomes quite fascinatingly translated into mathematics, but mathematics that everyone can understand. If a man is trying to run a 4.08 mile, which is brilliant time (Glenn Cunningham's smashing world's record for the mile is 4.06.7), and is careless of his pace in the first quarters, or too miserly and thoughtful of his bank balance and does the first two quarters at an average of 1.05 minutes each, instead of something more closely approximating 1.02, he is through, because he is then called upon to run those two final quarters in 59 seconds each to get his 4.08, and the man has not yet been born who can do that. When he is, we may see the long awaited, but never even approached four-minute mile.

It is a popular fallacy connected with track, and also with many other sports, that with the finish line in sight the champion calls upon some reserve of courage and spirit that overcomes exhausted muscles and carries him on to victory. "He finished on his nerve," sings the lyrical sports-writer. Physiologically there is no such thing. An exhausted muscle is dead, and nothing can bring it to life again but complete rest. The harder it is pushed, the more surely dead it becomes, until it is as inanimate a thing as a piece of wood, and just about as responsive to that mystery we call will-power.

What actually happens is that the poisoned, failing muscles begin to send out storm warnings long before the danger point or total stoppage is reached. The man of too vivid and sensitive an imagination might quit long before he needs to do so because his overactive brain translates the pain he feels, the terrible fire that rasps and scorches his chest and makes every breath burn as though he were inhaling steam, into approaching disaster. The throbbing head, the aching legs, all tell him that his number is up, that he has run a bad race, perhaps, and is through.

The champion with will-power, courage, and a resolute, fighting spirit doesn't believe it. It hurts like all fury to go on running, but he keeps on in spite of it, because he knows that he still has something left in the bank, only the bank officials are making a fuss about letting him have it because his account is beginning to run low. He has no power to go on after complete exhaustion has set in, but he has the power which his weaker or more temperamental or imaginative brother has not, to go on in spite of hell and high water as long as there is anything left in his body. He knows that as long as he can lift a leg, no matter how much it hurts him, he is not yet exhausted.

Under perfect conditions, to break a record and to have run a good race, an athlete should be close to a state of complete collapse two or three steps after he has passed the finish line. Sometimes you will hear of a runner shaking his head angrily after winning a race, and uttering one of the most expressive of all track phrases: "Hell! I finished too full of running." What he means is that he was much too strong and able to run at the finish of the race. He has too much left in the bank past the finish line, where it can no longer do him any good. The race is over at the tape. That surplus energy that remains to him, had it been wisely expended in lopping off fractions of seconds from the various quarters around the course, might have set up a new record.

Now, added to the great and ever-present duels against himself, are the races that the athletes run against their immediate competitors, who may number anywhere from three to twenty. It takes nerve and courage to let some pace-setter out to kill off the field open up a hundred-yard lead in the first quarter or so. The wise veteran lets him go because he knows that in the end nature will pull him back where he belongs. And yet the temptation to chase him is very strong, and the youngster is liable to succumb to that ever-present fear that grips every foot-runner at one time or another: "What if he *should* be able to maintain that clip? I'd better go after him." The veteran knows that if the mad pace-setter actually does maintain his speed for the full four quarters, he is looking at a miracle, not a foot-race, and there is nothing he can do about it.

Then there are the dangerous jockeying for positions and the ever-present peril of being pocketed and therefore unable to get out and meet a challenge at just the right moment, and the nervous tension of taking the lead, setting the pace and listening for footsteps closing in from behind—all are a part of the fascination of the foot-race. Position is highly important. Some runners work best from out front, others like to lay off the pace and move up gradually—Jack Lovelock is one of these. Others prefer to dog the leader and try to catch him napping with a sudden spurt near the tape.

Imagine if you can the tension there must have been at the start of the great Olympic 1,500-meter run, roughly equivalent to the mile, with a field that included such world stars as Glenn Cunningham, world's record-holder for the mile, Luigi Beccali, former Olympic champion, Jack Lovelock, the great New Zealand runner, Gene Venzke, holder of the indoor record for the mile, Eric Ny of Sweden, Phil Edwards of Canada, and San Romani of America, besides half a dozen others. Every type of miler was here represented. Lovelock had to set a world's record, 3.47.8, to win it, and Cunningham, who finished second, was likewise inside the world's-record time. This was the big thrill of the games. The men were pioneering in time, exploring fractions of seconds where no human being ever had been before. For instance, Beccali, the Italian, ran his race two whole seconds faster than when he won it at Los Angeles four years before, and still was only good enough to take third. For the last half, Cunningham ran where he likes to and is most dangerous—out in front. Lovelock kept creeping up, improving his position at every lap. And the stop watches were clicking off their tenths of seconds. Ambition, nerve, tension, worry, nerve tension, fear of defeat were all playing their parts in the running of that race, pouring their own toxins into the already fatigue-poisoned muscles of the men on the track. Only one of them could be right. Which? The final decision had a hundred thousand people fairly bug-eyed and hysterical with excitement. It was Lovelock who was perfect, and Cunningham who had made a mistake somewhere along the line and didn't have enough left to meet the final challenge of the winner.

And so it goes, not only in the mile, but right on through the whole little world of track and field competition, the long-distance grinds, the graceful hurdle races, and the field events, the weight-throwing, pole-vaulting, and jumping, the last being completely paradoxical in the manner of the competition; that is, the nearer the jumpers get to the finish and the more tired they ought to be, the higher they go.

If ever there was a sport that is seventy per cent mental and thirty per cent physical and therefore doubly interesting to see, it is high jumping or pole-vaulting. The paradox is explained by the fact that it takes time for a jumper's muscles to warm up and stretch to their fullest capacity, and when there is a large

number of competitors, the athlete is usually given a good rest
and time for recuperation between jumps. But it is his mind
that takes him higher and higher until he finally reaches his
muscle capacity of power over the inexorable pull of gravity,
that never gets tired, and he stops.

Supposing a high-jump bar is set at six feet four. The jumper
takes his run, leaps, and clears it safely. But he knows that he
has jumped more than six feet four. If he has cleared the bar,
he has done so by anything from three eighths of an inch to two
inches. If he had jumped exactly six feet four, he would have
knocked the bar off. And so when the cross-piece is moved
up to six feet four and one half inches, it holds no particular
terrors for him because he knows that he has already jumped
that height, and possibly more. It is when they get up to the
fantastic record heights of six feet eight or nine inches—a six-
foot man could walk under the bar wearing a top hat—and the
stick shivers and shakes after their passage and then decides
to remain put, that they know their number is up. The mental
lift is no longer there to help them over. And in addition to
that relentless pull of gravity the jumpers are also contending
with that deadly seductive three-trials-and-out hazard.

For full enjoyment of a symphony or an opera the devotee
takes the score into the concert hall with him. To open up a
new chapter in thrill and appreciation of the human mind and
body, take a stop watch and a record-book with you the next
time you go to a track meet, and keep tabs on how close the
boys come to stealing successfully from time and nature.

XXV

MORE

MISCELLANY

THE WORLD is full of a number of minor sports which have their devotees as either spectators or active participants and therefore deserve to be mentioned. A sports-writer runs across them all at one time or another, if only when he opens his mail and plucks forth a letter from Indignant Subscriber wanting to know why more space in the paper is not devoted to curling, or pocket billiards.

A partial list of this small fry includes hockey, ice and field, ice-skating, speed as well as figure, basketball, fencing, skiing, polo, fishing, handball, soccer football, rugby football, canoeing, bowling, billiards, badminton, table tennis, better known as ping-pong, sailing, lacrosse, water polo, rodeos, rowing, shooting, squash in all forms, trap shooting, and weight-lifting.

There will be bitter complaint at my listing ice hockey as a minor sport, since as a professional game organized into leagues in the manner of baseball and English football it entertains hundreds of thousands of people, but my cataloguing is purely arbitrary; it has never managed to entertain me. The game has the thrill of hard body contact, the beauty of speed and lovely, fluid movement, and the excitement of a more than occasional brawl, riot, or fist fight on the ice, but it lacks variety. There is only one way of scoring, which is to drive the puck into the net, and the rules have given the balance of power to the team that elects to play defensively. Also, because it is an artificial game, the action is too frequently stopped by officials enforcing rules, and rules the infractions of which are not apparent to any but the most expert in the audience. I have always suspected that the real appeal of hockey, and the reason for its immediate success when introduced from Canada to American audiences in 1925, are that it is a fast, body-contact game played by men with clubs in their hands and knives lashed to their feet, since the skates are razor-sharp and before the evening is over it is almost a certainty that someone will be hurt and will fleck the ice with a generous contribution of gore before he is led away to be hem-stitched together again. There is also an excellent chance of a free-for-all before an evening's exhibition is over, involving all the players of both teams and often including spectators as well as police, all swinging clubs, hockey sticks, and fists in merry riot. Cantankerous and short-tempered hockey-players are considered a great draw. The audience accepts them as villains in the same manner that they do the heavy, or menace, in wrestling, hisses and boos them, but flocks to the arenas when they come to town because they usually start something.

Some of these brawls are legitimate, as there are any number of delicate attentions invisible to officials as well as audience that one hockey-player can pay another with his skate or the butt end of his stick, and the succession of bruising shocks sustained during the evening has an accumulative effect upon the lowering of the threshold of acrimony. But occasionally when attendance at the games has fallen off, some of these lovely little riots have happened too apropos to look natural, and while the owners of hockey teams raise their hands in holy horror at these melees, I have always suspected them upon occasion of tipping the boys that a little scuffling wouldn't hurt the box office any and might even do it some good.

I love a good fight, but why call it hockey? Why not arm two groups of men with lethal weapons and turn them loose? I feel there is just a faint hypocritical note in the public's love

for ice hockey *per se*. Make it impossible for the players to injure one another or fight, and see how long the game would
last. I realize that I am in the absolute minority in not being
stirred by ice hockey, but after all what is the good of saying
good-by if you don't speak out your mind? As long as I was
working for a paper I could whoop up as much enthusiasm for
hockey as the next guy. That many customers must be right.
Certainly. I am a good deal of a hypocrite myself. That is what
always makes me so mad when I find the same trait in others.

Basketball is a brisk, mildly exciting game to watch, with
plenty of skill, speed, and hard body-contact. It has a tremendous following in the Midwest, but only lately has had the mis-
fortune to become almost a big-league sport in the East, attracting crowds of sixteen and eighteen thousand to double college
bills in Madison Square Garden. Financial success has always
preceded the ruination of any game or sport in one way or another. Basketball, which to date has had only a few minor
scandals due to the college amateurs playing a little alfresco
semi-pro ball to pick up a few dollars, is now headed for a major
one. It is making too much money, and the gamblers have
taken it up as a betting proposition.

Curiously, it is a game that above all others seems to appeal
to the temperament of Jews, and for the past years Jewish players on the college teams around New York have had the game
all to themselves. A good Jewish football-player is a rarity, but
Jews flock to basketball by the thousands. It is a good rough
game. A Jew, contrary to popular opinion, can take a licking,
depending upon the individual, as gamely as any other race,
vide the many successful Jewish prizefighters; but the reason, I
suspect, that it appeals to the Hebrew with his Oriental background is that the game places a premium on an alert, scheming
mind and flashy trickiness, artful dodging, and general smart-
aleckness. I am surprised that no one has ever advanced another
reason for the great success of the game. It is definitely psychically satisfying to see the ball, thrown or shot through the air,
drop through the hoop and net that seems barely big enough to

permit it to get through, and the longer the shot, the bigger the thrill. There is something vaguely sexual about it.

Fencing, combat with foil, épée, and saber, you may be surprised to learn, is on the upgrade in popularity after having been for years, like skiing, a sport indulged in by only a few enthusiasts. It is due to be taken up generally in the next few years as a game that is tremendously exciting and stimulating mentally, splendid exercise, cheap, and calling for not much more space than is afforded by an average apartment when the furniture is cleared and the rug rolled back for dancing.

It is the dullest of all sports to watch, perhaps, and the most exciting and thrilling one I know of in which to take part. It is dull as a spectator sport because it requires from four to six judges and a referee, who go into consultations lasting for minutes to decide whether or not there has been a touch, unless, like the épée duelists at the Olympic Games, the competitors are neatly wired for sound and ring bells and flash on lamps when a touch is scored. It is supreme as a participant sport, especially for the man who wants exercise and mental relaxation and has not much time to give, because an hour's fencing is enough to tucker even a man in the best possible condition. It carries the romance and excitement of naked steel even though the steel is protected with a button or a dulled edge; it calls for courage, speed, brains, craft, initiative, nerves, and combativeness, but the physical punishment is never severe, beyond an occasional scratch or a hard lick with a saber. It requires so much concentration that it is a complete antidote for any kind of brain fag. It has all the excitement of the personal-combat element of boxing minus the pain and the damage that the boxer sustains, no matter how clever. It is a means of expression, because no two men handle a weapon alike, and every trait and quirk of character is eventually disclosed at the end of an épée or a saber. Fence with a man and he stands revealed to you.

Of all the outdoor winter sports in which the average person can take part, skiing is the most fun—and the most dangerous.

Never forget it. You can get hurt more easily on skis than at any other sport, with the possible exception of polo. I remember arriving in Garmisch-Partenkirchen in Bavaria about a week before the start of the winter Olympic Games and noticing that it looked like a village behind the lines during war, what with most of the population hobbling along the streets with the aid of canes and crutches or even wheel chairs. In my youthful innocence I inquired immediately what had brought all those invalids to a winter resort devoted to the most violent kind of sport. Invalids nothing. They were all skiing casualties. And in skiing, as in flying, the greater the adept, the greater the danger. Ladies and gentlemen who slither down reasonable wide-open slopes do no more than twist their knee caps or sprain their thumbs and ankles or wrench their arches. It is when they get sufficiently proficient to thunder down near-perpendicular slopes studded with trees and rocks at fifty and sixty miles an hour that they break legs, lose eyes, and split their skulls open. Anyone who tries to ski without first taking lessons is a sucker. Anyone who doesn't ski if he or she possibly can is even a greater sucker, because of all the things one can do outdoors it is the most fun, thrill, and excitement.

Probably the most ludicrous game in the world when played by grown men in all seriousness for championships and titles is table tennis, or ping-pong, but it is only slightly more ridiculous than the attempts of the players to badger the sports editors into taking them seriously and reporting and publicizing the game as an adult sport. True, the experts perform prodigies of speed, judgment, and the quick eye, and heroes like William Tatem Tilden, Jr., have placed their stamp of approval on it; but no matter how fast they play or how grim their expressions or how copious the pools of perspiration they shed on the floor, it is still just two guys urging a small, hollow, celluloid ball about the size of a walnut back and forth on a table, over a net not high enough to trip a good-sized cockroach, using butter pats for weapons.

In all my fourteen years of sports-reporting I never once

heard someone say: "Come on, let's go some place and see a lacrosse game," though it was once introduced into Madison Square Garden in an indoor form, where it perished miserably after one or two showings. And yet it isn't a bad game to watch. When I went up to West Point or to Annapolis for football practice I used to like to wander off and look at the lacrosse-players instead.

The one game I would never in the world play as long as I had my reason and could run from it is water polo. There is one of the roughest, dirtiest games ever invented to try the stamina, courage, and spirit of man. The player must be able to swim like a seal and have the lung capacity of a sulphur-bottom whale. It is courting death by asphyxiation to lay your hands on the ball, because when you do they drag you down to the bottom and keep you there until you let it go. It is only a fair game to watch because the negligible speed of swimming makes it slow.

Handball and all its derivatives, squash, squash tennis, and rackets, are fine exercise and exciting games to play if you have the constitution for it. All those games are inclined to be a little tough on the ticker. Nobody ever goes to see them played, mainly because there is never any room for spectators in or about the courts.

Canoeists take themselves and their art very seriously and have annual races and championships, which are held practically in private unless they are free of charge. I once promoted and staged a canoe Marathon around Manhattan Island, which cured me.

Bowling has probably more quiet devotees among the common people than almost any other sport, with the possible exception of golfing and fishing. Thousands of people bowl for the fun of it and the mild exercise, and when the championships are held, there are from twelve to fourteen thousand entrants. For a thoroughly satisfactory male evening, there is nothing like collecting three fellow drunks and wandering over to the nearest parlor or alleys, there to remove the coat, roll up the shirt-sleeves, loosen the necktie and open the collar, light up a ten-cent cigar, holler for beer, and bowl until your arms ache. In the interim, while the other fellows are bowling, one can get excellent practice in spitting at garboons. The bowling alley is practically the last remaining stronghold of this early American cultural development.

The most overrated spectator sport I know of is college rowing, and how it manages annually to attract the vast crowds that go to see it has mystified me ever since in my early youth as number six in the Columbia shell I rowed four miles down the Hudson past banks solidly black with people. The regattas are difficult to get to and even more difficult to get away from. If you haven't a seat on the observation train—and the supply of seats is limited—you see perhaps one minute of the race. The Intercollegiate Regatta at Poughkeepsie sometimes turns up some pretty good dogfights between crews fighting for the lead, but the average Harvard-Yale race is a procession, with one or the other opening up a two- or three-length lead and holding or increasing it down the river. The only way really to see a crew race is from an airplane. Most of the spectators are pretty bored with them, but go for the party and in order to be able to say they've been. I can't think of any other reason.

The rodeo is now an annual fixture in the big cities of the East, the cowboys and cowgirls traveling three thousand miles or so away from where they belong to stage their trade championships. I went once and saw one of the steers used as guinea pigs break loose and try to climb into a box and kiss a dowager decked out in a lot of feathers and ermine, with whom it was apparently infatuated, and it took the entire flower of the Western plains nineteen minutes by the clock to catch it, rope it, and drag it back to where it belonged. I haven't been since, but a lot of people seem to like the sport. It is more or less of a sadistic performance, and the promoters always wisely tie it up with some charity to avoid criticism and trouble with the S.P. C.A. A half-dozen of the boys and girls competing usually wind up in Polyclinic Hospital across the way, and sometimes they die. I am probably too effete to appreciate this show.

There hasn't been a badminton championship held in the United States as yet, but it is coming. Whereas ping-pong looks like a sissy sport and is, badminton looks like one and isn't. Three fast sets of that, and you've had enough. This is the speedy game developed out of what your Aunt Martha used to play during her vacations up in Woonsocket or Stockbridge back in the rather dismal nineties, when it was known as "battledore and shuttlecock." It is the coming indoor winter sport in America.

The only excuse for watching a sailing race is to be aboard somebody's palatial yacht with plenty of caviar sandwiches at one hand and tall glasses, ice, soda, and whisky at the other, and nothing better to do. Actually, sailing or crewing small boats in races is grand fun, but who can afford it? The only American snob bigger than the tennis snob is the yacht-club snob.

Fishing is listed as a sport. It is, too. Hundreds of thousands of people fish, have fished, or want to fish. I have tried practically all kinds and get the biggest kick out of surf-casting which is as tantalizing and as hard to stay away from as golf. You feel that if you can just heave the lead out beyond the one spot you cannot seem to reach, that is where the big one is lurking. It has the grab-bag element of surprise, too. You never know what is going to be on the end of your line. Trout-fishing is too finicky for me. I haven't the patience to stalk a fish. And besides, it is bad for my complexes. A trout is admittedly the most intelligent of fish, but it is still just a fish, and to date I have always come off second best in my encounters.

One of the greatest of all spectator sports from the point of view of sustained action and wide-open play that anyone can understand is soccer football, and after you have seen it played in England or in Italy it is easy to understand why crowds of a hundred thousand turn out for it. But it doesn't appeal to the American, who prefers to have his football picked up and advanced concealed beneath a welter of rules and regulations that he cannot possibly comprehend. In soccer the ball is never out of sight, and the players are in action, running at top speed, for the full sixty minutes.

Speed skating is fairly interesting and colorful, but it gives one the curious effect of looking much slower than it actually is. A mile run, somehow, looks much faster than a mile skate. The contestants, bent over double, string out in a line, gliding with long powerful strokes, all apparently in the same rhythm. It is striding that wins skating races, which gives them their strange placidity.

The darling of all the blade and ice sports is the free skating phase of figure-skating, which is destined to become the joy and delight of the balletomanes of the future, because it is the ballet freed almost completely from the trammels of gravity and the limitations of the human body. The speed of steel on ice gives height, distance, and pure flight to leaps that cannot possibly be paralleled on foot, as well as the pure, flowing line of movement that is never broken.

For lovely, sustained, and rhythmic poetry of the human figure in motion, I have never seen anything more beautiful than the pair skating of Maxie Heber and Herbert Baier, the German world-championship pair, or that of the brother and sister Paussin, the two Viennese youngsters who bring the Strauss waltzes to new life and meaning on the ice, or the solo skating of Sonje Henie of Norway, or the ice-dancing of gleaming Maribel Vinson of the United States, or Vivi-Ann Hultane, the Swedish skater.

Figure-skating has still to free itself of ugly, formalized spins and meaningless whirls done in ungainly squatting positions. But these are being turned more and more into legitimate ballet pirouettes and blended into the ice dances rather given as exhibitions of ability to withstand centrifugal force and violent attacks of vertigo. Figure-skating more than any other sport has been shackled to its past, and in the past, free skating without reverting to acrobatics for the sake of acrobatics was unthinkable. One of the first great steps towards freeing the combination sport and art from these ungainly hangovers was realized at Garmisch during the 1936 Olympic Games, where for the first time in the history of figure-skating Baier and the lithe, elf-like Herber dance-skated their pair to music composed especially for them, and interpreted the music.

There is an amusing angle to figure-skating which nobody ever sees but the judges because it is unspectacular and a great bore, and that is the competition in the school figures, the rockers and loops and brackets and double threes and bracket-change-bracket, the back inside rockers, and all the rest of the stylized maneuvers that are judged by exactly what the name implies, the figures traced on the ice by the sharp edges of the skate. When the skater in the competition has completed the figure called for in the test three times, the judges solemnly stomp out onto the ice, teetering a little in their heavy overshoes, kneel down with all the hawk-like keenness of Sherlock Holmes looking for a footprint or some ash from a Trinchinopoli cigar, and examine the tracings.

There is also a sinister aspect to it all. International, and frequently Olympic, figure-skating competitions are for the most part as completely and joyously crooked and bought and sold as any prizefight or wrestling championship. Some of the European judges are as fine a set of scamps and vote-peddlers as you ever laid your eyes on. The sport is so completely commercialized abroad that it is vital to have the right people win it. The right people always do. It would be foolish, for instance, to have an American girl win a world championship, or an American pair, because that would entail a great deal of expense in bringing them over for those perennial European ice carnivals and exhibitions. The dressing-room of the American skaters in Garmisch was invaded by one of the European judges offering to do a little horse-swapping of votes. If the American judges would give Miss Whosit high marks, the European judges in return would see that the American, Miss Whatsit, would place higher than she would otherwise. They laughed at him and threw him out. The American figure-skaters didn't do so well at Garmisch.

Do I hear you inquiring plaintively: "Ain't nuthin' on the level?" I dunno. You tell me.

XXVI

THE

NEXT FIFTY

YEARS

THEY ARE wonders, all these heroes and heroines of mine, superlative, unsurpassed, and their deeds are certain to ring down through the ages—well, at least the next five or six years of these ages. Because, unless I miss my guess and the past is not an honest guide to the future, the records and accomplishments of these valiants are not carved in rock, but writ on sand. All things being equal and the nations refraining from destroying one another and their able man-power by gun-fire, chemicals, and high explosives, I suspect that there are equally great and even greater athletes and colorful performers in sports to follow, and that fifty years from now the deeds and records of Dempsey and Ruth, of Glenn Cunningham, Paavo Nurmi, Helen Wills, Bill Tilden, Bob Jones, and Jesse Owens will appear as musty and forgotten to that generation as those of the heroes of twenty-five and thirty years ago appear to me now.

About seven years ago, at which time Captain J. M. Patterson, publisher of the *Daily News*, was also publishing *Liberty Magazine*, I offered him an article to be entitled "The Golden Decade," listing and extolling the glories of the sports heroes of the greatest ten years of sports and great athletes the modern world had ever known, from 1920 to 1930. He said that he didn't think the heroes of the present time were so much better than those of his day, and turned the article down. And from his point of view he was quite right. One's real and permanent heroes are always those one grows up with in one's youth.

Thumbing the various record books, I can see that he was thinking of Cobb and Speaker, and Sisler, Napoleon Lajoie, Christy Mathewson, Honus Wagner, Iron-Man McGinnity, Three-Fingered Brown, Rube Waddell, Evers to Tinker to Chance, Eddie Plank, Home-Run Baker, Chief Bender, and other ballplayers who were famous and celebrated in their day. Year for year and record for record, except in home runs hit, Ty Cobb was a better man than Babe Ruth, and was as violently loved and hated in his time as Babe Ruth was in ours.

In boxing there were Ketchel and Fitzsimmons, Jim Corbett, Jim Jeffries, and Tom Sharkey, the superb boxing and defensive scientist Jack Johnson, Sam Langford, Joe Walcott, Joe Gans, Terry McGovern, Ad Wolgast and Bat Nelson, Willie Ritchie and Benny Leonard, Packy McFarland, Jack Britton, Young Corbett, and Jimmy Wilde, as great a galaxy of names and performers probably as the ring has ever known, now fading more and more into the forgotten past and already being supplanted in power and legend by the glamorous figures of those of the past ten or fifteen years, some of whom may not have even been so glamorous, but who are already beginning to acquire that fine patina that comes of being "remembered when" and compared to the upstarts of today.

There were tennis greats too. William A. Larned won the singles championship of the United States as often as did Tilden, seven times. And Maurice McLoughlin was every bit as colorful a figure as any of the latter-day players. From 1915 to 1926 Molla Mallory won the women's American singles championship eight times. Helen Wills in her time only achieved seven, though of course her Wimbledon record helps her to stand out. And Hazel Hotchkiss, later Mrs. George

Wightman, and Mary K. Browne were pretty good tennis-players even though the woman's game was not quite so fast then as it is today. But then, neither is the game of today as fast as that of tomorrow will be. Of the foreign tennis stars, Brookes and Wilding were real stars before the war.

In golf the ancient heroes are legion, and they played a much slower, shorter ball, with far less efficient clubs. True, no one in the past has equaled Bob Jones's grand slam, but it is quite possible that some phenomenal youngster, another amateur, will come along who will make a grand slam two years in succession. Oldsters admit that Jones was good, but they still like to talk about John Ball, Vardon and Ted Ray, Walter Travis and Jerry Travers, Frances Ouimet and Chick Evans, and a professional by the name of Willie Anderson who won the National Open Championship three years in succession, in 1903-4-5, something no one has managed to do since. They could all hit that ball up to the pin, those boys, putt like wizards, and they had no trouble-shooters like the modern sand-wedge to nullify bunkers.

There were foot-runners too—Jarvis, Archie Hahn, Alf Shrubb, Mel Sheppard, Johnny Hayes, and a host of others. They didn't run as fast as the fields run today, but they ran faster than anybody else of their time, which is always fast enough. If their records are all gone, it should not be forgotten that the apparently miraculous achievements of today will be dead lines of type chucked into the hellbox and long since melted fifty years from now. There were fast horses, great jockeys, bicycle-riders, swimmers, and jumpers before 1920, and there will be many greater ones to come.

When will the ceiling of human athletic endeavor be attained? Who can attempt to say at this time? After all, it took several billions of years to achieve the 4:06.7 mile.

We have happened to have a great run of champions and performers in the past fifteen years, at a time when the public, tired of war, death, and taxes, turned to sports as an outlet. There was money to spend on the shows and exhibitions, plenty of ballyhoo for the athletes to get the people to come and spend still more money, and increased circulation for the newspapers that printed entertaining stories about their deeds and personalities. All this brought this particular group of athletes into focus more sharply, perhaps, than any other similar group in the past.

When the heroes of the preceding generation were active, it must be remembered, prizefighting was in exceedingly bad repute, tennis wasn't considered a man's game; golf was, but only an old man's sport, and hadn't yet been taken up by the masses. None of the sports with the exception of horseracing, polo, and yachting were as popular or as fashionable as they are today. The upswing was a wide, rapid stroke. The pendulum may swing back again. Interest in sports nose-dived violently for a time during the depression, and many of us felt a little silly, still writing daily in the flamboyant post-war style of highly paid professional and amateur athletes at a time when most people were wondering where their next pay-check or meal was coming from.

There will always be interest in sports as long as the average citizen has a fair income, leisure time, and a reasonable amount of security. The trend at present is in the direction of participation in sports and games. More people are playing or learning to play games or indulge in some form of exercise than ever before. There seems to be a feeling that this wave of active participation as opposed to taking sport vicariously via the grandstand seat will kill off interest in amateur and professional championships, and the big gates along with them. But I feel that exactly the opposite will be the result. The greater the number of participants, the more customers eventually for the experts and champions. Every man or woman who has ever played a game wants to go to see the champions play, for purposes of comparison and study. They are curious to see how much they resemble the champions—if at all.

There are three general means of advancing a particular sport: improving the equipment with which it is played, improving the technique of play, and improving the people who play it. I believe that we have gone only a little of the way towards the peak of possible human achievement in any sport. We have been, it must be remembered, keeping records and measurements for such a short time. It is quite true that the Greeks, the Romans, the Etruscans, the Egyptians, and probably the inhabitants of ancient Ur, ran foot-races, jumped, boxed, wrestled, and played games with a ball, either throwing it or kicking it, but the records of their performances, if they kept any, have been lost, and the only standards we have for purposes of comparison with the future are little more than fifty years old. Pheidippides ran the first Marathon, a distance of twenty-six miles two hundred and eighty-seven yards, but nobody held a watch on him because, among other pertinent reasons, there were none to hold. It would take an extraordinarily egotistical frame of mind to believe that because in fifty years we have reduced the time for the mile from 4:20 to 4:06.7, this is the summum of foot-running and the end. True, somewhere, some time, there must be a ceiling beyond which no combination of human courage, skill, endeavor, and physique can rise. They cannot eventually run that hundred yards in nothing flat. But we flatter ourselves when we think that we have approached it in this generation. Fifty years from now, not a record now on the books will be left standing.

In sport, and advances made, a great deal depends on what you think you can do and what you are used to doing. When I was rowing on the Columbia crew back in 1916–17–20–21, the four-mile race at Poughkeepsie was rowed with a fast racing start of about 36 to 40 strokes a minute, then quickly dropped to 32, and then down to 28 for the long grind. There might be an occasional sprint when the stroke would be raised slightly for ten, but most of the time the boats slogged along at that pace, 28, relying on smoothness, power, and the driving kick at the finish to keep ahead of competing eights. The last half-mile we would whoop it up to 32 again and possibly hit 38–40 in the final scramble for the finish line, and then keel over.

The four-mile race rowed that way, was, as far as I was concerned, the absolute limit of my endurance. I was used to that, keyed to it, trained to it.

In my last year in the boat, 1921, Navy sent an eight-oared crew up to Poughkeepsie that rowed at 40 strokes to the minute all the time in practice. They were an object of considerable derision along the river, where the old-time crews, Syracuse, Cornell, Penn, Columbia, had their boat-houses and training quarters. We just let them go because we knew that before they had rowed a mile at that pace in the big race, they would collapse and be out of it. All of us, coaches and oarsmen alike, but especially those of us who yanked the oars, knew that it was impossible to row four miles swinging 40 strokes to the minute.

The Navy, however, did not seem to know that, because on regatta day they hit 44 at the start at Krum Elbow and then rowed 40 the whole four miles down the course to the finish line a mile below the bridge, and nobody was even close. Their stroke wasn't as long as ours and it wasn't as rhythmic and pretty. However, this wasn't a beauty contest, but a boat-race, and they finished 'way out in front and were sitting up in the boat after they crossed the line.

Today, all boat-races are rowed at a higher stroke and the oarsmen survive beautifully. And just as people interested in rowing were congratulating themselves on this new and final development of the sport, along came a Japanese crew to the Henley Regatta on the upper Thames in 1936 and rowed fifty-two, all the way down the Henley course. I happened to be on the Thames one afternoon and quite by accident ran across them out for a practice spin. From force of habit I clocked them and came away a little dazed, knowing that one of us must be crazy. They didn't win in the finals, because, fast as their stroke was, it was too choppy to be one hundred per cent efficient, but the amazing thing is that they could do it at all. Will a crew some day row sixty strokes to the minute, a stroke a second? Why not?

One broken record usually precipitates a whole host of them because the smashed mark immediately changes the mental attitude of the athlete towards the task of wrecking it further. We borrow a term from boxing and call it "softening up." A crack sprinter will run the hundred yards in 9.6, then world's record time, and never improve on it. Along will come a new phenom and lower the world's record to 9.4. The 9.6 man will suddenly, to his own great surprise, do it in 9.4 too. Why? Because he knows it can be done, has been done. The English Channel was an impassable barrier of water, wind, waves, and currents for women swimmers until Gertrude Ederle softened it up by making a successful passage under her own power. After that they had to have traffic cops to keep other women who succeeded in doing the same thing from swimming over one another.

By 1987 the hundred yards will have been run in 9.1, and possibly 9 seconds flat, the mile in 4:3, and high jumpers will be squirming over the bar at seven feet while the pole-vaulters do fifteen. The track coach may laugh at this as a physical and technical impossibility, but it will be the same kind of laugh as the one given three decades ago by track experts at the thought of a 4:07 mile, the 9:04 hundred, or a running jump over a bar placed at six feet nine and one eighth inches.

At the standard distance in yards, there isn't a single world's record now extant that was made prior to 1926, and the same is true of the metric distances with the exception of the 5,000-meter record made by Paavo Nurmi in 1924. The marks set by the heroes and champions of 1900 and 1910 are wiped off the books. They are forgotten. There is no reason for believing anything but that the same fate will overtake the present-day crop. We're good all right, but we're not perfect by any means yet. There is the valuable aid of the strange, spongy, gray matter that fills the tops of our skulls to be considered. It does play its part. If you need any further proof, look at the track records made by racehorses bred solely for speed and stamina. Some of them still go 'way back to 1899. The human being, bred at random, manages to develop faster.

Our equipment for all sports has been improving steadily, and will continue to improve. I doubt whether the golf-players of today on the whole are better men or better golfers than those of thirty years ago, though of course they play and practice more, because there is more incentive to win today than there was then. But there is only one proper way to hit a golf ball, and it is the same now as it was when the first Scot smote his feather ball with a crooked stick, over the Highland hills and the seaside sand dunes, except that we know more about the swing today because we have slow-motion pictures to analyze it for us. But modern ingenuity has given the player of today tools that are far more accurate and precise than those used fifty years ago. Whenever human perfection is approached in the game, it is matched by an approach to mechanical perfection, an accurate, tough, far-flying ball and powerful, properly balanced clubs. And there is no reason to believe that the golf equipment of the next fifty years will not be even better.

The tennis racket has kept pace with the increased speed and tempo and severity of the game. It had to do so. Compare the modern streamlined, taut, tournament racket of today, strung to a musical note, with the square-headed clumsy bat that was used in the nineteen-hundreds. And it is well known that the important balance of power between pitcher and batter in baseball lies not in the hands of the players, but with those who are charged with the specifications for the inner construction and manufacture of the ball used. When the public is in the mood for hitting, the lively ball appears, and doubles, triples, and home runs rattle off the ends of the bats. When the fashion switches to tight pitching, a slight change in the center of the ball and its manner of yarn winding, and those long flies that today clear the boundaries of the parks for home runs will settle gracefully into the hands of waiting outfielders, of put-outs. There isn't a single piece of sports equipment used in any game that has not been tremendously refined and improved in the last thirty years, nor a single item in which there is not room for further improvement.

And as long as human beings continue to make money out of sport, games and competitions of every kind will continue to advance technically; that is to say, form will improve as the mechanics of participation are studied and analyzed. There is a vast difference in attitude between people who do things for fun or relaxation and those who do them to eat. Any amateur who turns professional will tell you that he never really began to learn about his game until he took it up vocationally as a wage-earning profession. Even the amateurs today are competing much more fiercely than they ever did before, on account of the kudos and the titles which in some manner or other can be turned to cash or benefit or advantage. And all top-rank amateurs have their professional coaches and teachers who profit directly out of the records and victories of their pupils; so again there is the incentive to study the mechanics of sport.

No small part of the modern standards of track and field sports and the general excellence of today's competition compared to that of thirty years ago is due to the greatly improved technique of running and jumping, all tending towards efficiency and the elimination of waste motion. But it would be merely thick-headed to hold that we know all there is to know about such technique.

A first-class football team of thirty years ago wouldn't stand a ghost of a show on the field today with a fast, deceptive, modern team such as one will find at Southern Methodist, Colgate, Stanford, Yale, or Minnesota. The 1937 team, with its reverse plays, hidden-ball tricks, fake attacks, deception, forward and lateral passes, and, above all, speed and mobility, would run the old-style teams ragged. And the team of today would probably be just as badly off with the teams of the future. When football was merely a collegiate pastime, all hands were content to slog away with force and weight. When it became a huge money-making industry, with victory translated into bank-notes, teachers of the game began to study it and to make use of their brains. At the rate that it has been changing in the past ten years—even the shape of the football has been slightly altered to make it more adaptable to passing—fifty years from now it would probably be unrecognizable to the spectator of today.

As an example of what is made possible by changing styles in public approval, the development of the modern six-day bicycle race may be examined. Twenty years ago, when the teams used to ride in the old Madison Square Garden down on Twenty-sixth Street, one stolen lap was usually sufficient to win the race for the team that managed to pull it off, and stealing that lap—that is, riding around the field fast enough and long enough to catch up again with the tail-enders and thus gain a full lap—was a difficult feat. But the post-war six-day race fans wanted more action and began to stay away when they didn't get it. And so the promoters had to gear up the athletes to create more jams and try to steal more laps. They did. And the more they stole, the more the public wanted. Today, it is considered normal for a total of three to four hundred laps to be stolen during the course of one race.

Judging from the ephemeral quality of the swimming records for both male and female, the technique of swimming is apparently still in swaddling-clothes. There was a lot of nonsense written after the 1932 Olympic Games about the Japanese secret of swimming that enabled fourteen-year-old schoolboys to carry off most of the Olympic prizes in competition against grown men and mature athletes. There was no secret except that the Japanese had learned the most correct and efficient style of swimming yet developed, the American crawl, and then had taken the trouble to teach it properly and to insist upon practice with Oriental patience and thoroughness. But the technique of speed swimming is not yet completely developed, and few if any of the present-day records will be extant even ten years from now. Fifty years from today, when that generation reads about the time we used to make back in 1937, it will wonder whether we swam with weights tied to our ankles.

But this is an uncertain world. Civilizations have risen and fallen before. Our records, printed on rag paper, are less lasting than those of the ancients, who, if they kept them, inscribed them on parchment or chiseled them in marble. Not a scrap of theirs remains, and archæologists digging down through the rubble that may cover the cities of today a thousand years hence, will find not one single piece of evidence that in 1934, the mile was run in 4:06.7, or the hundred in 9.4, or that later generations improved upon these startling figures. A great social catastrophe involving the destruction of nations and the wholesale slaughter of peoples such as have been periodic in history may throw the development of sport out of gear, to be resumed later, perhaps at levels never dreamed of today. One is likely to forget that there was organized sport in Greece and Rome before Christ, track meets and games, and that with the fall of these nations there then was a hiatus of something like eighteen centuries before national and international sports competitions were resumed. For all we know, the Greek athletes of the great Hellenic period may have run the equivalent of the hundred yards in nine seconds flat and made our modern milers look like selling platers. One might well fancy running brought to the state of a high art in an age where it might more often than not mean the difference between life and death.

But we are not looking that far into the future. Conditions and nations and the state of affairs remaining what they are, the next fifty years will see the apparently inevitable sports cycles still faithfully revolving. Tennis is a fair example of the way things move in sports. England first had the balance of power in tennis and lost it to Australia. The United States took it over from the Aussies in the heyday of Tilden, Richards, and Johnston and then passed it to France, which held it during the prime of Borotra, Cochet, and Lacoste. It went to England again, and last summer finally returned to the United States. England seems now on its way to taking over the supremacy at golf that it used to have and that it held for such a long time.

In twenty years' time, when the new generation of youngsters, regimented and trained from infancy in Germany and
Italy and other Fascist states, come to maturity, the strangle-
hold that we have had for years on track and field athletics is
liable to be broken. The Opera Ballila, the Italian youth movement, and the Hitler Jugend, are undertaking the athletic and
military training of youngsters under ten years of age, teaching
them the fundamentals of sports and drill. The early sports
training may make them a nation of athletes far surpassing anything that we have ever known before—or it may make them
cannon-food.

Sport has the same tendency to repeat itself that history has.
Thus, there will appear again within the next fifty years a
mighty batter with a deadly eye, and he will hit more home runs
than Babe Ruth, and Ruth, the greatest of his age today in baseball, will have become simply a measuring-stick, somebody, as
the Brooklynite would put it, that somebody else hit more
home runs than. And there will appear likewise a baffling
pitcher, a phenom at delivering the ball, who will be called the
greatest the world has ever known because he will have pitched
two or three no-hit games in one season.

There will be a heavyweight champion of the world at 160 or
170 pounds, because in the cycle of boxing and boxing champions it is nearly time for one of those big little men like Bob
Fitzsimmons or Joe Walcott to show up again, and there will
also be a heavyweight fighter who will be called unbeatable and
a superman and superfighter by a new crop of sports-writers and
experts who never will have heard about what happened to
present-day experts, long dead and buried, who applied those
terms to a Negro heavyweight by the name of Joe Louis.

There will be a lady tennis star who will combine beauty with
talent and who will probably be an accomplished torch singer
as well as an unbeatable champion. This generation managed
to combine those sterling qualities, as we know, in a backstroke
swimming champion. There will be a golfer who will play nine
holes in birdies, and another who will win the Open Champion-

ship of America and Great Britain three times in a row. Where this generation measured its affluence and spending power with a three-million-dollar prizefight gate, fifty years from now there will have been a seven-million-dollar gate that will make ours look like chicken-feed. Well, high-grade chicken-feed, then. There will be super-horses, super-jumpers, super-athletes of every description, and the men who drive the thundercraft, the racing craft, motorboats and planes, will laugh at the junk piles of yesterday that wouldn't do more than 130 on land or sea, and a piffling 300 through the air.

I shall not be here to see them, which doesn't matter greatly, because after the fourteen years spent celebrating the heroes and heroines just passed into the wings, I should not have sufficient adjectives left to do them justice. It might be pleasant to be able to get a glimpse of the record-books of 1987 and see what the boys are running the mile in, or pick up a paper and learn whether the stumble-bums have developed any more potent way of rocking a man to sleep than by hitting him on the point of the chin or swatting him in the solar plexus, but in my own generation I figure that I have seen about all that there is to see in sport and said all that I have to say upon the subject. I am, at this end, content to say good-by and leave the field and its marvels to be rediscovered by the new generation of sports-writers.